Italy and EC Membership Evaluated

Italy and EC Membership Evaluated

Edited by Francesco Francioni

 Pinter Publishers
London

First published in Great Britain in 1992 by
Pinter Publishers Limited
25 Floral Street, London WC2E 9DS

British Library Cataloguing in Publication Data

A CIP catalogue record for this book is available from the
British Library

ISBN 0-86187-000-0

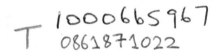

Typeset by Koinonia Limited, Manchester
Printed and bound in Great Britain by Biddles Ltd, Guildford and Kings Lynn

Contents

PART III: POLITICAL AND LEGAL SYSTEMS

PART IV: SOCIAL POLICY

List of contributors

Grazia Atanasio, Dr. in Political Science, University of Siena; Diploma, College of Europe. Visiting Researcher at Columbia Law School, USA.

Silvia Bartali, Dr in Political Science, University of Siena; Diploma, College of Europe. Administrative Officer, D. G. 11, EEC Commission.

Andrea Bianchi, Dr. in Political Science, University of Siena; LL.M. Harvard Law School. Assistant Professor of International Law, University of Siena.

Paolo Cesarini, J. D., University of Siena; Diploma, College of Europe. Formerly Legal Officer at the International Labour Organization and currently Legal Officer at the Directorate-General for Competition at the EEC Commission.

Maurizio Cotta, J. D., University of Rome; Professor of Political Science, University of Siena.

Elisabetta Croci Angelini, Graduate in Economics, University of Siena; Ph. D. in Economics, European University Institute. Assistant Professor of Economics, University of Siena.

Francesco Farina, Graduate in Economics, University of Naples. Professor of Economics, University of Siena.

Luigi Vittorio Ferraris, Former Ambassador of the Italian Republic. Currently a Member of the State Council.

Francesco Francioni, J. D., University of Florence; LL. M., Harvard Law School. Professor of International Law, University of Siena; Visiting Professor of Law, University of Texas at Austin.

Carlo Garbarino, J. D., S. J. D., University of Genova, LL. M., University of Michigan, Visiting Professor of International Taxation, University of Siena.

Giovanni Grottanelli de' Santi, J. D., University of Siena; Diploma, College of Europe; LL.M., Yale Law School. Professor of Constitutional Law, University of Siena.

Francesca Martines, Dr. in Political Science, University of Florence; Doctoral Candidate, European University Institute.

Series introduction

This volume is one in a series entitled *European Community Membership Evaluated*. The series comprises eleven volumes and examines the gains and losses of European Community (EC) membership for each of the twelve states.

Over the entire period since the first steps in European integration were taken, with the formation of the European Coal and Steel Community, the impact of membership upon the individual states has been both a matter of importance to, and an issue for evaluation by, the political parties, interest groups, government, elites, researchers and, increasingly, the public at large. The renewed dynamism of the EC in the period following the signing of the Single European Act in 1986 and the approach of the completed internal market by the end of 1992 have raised awareness of EC membership to new heights.

It is against this backdrop that the project leading to this series was undertaken. Policy-makers and the European electorate alike require the information to make informed judgements about national gains and losses (or costs and benefits) arising from EC membership.

— How far have the EC's economic policies brought gains?
— Does EC membership impose constraints on the powers of national and regional/local government, or on the legal system?
— What have been the effects of the hitherto somewhat disparate EC activities in the social, cultural and educational policy areas?
— What are the gains and losses of foreign policy co-operation among the member-states?
— How pronounced are the specific national interests of the individual member-states?

In order to answer questions such as these, each volume brings together a team of specialists from various disciplines. Although the national teams are composed predominantly of academics, the series is aimed at a readership beyond the confines of the education world. Thus each volume seeks to present its findings in a manner accessible to *all* those affected by, or interested in, the EC. Extensive footnoting of academic literature is avoided, although some guidance is offered on the legal bases of EC policies; a bibliography at the end of each study gives guidance on narrower sectoral impact studies and on further reading.

A distinctive feature of the series as a whole is that a common framework has been followed for all eleven studies. This is aimed at facilitating comparison between the national studies. No systematic international comparative study of this kind has been attempted before. Indeed, for some member-states there exists no study of the impact of EC membership. The absence of such a series of studies initially seemed rather surprising. However, as the project progressed, the reasons for this became clearer. It is by no means easy to find a common framework acceptable to the academic traditions of all the member-states *and* all the policy areas and academic disciplines involved.

The project co-ordinators experienced these tensions in a striking way. Their international 'summit meetings' meant reaching compromises acceptable to all the diverse academic traditions of the countries involved. Then the individual national contributors had to be convinced of the merits of the international compromises! These negotiations brought many insights into precisely the type of problem faced by EC policy-makers themselves! Hence academic perfectionism has been subordinated to some extent to pragmatism and the wish to address a wider readership.

In some countries, for instance the Netherlands, Great Britain, Portugal and the Federal Republic of Germany, up to thirty scholars of various disciplines make up the national team. In other countries, such as Ireland, a team numbers less than ten authors. In the latter, *one* author deals with several parts of a subject-group or even with the whole of a subject-group. In either case, however, authors have assured comparability by making cross-references to subsections of policies.

The basic principle of the project has been to assess the gains and losses of EC membership for the individual state, with the hypothetical alternative in mind of that state leaving the EC. This alternative may be deemed to be somewhat simplistic but it is far more manageable than making assumptions about where individual states would be, had they not joined the EC in the first place. Such speculation is virtually impossible scientifically and would undermine efforts to make the findings accessible to a wider readership. The terms 'benefits', 'gains' and 'positive effects', and 'costs', 'losses' and 'negative effects', respectively, are used synonymously.

The activities of the EC, together with the foreign policy co-operation process EPC (European Political Co-operation), are grouped under four broad headings in the project (see Table A at the end of this Introduction). *Economic policy* covers a range of EC policies: from the internal market to the Common Agricultural Policy but also including environmental policy. *Foreign relations* comprise not only European Political Co-operation but also the EC's external trade policy and security policy. *Social and educational policy* brings together the rather disparate measures taken in a range of areas, some of which are now coming to be regarded as forming the 'social dimension' of the EC. Finally, the subject area *political and legal system* refers not to EC policies but rather to the EC's impact upon the principles and practices of government (for a list see Table A).

Each of the EC policy headings is assessed following a common approach. The objectives of the EC policy, and the accomplishments thus far, are assessed against the equivalent set of national policy goals and legislation, many of them common to all countries, some of them are obviously national ones. The idea, then, is to arrive at a 'balance sheet', both at the level of the individual policy area or sector and, at the macro level, for the member-state as a whole. Drawing up the individual sectoral balance sheets has to involve a rather flexible approach. The 'mix' of quantitative and qualitative assessments varies according to the subject matter. There can be no quantitative data on how far foreign policy co-operation has brought gains to national foreign policy; figures may be available, however, on the impact of EC trade policy on national trade patterns. In the case of quantitative data it is important to note that very little, if any, primary statistical research was involved in the project. In consequence, quantitative assessments generally present available evidence from previous studies; they follow no consistent methodological approach, while qualitative assessments are often arrived at for the first time. One further point must be made with regard to the common approach of the project: it is clear that the importance of individual EC policy areas varies from one member-state to another.

It follows, therefore, that the weighting, and in some cases the categorization, of EC policy areas will vary between the national studies. To assign the same weight to fisheries policy in the British and Luxembourg cases, for instance, would be irrational. Some national policy goals and national interests are related to specific interests of some member countries. For instance, the German question and the problem of Northern Ireland are specific to the Federal Republic, Ireland and the United Kingdom respectively.

The whole project has been brought to fruition under the auspices of Europe-12 – Research and Action Committee on the EC. Created in 1986, Europe-12 brings together academics of all disciplines and from all member-states, as well as policy-makers and senior politicians. It aims to inform the policy debate through collaborative research and to raise public awareness of the important issues raised by European integration.

As with any such project a large number of acknowledgements must be made. A number of the participants took on the additional task of horizontal co-ordination, i.e. seeking to ensure consistency of approach across the national studies. For *economic policy* this was undertaken by Detlev Karsten, Bonn, and Peter Coffey, Amsterdam; for *foreign relations* by Carl-Christoph Schweitzer, Bonn, and Rudolf Hrbek, Tübingen; for contributions on the *political and legal system* by Francesco Francioni, Siena, and K. Kellermann, The Hague; finally, for *social and educational policies* by Bernard Henningsen, Munich, and Brigitte Mohr, Bonn. Sadly, Guenther Kloss, a co-ordinator of the British volume, died during the preparation of the series.

Last but by no means least, we are indebted to the Commission of the EC and to those bodies supporting the project: the German foundations, Stifterverband für die Deutsche Wissenschaft, Essen; Bosch GmbH, Stuttgart; Ernst Poensgen-Stiftung, Düsseldorf; as well as the Government of the Saarland and the Federal Ministry for Science and Technology, Bonn. The British and German Studies were made possible by the support of the Anglo-German Foundation for the Study of Industrial Society, London.

Carl-Cristoph Schweitzer
Bonn

Table A: Project's categorization of EC policies and structures

---

I   Economic policy

Internal market policy   Agricultural policy
Competition policy   Environmental policy
Industrial policy   Fiscal/taxation policy
Technology policy   Monetary policy
Transport and communications policy   Regional policy
Energy policy   External trade policy

II   Foreign relations

Foreign policy co-operation   Development policy
Security policy

III Political and legal system

sovereignty   National legal system
Parliamentary control of the   Judicial procedures
    executive
Electoral system   Maintenance of public order
Political parties   Protection of fundamental rights
Regional and local government   State organization
Policy-making process

**IV   Social, educational and cultural
      policies**

Manpower (employment/   Consumer protection
    unemployment)
Movement of labour and migrant   Education and training
    workers
Industrial relations   European identity and
Social security and health   cultural policies
Equal treatment of men and women   Media policy

Note: This list was a schematic guideline for the project; not every sub-section will be dealt with individually and the sequence is purely illustrative.

EUROPE–12:
Action and Research Committee on the EC

Hon President:
Lord Jenkins of Hillhead
Chancellor of the University of Oxford
H E Emilio Colombo
Minister Rome

Board:
Chairman: Former Minister Dr Ottokar Kahn
Senior Advisor, EC Commission, Brussels

Vice Chairmen:
Prof Dr Hélène Ahrweiler
Rector and Chancellor, University of Paris
Enrico Baron MEP
President European Parliament Brussels, Madrid
Piet Dankert
Undersecretary, Foreign Office, den Haag
Dr Garret Fitzgerald
former Prime Minister, Dublin.
Niels Anker Kofoed MP
former Minister, Copenhagen
Dr Hans Stercken MP
Chairman Bundestag Foreign Affairs Committee, Bonn
Franz Ludwig Graf von Stauffenberg **MEP,**
Representative of the President of the European Parliament

Senior Economic Advisor
Dr Otto Graf Lambsdorff **MP**
Former Minister of Economics, National Chairman FDP,
Bundestag, Bonn

Co-ordinator of Committees:
Prof Dr C C Schweitzer
University of Bonn, Political Science

Steering Committee:
Spokesman: Dr Renate Hellwig MP
Bundestag, Bonn, Chairman Sub-Committee on Europe
Dr Peter Baehr
Netherlands Scientific Council, The Hague
Prof Dr P D Dagtoglou
University of Athens, Law
W Dondelinger MP
Chairman Foreign Affairs Committee, Luxembourg
Prof Dr Francesco Francioni
University of Siena, Law
Fernard Herman MEP
Chairman Institutional Committee, EP, Brussels

Dr J Silva Lopes
Caixa General de Depositos, Lisbon, Economics
Anthony J Nicholls MA
Senior Fellow, St Anthony's College, Oxford
Dr Hans-J Seeler
Chairman FVS Foundation, Hamburg
Georges Sutra de Germa MEP
former Vice-Chairman, Institutional Committee, EP,
Pezenas, France
Prof Count L Ferraris
Council of State, Rome
Jacques Maison Rouge, ex Vice President
IBM, Paris
Dr Claude Treyer
Director, European Affairs, IGS, Paris

Research Committee:
Dr Simon Bulmer
University of Manchester, Dept of Government
Gerry Danaher
Secretary, Irish National Economic and Social Council,
Dublin
Prof. Alfonso Ortega
Political Science, University Pontifica Salamanca, Spain
Prof Dr Grotanelli de Santi
University of Siena, Law and Political Science
Prof Dr R Hrbek
University of Tübingen, Political Science
Prof Dr Detlev Karsten
University of Bonn, Economics
Prof Dr M A G van Meerhaeghe
University of Ghent, Economics
Prof Dr Stavros Theofanides
Panteios School of Pol. Science, Athens
Prof Dr Christian Tomuschat
University of Bonn, International Law

Media Advisors:
Rolf Goll
Chairman, Communications and Marketing, Ansin-Goll,
Frankfurt
Prof Dr E G Wedel
Chairman, European Media Centre, University of
Manchester

Hon Secretary:
Dr Hartmut Schweitzer, Bonn

Preface

When the idea arose in the late 1980s to collect in a single volume a series of papers on costs and benefits Italy would derive from membership of the EC, the task appeared to be rather ambitious and not without hurdles. The main difficulty was that of securing a team of qualified scholars and practitioners within a relatively short period of time, as required by the publication agenda for the Europe-12 series. However, this task was facilitated by a series of inter-disciplinary workshops organized within the group of Europe-12.

These workshops offered an invaluable opportunity for intellectual exchange, which provided the stimulus for completing the project by the beginning of 1991. All but one of those invited were able to accept our proposal to undertake this research and to draft a paper in a fairly short time frame. The research, drafting, coordination and final editing of each text in English was done without subsidies or other financial contribution from the EC or other sources public or private. This is a reason for pride for the whole Italian team, which worked in a regime of Franciscan poverty, a rather unusual condition compared with the contemporary lavish support that scholarly research enjoys in the European Community. These remarks are meant to highlight the generosity of the authors and their readiness to devote unselfishly their time and effort to the completion of this common endeavour. In no way should they be interpreted as pleading indulgence for any defects or shortcomings of this book

Francesco Francioni
Siena, November 1991

PART I: ECONOMIC POLICY

Chapter 1

Monetary policy

Francesco Farina

1.1 Introduction

The acceleration given by the European Community (EC) to its economic and monetary unification process calls forth a further change in monetary and foreign exchange policies. New 'rules of the game' have been set up for the phases 2 and 3 which will lead to the establishment of a European Central Bank and to the introduction of a single currency. The implementation of these new rules will impinge on the working of the exchange rate mechanism (ERM) of the European monetary system (EMS) and will affect the choice of instruments by the Bank of Italy. However, the move towards the European monetary unification (EMU) should not modify the general strategy, followed by the Italian monetary authorities during the 1980s, to utilize the growing exchange rate stability brought about by the lira participation in the ERM to force a real adjustment in the economy. In fact, the 1980 switch to a tight monetary stance mainly originated from the objective to curb the inflation process which in the late 1970s – as will be argued in section 1.2 – had been worsening the performance of the Italian economy with respect to the other OECD countries.

The most difficult problem now facing the Bank of Italy is the need to reconcile the degree of autonomy so far retained – in the inception phase of the EMS, through the combination of administrative controls and devaluations, and, in the 'second and third phase', by maintaining a positive domestic–foreign interest rate differential (as described in sections 1.3, 1.4 and 1.5 respectively) – with the relinquishment of monetary independence required by the new obligations.

In so far as the evaluation of the EMS presented in section 1.5 is agreed, the benefits accrued to Italy from the relevant slowdown of inflation and the costs in terms of the huge public debt due to the high interest rates' level raising the debt service and of the rise in the unemployment rate caused by the stringent output-inflation trade-off are more or less balanced. Yet, as the final section of this chapter will maintain, the additional costs that the Italian economy must incur as a result of the leap forward towards economic and monetary unification (EMU) cannot be under-rated. Structural changes such as the convergence process required by policy co-ordination during Phase 2 and the increase in competition triggered by the 1993 completion of the European market might aggravate the conditions of the Italian balance of payments and prevent the achievement of a more acceptable unemployment rate. Later on, with the passage to irrevocably fixed exchange rates and the introduction of the European common currency, the de-industrialization problem might even arise.

1.2 The Italian economy's divergent path in the late 1970s

In the second half of the 1970s, higher inflation rates triggered by the first oil shock caused the monetarist theory to gain considerable ground. Central banks across the world began to believe that, contrary to the Keynesian model, the IS curve had to be considered less stable than the LM curve. Be that as it may, there is no doubt that by pegging the nominal interest rate despite higher inflation, the monetary authorities had in fact forced the real interest rate to become smaller and smaller, so that the growth rate of the money supply had been left to rise, which in turn fuelled inflation. Thus, the political and academic opinion turned to the conviction that monetary stability had to be ranked as the first objective if private- and public-sector balance sheets were to be re-equilibrated and the degree of uncertainty of economic decisions reduced. Accordingly, the monetarist rationale was pointed out according to which prices climbing along an almost vertical aggregate supply curve were the only durable outcome of 'activist' policies. Monetary policies then began to switch from monitoring nominal interest rates to controlling the growth rate of the money supply.

Italy's economic trend of the second half of the 1970s appears to diverge sharply from this anti-inflationary turnabout. Here the political and intellectual opinion had been inclined to believe that welfare and redistribution goals should not be subordinated to the achievement of monetary stability.In the early 1970s, public expenditure had increased to a permanently higher level because of welfare-oriented laws (dealing with pensions, housing, trade unions, rights, etc.), and in 1975, only one year after the first oil shock, a large indexation of wages and salaries had been introduced. In the face of sharp competition triggered by soaring trade deficits across Western non-oil-producing countries, Italian industry chose to rely upon the devaluation of the currency, different forms of public transfers and the expansion of the small-size hidden sector, rather than to boost technological change and promote productive restructuring towards the vastly expanding markets for advanced goods. For its part, the strategy of the monetary authorities was reflecting this attitude in that domestic monetary and foreign exchange policies were oriented to the nominal accommodation of the worsening wage rate and productivity-per-hour differentials with respect to the major competing economies. With regard to this, a major role was played by the poor performance of the 'Domestic Total Credit' (hereafter, DTC), the intermediate target agreed on with the IMF by the Italian government since 1974, which proved itself unable to control the expansion of the money supply and the consequent rise of the inflation rate.

The divergent path of the Italian economy in the late 1970s can be thought of as the failure of the Bank of Italy's attempt to insulate the domestic economy from external shocks by choosing its own inflation rate in the flexible exchange rate regime. By fixing a 'ceiling' in terms of DTC – total financing of the public sector, plus the loans granted to the private sector by the commercial banks and by the Special Credit Institutions (hereafter, SCI) appointed to firms' investment financing, plus bond purchases (see Hodgman and Resek, 1989, pp. 68–71) – the Italian monetary authorities intended to pursue a sustainable balance-of-payments final target. The DTC intermediate target, in so far as it was supposed to limit the domestic 'absorption' by linking the demand for money stock to a tight evolution of the monetary aggregates, might appear to be inspired by the 'Monetarist Approach to the Balance of Payments'. Yet the Bank of Italy has been presenting the choice of this instrument as derived from its own version of the 'Portfolio Choice Model', expressly adapted to the traditional Italian financing model based on non-price credit rationing (stock-market financing is still nowadays of trifling importance to Italian firms). According to the view of the Bank of Italy, the lack of direct control over the monetary base implicit in the DTC targeting would not have been remedied by stressing the indirect mechanism of substitution effects. Quite the contrary, the regulation of aggregate demand and balance-of-payments levels should have been mainly pursued by monitoring the expansionary wealth effect on households' consumption demand due to the increased amount of government bonds issued to finance the budget deficit, so that the contribution of the balance of payments to the adjustment of the monetary base could be obtained. The theoretical rationale was thus put forward according to which the stability of the demand for financial assets (high-powered money, plus bank deposit, plus government bonds) would be guaranteed by commercial banks. These credit institutions were in fact supposed to reshuffle in their portfolios the bank deposits and the excess supply of government bonds poured into the market by the Bank of Italy's restrictive open-market operations so that the households' demand induced by the wealth effect were sterilized and the credit accruing to the firms rationed. Due to the Italian peculiarity of interest-bearing bank deposits, the variations in the interest rates, if anything, would have been limited to the commercial banks' willingness to react to a shortage of liquidity by increasing the rate of interest they paid on deposits (Caranza and Fazio, 1983, pp. 67–8).

The special role thus assigned to the commercial banks to smooth the way between supply and demand in the financial market resulted in the strengthening of their oligopolistic position in the transfer of liquidity from savers to both private and public sectors. The increased influence of commercial banks on the interest rate level created a threat to the performance of financial asset prices acting as an efficient signal in the capital market. To enable the interest rate to remain constant, despite the soaring amount of T-bills issued in the market, a portfolio constraint aimed at enforcing the absorption of bonds by the commercial banks had to be introduced. The consequent fall in the *real* interest rate along with the upward trend of inflation brought about two unwelcome effects. The households' traditional restraint to buy government bonds was even more acute because of the rise in liquidity preference. And firms' demand for funds, which had been inflated by the soaring cost of imports and by the price–wage spiral, went up. Consequently, the outstanding credit 'ceilings' imposed on the commercial banks were not

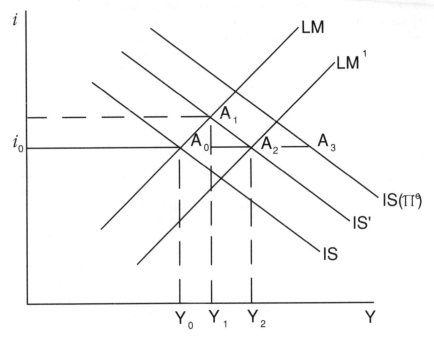

Figure 1.1

effective in restraining the working of the monetary multiplier. In fact, since the commercial banks increased the demand for Central Bank discounts and advances, and their liabilities with foreign financial institutions, the credit expansion was boosted. The ultimate reason was that the DTC target, being matched at different equally compatible proportions between financial assets and monetary base, was not providing a limit for the accommodation by the Bank of Italy of the augmented demand for monetary base, so that the acceleration in the growth rate of money supply ignited inflation to higher rates.

The inflationary escalation in the money supply growth can be sketched in graphical terms (see Figure 1.1) by considering the increase in aggregate demand provoked by the jump in the costs of production as a 'goods market shock' which shifts the IS curve rightwards to IS'. Due to the policy of pegging the interest rate, the new IS–LM short-run equilibrium will be established at A_2 (instead of at A_1). For the LM curve to move down to LM' and intersect the IS' at A_2, the monetary authorities have to let the money supply rise. But this monetary expansion calls forth an increase in price expectations (Π^e), inasmuch as the firms' attempt to enlarge their profit margins has been anticipated. The IS curve shifts then rightwards again (to IS (Π^e)) and the instability process will continue: in fact, for the new short-run equilibrium at A_3 to be reached, another increase in the money supply will be needed.

The Bank of Italy's foreign exchange policy was oriented, after the crisis of the lira in January 1976, to manage the lira's exchange rates upwards with the US dollar to curb the imported inflation, and downwards with the Deutschmark to boost exports. This strategy was in the short run successful in defending the competitiveness of the Italian manufactures and in sustaining firms' profit margins. Yet the inflationary environment sparked off by the unsuccessful working of the monetary mechanism was throwing the economy into the vicious circle of price inflation and currency depreciation, as the automatic transfer of price increases in higher nominal wages continuously annulled the real effects of the devaluation of the lira *vis-à-vis* the other European currencies. Even though no econometric estimate shows a clear causal relationship between the relative consumption prices (internal/foreign) and the exchange rate, a Granger-causality between the exchange rate and the price level due to expectations of future depreciations of the lira should at least have occurred.

It was then clear that the choice of a monetary mechanism based on the pegging of the nominal interest rate rendered extremely loose, despite the administrative controls, the monitoring of the growth rate of the monetary aggregates by means of the DTC intermediate target. Accordingly, the managed exchange rate policy which had been pursued after the lira had previously failed twice to take part in the 'snake' (the first European initiative for an exchange rate co-ordination set up by the countries belonging to the so-called 'DM area') was jeopardized, since the real wage rigidity had been forcing the currency to bear the whole burden of the adjustment.

1.3 Reshaping the monetary mechanism at the inception of the EMS (1979–83)

The switch to an anti-inflationary monetary stance was announced by the Italian monetary authorities in June 1980. This announcement was presented as the necessity to break away from the Treasury, that is to free the Bank of Italy from the requirement to provide unlimited financing of the public deficit. However, the monetary authorities' criticism of public deficits as the main source of instability for the Italian economy cannot be taken for granted.

Even though public expenditure had increased in the 1970s, the hidden taxation brought about by the inflation-induced increases of income levels in nominal terms (the so-called 'fiscal drag') greatly augmented government revenues; therefore, in the second half of the 1970s the public deficits did not exceed 10 per cent of the GNP. As for the financing of these deficits, despite the automatic Central Bank credit extended to the Treasury (up to the limit of 14 per cent of government expenditure) and the obligation of the Bank of Italy to act as the residual purchaser of government bonds, the Treasury's contribution to the monetary base formation showed no signs of rising, since the recourse to restrictive open-market operations allowed the Bank of Italy to reduce its share of public debt to a low of 23.9 per cent in 1979. The additional burden imposed on the bond financing was nonetheless affordable, once the shrinking effect on the Public Sector Borrowing Requirement (PSBR) of the negative real interest payments to bond-holders had been taken into account. Nor could a private sector 'crowding out' effect be claimed, since the cost of credit had been falling in real terms and private firms' investment financing by the SCI had been producing a rationing effect on the credit to the public sector (due to substitution of the loans to the public sector with SCI bonds in the commercial banks' balance sheet).

In fact, the real problem was that both the monetary policy's accommodation of the profit margins' recovery and the fiscal policy's support to households' income levels through public transfers were at odds with the trend towards a strengthened market efficiency that anti-inflationary policies were spreading from the United States and Germany to the other major Western economies. Therefore, the real adjustment of the Italian economy could no longer be postponed.

The accelerating impulse for a radical change in the monetary stance came from two shocks that aggravated an already unstable situation only a few months after the adherence to the EMS: the second oil shock (even worse than the first), and the start of the upward trend of the US dollar (which would last until 1985). The consequent rapid deterioration of the balance of payments (due to the soaring cost of raw material imports and to the tendency of Italian firms to transfer more than one-half of the increases in import prices to the level of manufactures' prices) left no doubt that, given the conditions of the Italian economy, the depreciation of the domestic currency turned rapidly to a 'J curve' effect.

Thus the anti-inflationary strategy put forward by the Bank of Italy stems from long before the commitment to fulfil the obligations implicit in the ERM of the EMS, the reluctant approval of which resulted in the negotiation for the lira of the wider margin of ± 6 per cent (instead of the normal ± 2.25 per cent) since the outset of the system. The preliminary condition to be met for the success of this strategy consisted in the enhancement of the monetary policy's effectiveness by removing inefficiencies both in the financial and the productive structures.

The first objective of the monetary authorities was to set in motion a process of curbing commercial banks' powers of intervention through the creation of a large money market in which the monitoring of the interest rate fixed by demand and supply for funds would supersede the dominant role of commercial banks in the liquidity transmission mechanism. Their expansionary attitude towards the monetary multiplier would then be restrained by the loss of bank deposits provoked by a higher propensity on the part of households to purchase government bonds, the increase of which as a share of the overall PSBR was equally necessary to curb the other domestic channel of monetary base expansion, the Treasury's autonomous creation.

This process was started up by the sharp monetary base restriction implemented from the second half of 1980 (see Table 1.1). In fact, the financial innovation introduced by the Bank of Italy with the creation of two types of T-bills – the short-term BOT (Ordinary Treasury Bill) in 1975, and the medium-term CCT (Treasury Credit Certificate) in 1977, the returns on which were indexed to the return on the BOT, plus a spread, so that capital loss expectations were minimized – was eventually able to foster the enlargement of the money market. Once the average nominal interest rate on the BOT was suddenly pushed up to 19.7 per cent in 1981 (in 1979 it was still only 12.5 per cent), causing the average real interest rate to become positive (in only eighteen months, from June 1980 to

Table 1.1 *Italy: monetary base (MB) and M2A[1] (annual and quarterly[2] % changes)*

		Nominal		Real[3]				Nominal		Real	
		MB	M2A	MB	M2A			MB	M2A	MB	M2A
1979		13.8	20.6	-3.5	3.5	1983	I	21.0	16.6	4.5	0.4
1980		13.9	12.7	-10.8	-11.7		II	18.0	16.1	3.3	1.4
1981		13.3	9.9	-5.4	-8.8		III	15.8	16.6	0.9	1.7
1982		13.4	16.9	-2.3	1.2		IV	15.0	11.5	1.0	-2.5
1983		15.0	11.5	1.0	-2.5	1984	I	12.0	11.9	-1.1	-1.2
1984		14.3	11.2	6.1	3.0		II	12.1	11.3	-1.4	-2.2
1985		17.3	10.0	9.5	2.3		III	12.2	10.7	3.3	1.8
1986		7.1	8.1	0.2	1.2		IV	14.3	11.2	6.1	3.0
1987		10.0	6.8	4.5	1.1	1985	I	16.1	13.0	4.9	1.8
1988		8.5	4.4	2.5	-1.6		II	16.9	13.2	6.3	2.6
1989		12.4	7.4	6.1	1.1		III	17.3	12.9	4.2	-0.2
							IV	17.3	10.0	9.5	2.3
1979	I	13.4	20.7	-1.8	5.6	1986	I	13.0	8.5	4.8	0.3
	II	16.2	20.2	-1.7	4.7		II	10.3	7.6	2.7	-0.1
	III	17.0	20.0	-1.5	4.5		III	8.9	7.3	1.7	0.1
	IV	13.8	20.6	-3.5	3.5		IV	7.1	8.1	0.2	1.2
1980	I	16.4	17.4	-4.5	-3.5	1987	I	8.9	8.5	2.1	1.7
	II	16.0	15.0	-5.6	-6.6		II	11.3	10.2	5.9	4.8
	III	14.9	11.9	-4.7	-7.7		III	12.7	9.2	7.2	3.6
	IV	13.6	12.7	-10.8	-11.7		IV	10.0	6.8	4.5	1.1
1981	I	16.0	12.6	-0.9	-4.3	1988	I	8.8	4.9	1.9	1.0
	II	16.2	11.1	-1.6	-6.4		II	7.5	4.8	1.5	1.2
	III	13.6	10.0	-2.4	-6.0		III	9.7	6.0	3.6	-0.1
	IV	13.3	9.9	-5.4	-8.8		IV	8.5	4.4	2.5	-1.6
1982	I	10.5	8.7	-7.3	-9.1	1989	I	10.7	6.3	4.8	0.4
	II	11.4	10.6	-7.0	-7.8		II	10.4	6.0	3.9	-0.5
	III	13.2	14.2	-6.5	-5.5		III	11.1	4.6	4.7	-1.8
	IV	13.4	16.9	-2.3	1.2		IV	12.4	7.4	6.1	1.1

Notes:
[1] The M2A definition was introduced in 1983; previously, it coincided with the M2 definition.
[2] Quarterly changes refer to the previous years' quarter.
[3] The real values have been calculated by the percentage change in the GDP deflator.
Source: Bank of Italy.

December 1981, it rose from -4.6 to 3.6 per cent), households started switching from bank deposits held as a 'buffer' stock to the now remunerative T-bills (the degree of substitutability with bank deposits is fairly large due to high liquidity and low risk), so that their share of public debt soared from a low of 21.2 per cent in 1989 to 38.3 per cent in 1981. However, even though the intensification of the open-market operations were successfully countering the autonomous Treasury's monetary base creation through its account at the Bank of Italy and the commercial banks' reliance on Bank of Italy's discounts and advances had been curbed by fixing the discount rate above the market rate (so that it turned out to be a 'penalty rate'), the inflationary mechanism was still working (see Chart 1.1).

Table 1.2 *Economic Indicators: France, Germany and Italy*

	Gross product (constant prices) Index numbers: 1980=100 Seasonally adjusted			Gross product per person employed Index numbers: 1980=100 Seasonally adjusted			Unemployment rate (Standardised) Index numbers: 1980=100 Seasonally adjusted			Consumer prices Index numbers 1980=100 Seasonally adjusted			Volume of exports Index numbers: 1980=100			Volume of imports Index number: 1980=100		
	France	Germany	Italy	France	Germany	Italy	France	Germany	Italy	France	Germany	Italy	France	Germany	Italy	France	Germany	Italy
1979	98.4	98.6	95.9	98.1	99.7	96.6	5.9	3.2	7.6	87.9	94.9	82.5	97	104	108	94	98	97
1980	100.0	100.0	100.0	100.0	100.0	100.0	6.3	3.0	7.5	100.0	100.0	100.0	100	100	100	100	100	100
1981	101.2	100.0	101.0	101.6	100.6	100.7	7.4	4.4	8.3	113.1	106.3	117.8	104	107	105	96	95	89
1982	103.8	99.1	101.3	104.3	101.5	101.3	8.1	6.1	9.0	126.6	112.0	137.2	100	110	106	99	96	89
1983	104.5	100.9	102.4	105.8	105.1	102.2	8.3	8.0	9.8	138.6	115.7	157.3	104	109	109	98	100	89
1984	105.8	104.2	105.5	107.8	108.3	104.9	9.7	7.0	10.2	149.2	118.4	174.3	109	120	116	101	105	96
1985	107.8	106.3	108.3	110.1	109.6	107.2	10.2	7.2	10.1	157.9	121.0	190.4	112	128	124	106	110	110
1986	110.3	108.7	111.0	112.5	111.0	109.4	10.4	6.5	10.5	161.9	120.7	201.4	112	129	127	114	117	116
1987	112.5	110.6	114.3	114.4	112.0	112.8	10.5	6.3	11.2	167.2	121.0	211.0	117	132	129	124	122	127
1988	116.3	114.6	118.8	117.4	110.4	115.9	10.0	6.2	11.3	171.4	122.5	221.7	125	141	136	135	130	136
1989	120.3	119.1	122.1	119.2	114.0	115.9	9.6	5.5	10.9	177.7	126.1	236.3	136	153	148	145	140	147

Source: MEI, OECD, IFS, UNMBS

Indeed, the increased oil price and the US dollar appreciation had been putting an additional burden on the manufacturing sector, whereas the wage rate indexation still triggered the price–wage spiral. Although the inflation rate had decreased from 13.0 per cent in 1981 to 14.2 per cent in 1983, the inflation differential with Germany, which was of 13.1 points in 1981, remained as large as 11 points, and even that with France, the other initially weak-currency and high-inflation country of the ERM, amounted to 5 points (see Table 1.2). In the face of the permanently sustained demand for funds by firms, the implementation of the administrative measures decided by the Interministerial Committee on Credit and Savings in December 1982 (the rise of the reserve requirement and its extension to a wider range of banking activities) was ineffective in weakening the ability of the commercial banks to expand loans to and beyond the monetary multiplier ceilings. In fact, the banking institutions were reacting to the 'disintermediation' process in a number of ways: by obtaining liquidity from abroad; by offering new instruments bearing higher returns than the bank deposits (financial innovations such as certificates of deposit, bankers' acceptances, repurchasing agreements); by selling government bonds; and finally – but to a lesser extent, due to the non-price credit rationing – by adjusting the interest paid on bank deposits to the variations of the market rates on T-bills.

On the other hand, for the reduction in the unit cost of production to take place a longer period of time was needed by firms to achieve a faster productivity growth (through capital for labour substitution and workers' mobility) and to take back the real wage flexibility (through the relaxation of the wage indexation). Meanwhile, the weakness of the balance of payments was impinging upon the commitment to the exchange rate pegging. The lira's exchange rates had then to be renegotiated in the four revisions of the ERM parity grid implemented from 1979 to 1983 (see Table 1.3). Surely, according to the inflation differentials, the devaluation of the lira would have been even more frequent if the change of the monetary mechanism from administrative controls to the market forces had not been slowed down by the 'ceiling' on the commercial banks' loans which was maintained until 1983) and, most of all, if the capital controls had not discouraged speculative assaults against the currency.

The extent to which capital controls have allowed the Bank of Italy to retard the upsurge of the realignments (and to devaluate the currency to a lesser degree than the inflation differentials would have required) can be appreciated by analysing the 'interest parity condition' (hereafter, IPC) between Italy and Germany. This condition, which represents the difference between the domestic-foreign differential and the per cent change of the exchange rate, can also be expressed as the sum of the 'covered' interest differential and the difference between the forward discount and the per cent change of the exchange rate.[1]

The estimate of the IPC relative to the inception phase of the EMS presents negative values, thus showing that the rate of depreciation of the lira with respect to the Deutschmark has continuously fallen short of the nominal interest differential (see the IPC equation in note 1 and data in Table 1.4). These deviations from the equilibrium IPC are mainly determined by the negative sign of the 'covered' interest differential. In fact, the high levels of the forward discount lira/

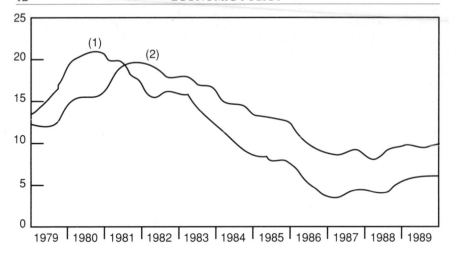

Chart 1.1 *Italy: Inflation rate(1); BOT interest rate (2)*
Source: Bank of Italy.

Table 1.3

Dates of realignments	24/9 1979	30/11 1979	22/3 1981	5/10 1981	22/2 1982	14/6 1982	21/3 1983	21/7 1985	7/4 1986	4/8 1986	12/1 1987
Belgian franc	0.0	0.0	0.0	0.0	-8.5	0.0	+1.5	+2.0	+1.0	0.0	+2.0
Danish kroner	-2.9	-4.8	0.0	0.0	-3.0	0.0	+2.5	+2.0	+1.0	0.0	0.0
German mark	+2.0	0.0	0.0	+5.5	0.0	+4.25	+5.5	+2.0	+3.0	0.0	+3.0
French franc	0.0	0.0	0.0	-3.0	0.0	-5.75	-2.5	+2.0	-3.0	0.0	0.0
Irish punt	0.0	0.0	0.0	0.0	0.0	0.0	-3.5	+2.0	0.0	-8.0	0.0
Italian lira	0.0	0.0	-6.0	-3.0	0.0	-2.75	-2.5	-6.0	0.0	0.0	0.0
Dutch guilder	0.0	0.0	0.0	+5.5	0.0	+4.25	+3.5	+2.0	+3.0	0.0	+3.0

Source: EC.

Deutschmark have reflected the lack of confidence that inflation expectations has
been causing in the lira's exchange rate expectations. Owing to the sharp restriction in the money supply pursued by the Bank of Italy, the Italian money and
financial markets joined the upward trend of the German rates of return aimed at
following the soaring US interest rates (the Federal Reserve's monetary tightening
augmented the prime rate – in nominal terms and in real terms, respectively, from
12.7 and 6.0 per cent in 1979 to 18.8 and 10.1 in 1981). However large was the
jump in the Italian rates of return, the interest differentials with Germany were in
those years not as large as needed to match the forward discount values (see Table
1.4).

Table 1.4 *Interest differential, forward discount and exchange rate (Italy – Germany)*

	$(i-i_G)$	FD		$\dot{s}$
1979	3.3	7.1	80/79	3.9
1980	6.4	11.5	81/80	6.7
1981	7.6	11.2	82/81	10.8
1982	10.5	13.4	83/82	6.7
1983	12.1	12.6	84/83	3.8
1984	9.3	9.9	85/84	5.4
1985	8.5	8.5	86/85	5.6
1986	7.1	8.2	87/86	5.1
1987	6.2	6.9	88/87	2.8
1988	5.4	6.3	89/88	- 1.6
1989	3.9	5.0	90/89	0.3
1990	2.2	3.4		–

Notes: i: three-months BOT interest rate (net of tax); i_G: German three-months interbank rate; FD: forward discount lira/Deutschmark; $\dot{s}$: ex post per cent change in the lira/Deutschmark exchange rate.
Source: Bank of Italy

The negative 'covered' interest differentials with Germany cast light on the effectiveness of capital controls by permitting the decouplement of the Italian from the foreign interest rates. Since outflows aimed at exploiting the outward arbitrage opportunities were in fact impeded, domestic rates of return did not need to soar and were then shielded from excess volatility (Giavazzi and Giovannini, 1989, pp.172–79).

1.4 The nominal and real adjustment during the second phase of the EMS (1984–86)

The U-turn towards a tight money creation eventually succeeded in reversing inflationary expectations. The credibility of the Bank of Italy's strategy was in fact established when the two necessary structural changes in the financial and in the productive sectors took place almost at the same time.

As for the first, the key-rate on T-bills, which had re-ascended to positive values in real terms since 1981–82, stimulated the reshuffling in households' portfolios from bank deposits to government bonds. The consequent growth of the money market permitted a sharp reduction in the money financing public deficits and eased the introduction in 1984 of a second intermediate target, dubbed

M2A. Since this target represents the monetary aggregate closer to free reserves (it includes the monetary base, bank deposits and the liquidity raised by banks through short-term operations with the public), the monetary authorities were finally able to take back a sufficient degree of control on the money supply growth (see Table 1.1). From then on, the Italian monetary authorities have controlled the LBN (Net Bank Liquidity, the free reserves net of the amount drained by the Bank of Italy) by absorbing the excess liquidity through the OPCT (*pronti contro termine* operations, that is temporary sales to the banks of government bonds at the market interest rate on the T-bills), so that the commercial banks' liquidity has been stabilized at a constant level. As the expansion of free reserves pursued by the commercial banks was restrained, the discontinuity between the newly created money market and the credit market was brought to an end, and the credibility of the anti-inflationary monetary stance was strengthened.

As for the second, the most significant fall in the inflation rate occurred just after the tough stance taken in 1984 by the Italian government towards wage indexation. The growth of CPI decreased from 14 per cent at the end of 1983 to 5 per cent at the end of 1986; in addition, the rate of change of the cost of labour per production unit went down from 17.8 in the period 1981–83 to a low of 6.4 in the period 1984–88. The smaller fall registered in the cost of labour per unit (from 17.6 to 9.2) indicates that the rationalisation in the use of the labour force played an important role. In fact, the rate of change of the productivity of labour, which had been negative in the first period (-0.1), shows a positive value (+2.6) in the second one. The real wage downward adjustment and the consequent decrease in the inflation expectations brought about a slowdown in the devaluation process (see Table 1.3), which squeezed firms' profit margins and put under pressure the competitiveness of the manufacturing sector. Yet, as the low unemployment cost of the deflation demonstrates (the rise of the unemployment rate measured as a percentage of the reduction obtained in the inflation differential with Germany amounted to only 1.96 in the period 1980–87), the profit cushion set up by firms during the years of accommodating monetary policy provided them with a sufficient amount of liquidity to face credit rationing and prevented unit costs of production, still exceeding the slow productivity recovery, from tipping the economy into a recession (Giavazzi-Spaventa, 1989, pp.151–7).

The fall in the inflation rate (see Chart 1.2) determined by the nominal and real adjustment was registered only partially by the nominal interest rates. The BOT rate kept rising in real terms and the 'covered' interest differential with Germany became on the annual average no more than one point lower than the forward discount lira/Deutschmark, which drastically fell to a lower level beginning from 1983–84 due to the slowdown in the lira depreciation expectations (see Table 1.4). From then on, the deviation from zero of the IPC reversed from a negative to a positive sign, thus corresponding to positive values in the second term of the equation; that is to say that the forward exchange rate lira/Deutschmark has been a biased indicator of the future spot exchange rate.[2]

Interest differentials were larger than the lira's *ex-post* exchange rate variations not only with respect to Germany but also *vis-à-vis* the United States and most of the EMS countries. A possible reason for these deviations from the IPC is the

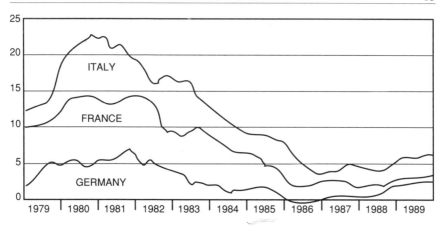

Chart 1.2 *Inflation rates (annual per cent change)*
Source: Bundesbank, Banque de France, Banca d'Italia.

presence of a risk premium (Artis and Taylor, 1989, p.203). In fact, since 1984 the values of the forward discount lira/deutschmark have exceeded the *ex-post* per cent lira depreciation, thus indicating that financial markets did not have faith in the lira's parities. Moreover, even though the annual mean values of the forward discount appear to have slowly decreased (see Table 1.4.), on the occasion of the two major speculative attacks against the lira in the period 1985–87 the forward discount sharply peaked (Farina, 1990 b, p.374). Therefore, it can be said that the capital movements' liberalization process, which began in 1985, was not considered in the Euromarkets as the sign of an augmented monetary stability in Italy. In order to counteract exchange rate speculation, the Bank of Italy has often made recourse to the restoration of current account restrictions.[3]

However, the dismantling manoeuvre of the capital restrictions was also slowed down by the need to curb the external creation of monetary base due to the commercial banks' tendency to obtain loans from abroad in the attempt to overcome the ceiling on the Nel Bank Liquidity imposed by the Bank of Italy. In fact, the administrative control of the PNEAC (the Net Foreign Position of the Commercial Banks) was reintroduced in 1986 and 1987 for short periods of time, and then replaced – due to capital movements' liberalization process – by the extension of the reserve requirement to the commercial banks' fund-collecting in the foreign money markets. The presence of potential arbitrage opportunities relative to inward capital movements suggests that the interest differentials are also to be traced back to the Bank of Italy's strategy aimed at the fulfilment of the final targets of monetary stability and balance of payments.

The continuous recourse to relevant open-market sales of government bonds through which the money supply control was pursued throughout the 1980s by the Bank of Italy – more than a risk premium raising the rate of return of the high share of government bonds held in the portfolios[4] – seems to provide a reason for the high level at which the short-term interest rate has maintained (See Chart 1.1

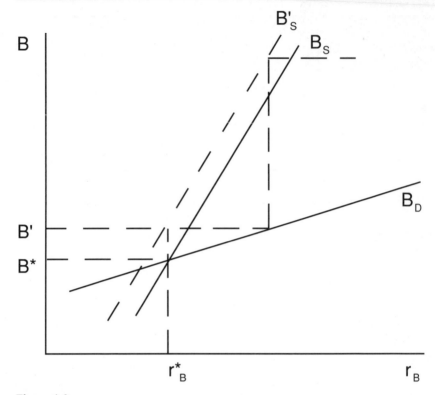

Figure 1.2

Table 1.5 *Italy: capital movements (balance) (bn. lire)*

	Banking capitals	Direct investments	Investment in financial assets	Private loans	Public loans	Other non-banking capitals	Total
1980	6.932	- 145	- 793	2.050	3.081	-1.691	9.434
1981	-1.521	- 310	- 460	6.440	5.045	510	9.704
1982	-3.062	- 567	- 509	4.705	3.204	-1.899	1.872
1983	4.996	-1.418	353	411	2.789	- 522	6.609
1984	5.138	-1.199	173	-2.055	4.465	-1.321	5.201
1985	-5.299	-1.430	717	351	4.392	2.162	893
1986	6.454	-3.987	-1.555	109	2.733	-1.515	2.239
1987	5.573	2.341	-9.618	5.169	5.788	2.850	12.103
1988	10.224	1.729	430	6.045	2.869	340	21.637
1989	14.979	63	4.750	16.842	1.303	-2.620	35.317

Source: Bank of Italy.

and Table 1.4). Since the presence of the Bank of Italy as a buyer of T-bills in the auctions has continued despite the so-called 'divorce' from the Treasury, the negative balance between purchases in the auctions and sales in the secondary market has often brought about a large restriction in portfolio liquidity; consequently, at the opening of the successive auction the Treasury was forced to push up the whole structure of interest rates. The uneven upward trend followed by the interest rates suggests that a process of 'financial instability' was then established in the T-bills market, depending on the high ratio of bond-financing of the PSBR. As the increase in the rate of return implied an almost proportional increase in the amount of T-bills that has to be issued to service the outstanding (and the currently created) debt, in the bond/interest rate plan (sketched in Figure 1.2), the interest elasticity of the supply of bonds (B_s) is positive and higher than the interest elasticity of the demand (B_D). Therefore, each restrictive impulse triggered by an open-market operation ends up in a multiple increase in the interest rate needed for the automatically augmented supply of bonds to be matched by the demand for bonds. In Figure 1.2, the upward shift of the supply curve to B'_s caused by an open-market restrictive operation determines – at the equilibrium interest rate r^*_B – the augmented supply of bonds B'_s. But this larger amount of T-bills poured into the market could be matched by an equal demand only at a higher interest rate, thus automatically raising the supply of bonds

1.5 The monetary management in the third phase of the EMS (1987–91)

The tentative explanation can be put forward according to which the fulfilment of the intermediate target represented by a tight money creation has been too much pursued by means of the operative instrument of T-bills open market operation. High interest rates in Italy appear less as the result of the exogenous determination of the interest rates' level in a 'small open economy' like Italy once the financial liberalization process was accelerated, and more due to the utilisation of a unique instrument – the interest rate – for the pursuit of two targets, the monetary base and the exchange rate targets (Farina, 1990a, pp.205–6).

In fact, the interest rates of the money market have been raised above the level needed for the sustenance of the balance of payments, that is to compensate the loss of competitiveness of Italian exports created by the lira's overvaluation. This overshooting of the interest rates is demonstrated by the amount of capital inflows attracted by the broad Italian interest differentials, which became larger than the gap to be filled in the trade account. Beginning in 1987, not only has the credit obtained by commercial banks in the foreign financial markets (Banking Capitals) triggered the continuous rise in the external channel of monetary base creation, but so, too, has the arrival of foreign private investments – loans to Italian private and public companies and, more recently, investments in financial assets such as purchases of government bonds (see Table 1.6).

In effect, the nature of the EMS has evolved in the last years of the eighties, mainly as a result of capital flows moving towards the divergent countries' financial markets. Since in initially high inflation and weak currency countries – first of all, France and Italy – monetary policy has gained growing credibility and a positive shift in the exchange rate expectations held in the European financial markets has occurred.

The strengthening of the Italian currency inside the ERM, while smoothing the transition to the complete deregulation of the capital market, has called for an augmented control on the domestic money creation. Faced with growing capital inflows, the Bank of Italy's monetary management aimed at limiting the growth of M2A within the programmed range target of 6–9 per cent by alternating two manoeuvres: the sterilization of excessive increases in the monetary base caused by capital inflows and the non-accommodation of excess demand for lira. The first manoeuvre consisted of allowing the accumulation of foreign currencies (first of all, the base currency of the EMS) in the international reserves of the Bank of Italy, but draining from the domestic channels of money creation, so that money supply growth was rigorously controlled and the domestic-foreign differentials were not affected. The second one consisted in impeding the accumulation of excess demand for lira, thus letting the currency appreciate on the upper side of the bilateral band, provided that the competitiveness of Italian exports did not markedly diminish. Whether the absorption of the excess supply of foreign currencies was promptly impeded or subsequently compensated through sterilization, the monetary management was anyway orientated towards the restriction of the monetary base, as negative per cent variations in all the quarters of 1988 and in two quarters of 1989 demonstrate (see Table 1.1). Given the stability of the lira parities and favourable external conditions like the oil counter-shock and the US dollar depreciation, there was probably some room in 1988 and 1989 for the achievement of a higher GNP through the determination of lower interest rates level.

Beginning in 1990, the shrinking of the interest differential with Germany started, as the combined effect of the structural changes consisting in the positive reaction of the lira's exchange rates to the integration in the European financial markets and the German unification process. The reduction in the lira/ Deutschmark forward discount along with the fall in the risk premium required in the Euromarket started with the augmented credibility of the Bank of Italy's commitment to stability of exchange rates and has continued after the further positive signal given by the lira joining the narrow bilateral band of the ERM in January 1990 (Farina, 1990b, pp.381–86). The diminished uncertainty on the lira's parities transmitted to the domestic financial market also by virtue of the completion of the financial liberalization in the first half of 1990.

The full abolition of capital controls has caused the quantity of money to be endogenously determined in the fixed exchange rates regime, so that the monetary authorities' control of the overall money creation has sharply reduced. The Bank of Italy's sterilization manoeuvre of foreign financial investments and funds collected abroad by the Italian firms and banks (because of the lower cost of money) became less effective, and short term interest rates started moving downward. Finally, after the German unification shock caused the money supply to grow faster, the Bundesbank has regulated the rise in interest rates triggered by the

Table 1.6 *Italy: monetary base creation (variations; bn. lire)*

	Foreign	Treasury			Advances to commercial banks	Other factors	Total
		PSBR	Non-money financing	Total			
1980	708	37.018	27.278	9.740	-2.576	-3	7.869
1981	25	53.293	39.060	14.233	119	-5.738	8.639
1982	-5.647	72.799	60.123	12.676	638	2.669	10.336
1983	8.840	88.260	83.746	4.514	-3	-747	12.604
1984	5.141	95.695	85.668	10.027	-218	-1.103	13.847
1985	-13.677	122.613	95.094	27.519	5.880	-646	19.076
1986	3.543	110.159	99.165	10.994	-4.334	-1.003	9.200
1987	6.756	114.250	105.078	9.172	-729	-1.253	13.946
1988	10.947	125.643	122.895	2.748	-30	-708	12.957
1989	14.971	133.798	127.416	6.382	1.203	-2.019	20.537

Source: Bank of Italy.

increase both in the private and public demand levels. The consequent further reduction in the interest differential with Germany has then drastically narrowed the degree of autonomy in monetary and foreign exchange policy so far retained by the Bank of Italy.

1.6 The impact of the EMS on Italy's macroeconomic performance

Let us begin by observing that, had the EMS not been introduced, higher price instability and a slower growth rate would probably have prevailed in Europe. As for price instability, if the flexible exchange rates regime had continued and the divergent countries had kept choosing their own monetary targets, inflation rates in Europe would have been much higher than the ones corresponding to the natural rate of unemployment: in a model simulating the non-cooperative free floating among the ERM currencies, inefficient economic performances have in fact been obtained (Begg and Wiplosz, 1987, pp. 201–3). Moreover, the inflation rate of the best performer would have also been affected: the comparison between a game in which Italy commits its money supply to fixing the exchange rate with Germany and a game in which Italy takes it as an instrument (that is, no commitment to defend the exchange rate is announced), shows that in the second case an anti-inflationary money supply targeting pursued by Germany results in being completely undermined (Canzonieri and Henderson, 1988, pp.115–21). As for the output-inflation trade off, it would not have improved either. In the case of divergent countries autonomously pursuing deflationary policies, disruptive competition would have probably arisen among members each simultaneously trying to impose its own monetary tightening at the expense of the others. It is not surprising that a non–cooperative game modelled between Germany and a weak-currency country like France and Italy ends up in a competitive deflation, with losses in output much larger than in the case of a currency agreement or a bargaining in which Germany dictates monetary policy (Collins, 1988, pp.119–23).

The question whether a free floating of the lira *vis-à-vis* the ERM currencies was a viable alternative for Italy might also be asked. Owing to the prerogative to choose its own inflation rate guaranteed by a flexible exchange rate, a lower unemployment rate could have been selected by the political process and implemented by the Bank of Italy. Had then Italy adopted a managed exchange rate, higher employment and growth rate levels might have been reached. Indeed, the pegging of the lira to the Deutschmark brought about the transfer to Germany not just of monetary policy but also the production and distribution decisions which are strictly connected to the choice of the price standard. Moreover, the lira's real over-valuation contributed to trigger the rise in German exports, thus facilitating the strengthening of the oligopolistic position of the German industry inside Europe, and worsened the Italian current account as a percentage of the GDP.

Anyway, no alternative view happened to be more convincing than the theoretical underpinnings of the Bank of Italy's decision to make monetary stability the first priority so that cost and productivity differentials of the Italian economy *vis-à-vis* its major competitors could be reduced. Against the view supporting an output-inflation trade off autonomously chosen by Italy, the Italian monetary authorities have repeatedly pointed out that in the case the Italian economy had not bound to the Bundesbank's restrictive monetary stance, higher employment and welfare levels allowed by an accommodating money creation could not have lasted beyond the short run. Quite the opposite, an inflationary environment would have established in Italy and a run on the lira would have soon followed in the European financial markets.

The outlook with regard to the Italian performance after more than a decade of involvement with the EMS is mixed. Since the stagnation suffered during the inception phase (1979–84), Italy's GNP growth recovered during the second phase at annual rates above 3 per cent in real terms. Yet the trend of a number of important variables is worrying. Although the productivity growth has improved along a smooth course, the slow acceleration in the productive investment growth rate has not proved sufficient to absorb at least part of the high level to which the unemployment climbed since 1982–83. Meanwhile, after having fallen in the period 1984–87, the inflation rate has remained in between 5 and 7 per cent with a differential with Germany and France of around 3 points (see Chart 1.2). On the other hand, the T-bills rate increases caused the debt service to reach three-quarters of the overall public deficit. Thus, the public debt now amounts to the 103 per cent of the GNP and the ratio public deficit/GNP still exceeds 10 per cent despite repeated cuts in public expenditure.

As for the trade account, the recent improvement in the Italian share of world trade cannot be taken as a long-run trend which might further the re-equilibration in the current account balance. Italy's propensity to import remains very high, and the rise in exports since 1988 have been limited to the traditional consumer goods. Moreover, the Italian science-based sectors are still unable to withstand the non-price competition taking place in the high-tech goods markets (the high-tech goods/overall manufactured goods ratio of the Italian exports is presently one of the lowest in Europe at 7.8 per cent). Therefore, as a result of the larger convergence of the French economy on Germany's figures, Italy's performance in comparison to the French one appears to be slightly better only with regard to the GNP growth rate, this is much less satisfying when one considers the unemployment rate, the inflation rate and the public debt/GNP ratio.

It is hard to disentangle the direct influence of the EMS on the Italian macroeconomic trend of the 1980s, and even more difficult to assess how much of the lower inflation and exchange rate stability may be considered as benefits accruing by means of the EMS, and how much of the rise in the unemployment rate and of the exploding public debt due to interest payments are costs to be attributed to it. To answer these questions, the issue of the nature of the co-ordination between the two initially large high-inflation and weak-currency countries of the ERM or of the EMS (France and Italy) on the one side, and the so called Deutschmark zone (Germany and the small countries highly integrated with this centre-country) on the other side, has to be tackled.

The EMS has alternately been evaluated, by means of game theory applications, either as a system of exchange rate co-operation (e.g., see Fratianni and Von Hagen, 1990) or as an instrument of monetary discipline, that is the choice of trading away monetary sovereignty to the Bundesbank in order to take advantage of its unquestioned anti-inflationary reputation (e.g., see Giavazzi and Pagano, 1988). Both these proposed interpretations appear too extreme to accommodate the complex interplay among the features of the EMS.

According to the co-operation view, two main goals may be attributed to the partners of the EMS: to internalize the overspill effects of uncoordinated monetary stances, and to set up a coordinated response of the European currencies to the US dollar fluctuations. The conservation of monetary sovereignty by all countries is then assumed. In the case of Italy, this assumption fits with the situation that the drift towards the anti-inflationary strategy was an autonomous decision of the Italian monetary authorities and the reversal of price expectations arose out of the structural changes which occurred in the internal labour and money markets. As previously argued, by means of delay, less than 'purchasing power parity' and restoring devaluations the Italian monetary authorities succeeded in obtaining the revision of wage indexation and by putting the industrial sector under pressure of the deterioration of price competitiveness, and by means of the reformed money market mechanism to regain control over the monetary multiplier.

Yet, monetary sovereignty is at odds with the lira's experience inside the ERM. The trend towards monetary stability would probably not occur if the Bank of Italy had not utilised the fixed exchange rate regime as the external constraint on their monetary management. Once the influence of the wage and interest rate signals were restored in the labour and money markets, respectively, lower inflation and the reduction in the risk premium on the lira permitted the passage from a frequently adjusted to the growingly stable exchange rate. Even though the progressive rise in the Italian interest rates has been endogenously determined, the management of the interest differentials helped in the defence of the lira parities despite the progressive abolition of capital controls. Thus, the co-operation view has to be rejected, inasmuch the monetary independence has been fully retained only by the Bundesbank. Besides, the objective of a co-ordinated response of European currencies to US dollar fluctuations mainly reflected the interest of Germany, whose financial market was the more exposed to the instability provoked by speculative capital flows originating in the US dollar area.

Quite the opposite with respect to the previous view, is the monetary discipline view which maintains that was just the stringency of the convergence mechanism embodied in the EMS rules of the game to allow Italy's and France's monetary authorities to 'import' the Bundesbank anti-inflationary reputation and gain credibility for their monetary management. However, as shown by the Bank of Italy's reliance, in the first phase of the EMS on devaluations and internal (credit market) as well as external (capital market) controls and in the second and third phases on the maintenance of an interest differential with Germany larger than the one required by the IPC, the high-inflation members were not subjected to binding regulations. In other words, the commitment to monetary stability did not imply full surrender of monetary policy autonomy.

A more appropriate characterization of the EMS may be the following. Whenever a currency agreement is plagued by large cost differential performances, even if the divergent countries participate after having made the decision not to accommodate the internal distributive conflict by recourse to money expansions and devaluations, a credible price standard to which peg currencies is needed. It can then be understood why the 'redundancy problem' typical of this and of every fixed exchange rate regime (all but one country must peg their exchange rates, so that there is an extra instrument with respect to the number of policy targets) has been solved by singling out the Deutschmark as the core-currency. However, the additional requirement of asymmetry in the functioning of the system cannot be done without. In fact, if the setting of the currency agreement is symmetric, it can happen that the central bank of a divergent country proves itself unable to resist the output–inflation trade off resulting from the domestic distributive conflict, and the central banks of the other countries co-operate and allow the needed monetary expansion (Rogoff, 1985).

In the EMS case, this possible counterproductive outcome of monetary cooperation agreements was avoided not only by the precondition represented by the Bundesbank's reputation to stick to a deflationary monetary growth but also by the recourse to asymmetric obligations among the members (Farina, 1991, pp.444–49). So that the Deutschmark's function of nominal anchor could be carried out without disturbances, the privilege has been granted to the Deutschmark nominally not to move its ECU parity in the event of realignments, and the faculty of the Bundesbank to fix in full independence its monetary stance and not be affected by the other members' increasing use of the Deutschmark for reserve holdings and interventions.

Therefore, contrary to the monetary discipline view which underestimates the room for manoeuvre allowed by the EMS rules of the game, it can be said that the slow convergence to the Bundesbank's tight monetary stance met both the divergent countries' problem to cope with the sluggish adjustment of cost differential performances and the interest of Germany's highly integrated corporate and banking system.

As for the first, central banks in the divergent countries like France and Italy utilized the exchange rate as an external constraint. This strategy was smoothed in the inception phase of the EMS by frequent devaluations, means of capital controls and afterwards mainly by interest differentials, aimed not only at counteracting the exchange rate devaluation expectations but also to manage the convergence process to the Bundesbank restrictive monetary policy. As for the second, the consequent Deutschmark real devaluation boosted Germany's export-led growth, while the consolidation of the German financial market was triggered by the accumulation of foreign reserves. The asymmetry embodied in the EMS mainly consisted of the Bundesbank's autonomous monetary policy: interventions in US dollars in order to defend the Deutschmark/dollar parity have been very frequent, while intramarginal interventions in lire or in other ERM currencies have rarely been carried out and have always been promptly sterilized by open-market operations (Russo and Tullio, 1988, pp. 310–7). The monetary discipline view is flawed by not providing a reason for German interest in the EMS and by not taking into account that margins of monetary policy autonomy have been retained by the divergent countries (Farina, 1990b, pp.376–81).

The EMS can then be regarded as a co-operative agreement but based on asymmetric obligations. The co-operative feature of the EMS consisted of the exchange between Germany providing the public good of low inflation through the Deutschmark as the nominal anchor and the divergent countries helping Germany to counteract the dollar fluctuations *vis-à-vis* the Deutschmark by the commitment to monetary stability. As for the asymmetric functioning of the EMS, the so called 'German leadership' has to be considered a structural condition of the EMS functioning. The political decision taken by the divergent countries to meet and even out the cost and price differentials implied the acceptance of asymmetric obligations in participating in the ERM of the EMS. As is well known, the divergence indicator designated to single out the divergent currency on which to impose the burden of adjustment has never been employed, and in all the realignments, except the 1987 one, the other currencies have been required to devaluate *vis-à-vis* the Deutschmark.

In this respect, the case of Italy is particularly telling. The political choice to stop the wage-prices spiral and the money financing of public deficits has found in the slow monetary growth dictated by the Bundesbank the external constraint needed for imposing internally the output-inflation trade off required by the need to resist devaluations. Instruments like capital controls and interest differentials have been used not as a substitute but as a complement for the anti-inflationary monetary stance which has stimulated the restructuring and the consequent gains in productivity inside the manufacturing sectors (Farina, 1990b, pp.386–90).

Therefore, it can be said that the evolution of the EMS towards virtually fixed exchange rates was favoured by the overlapping of the German national interest with the general interest to create an area of monetary stability in Europe. From the viewpoint of a divergent country like Italy, the real question to be answered then lies in the evaluation of the EMS impact on the adjustment strategy decided by the Italian monetary authorities. In other words, the asymmetric functioning of the EMS calling forth a degree of deflation sharper than that autonomously planned by the Bank of Italy may have provoked a smaller GNP growth rate.

The thesis has been put forward that the performance of the Italian economy has been aggravated by the German strategy to strengthen its leadership in the EMS. On one hand, the independence retained by Germany in fixing the monetary stance has been questioned on the grounds that restrictive money creation enables Germany to sustain a non-inflationary growth through trade surpluses at the expense of the growth rates of the other EMS countries (De Cecco, 1989, pp.92–6). On the other hand, the hegemonic status of Germany is neither supported by a demand-pull function (as in the United States by means of their structural deficit in the Bretton Woods system) nor by a financial role (Germany's universal bank and institutional intermediaries are far from being financial centres generating liquidity for the other EMS members) (Guerrieri and Padoan, 1989, p.12).

It is true that Italian trade imbalances with Germany turned out to be sustainable by means of external circumstances: the rise in the US growth rate and the US dollar appreciation until 1985 was of great importance especially to Italian exports. Italy, among the ERM countries, has in fact the highest expenditure elasticities and is the only economy with a larger export responsiveness to changes in price competitiveness with the non-ERM OECD countries than with the ERM ones (Vona and Bini Smaghi, 1988, p.151). Yet, a faster GNP growth rate would have been incompatible with goals to control the wage and price dynamics and to contrast the deterioration of the terms of trade. As previously argued, only in the last years a higher GNP expansion would have been allowed by the growing stability of the lira parities. Therefore, however sluggish, German demand growth has impinged upon the Italian trade balance, which is deteriorating following a 1 per cent reduction in the level of German domestic aggregate demand, just as if a 6 per cent devaluation of the lira had occurred (Bini Smaghi and Vona, 1988, p.307). However unequally distributed the burden of the adjustment has been in the event of realignments (with the consequent overall loss of competitiveness amounting to 12 per cent with respect to Germany) the existence of an additional cost such as a slower growth rate inflicted by the EMS participation in the Italian deflationary process seems to be excluded.

The lack of an engine of growth was anyway a major weakness in the EMS members' expansionary trend and might even aggravate on the road to EMU. Whereas the role of the United States as a creator of demand for the European Community with further decline due to the need to sustain exports by means of a depreciated dollar, Germany is not willing to renege price stability as the prior objective of its monetary policy.

1.7 Italy's monetary policy and the economic and monetary unification process

The German unification process, by obliging the Bundesbank to cope with the problem of growing monetary instability, has accelerated the tendency towards a more symmetric EMS which began in 1987 with the strengthening of the divergent countries' currencies inside the ERM parity grid. These developments are heavily impinging on Phase 2 of the transition to EMU which started on 1 July 1990. As previously said, the German real interest rate has risen, due to the sharp augmentation in investment demand brought about by the restructuring of the Eastern landers' economy and the Bundesbank has been obliged to make recourse by raising the nominal rates, in order to curb the increase in the inflation rate caused by the looser control on money creation by the Bundesbank. Quite the opposite with respect to the downward line-up of inflation and interest differentials towards German figures was expected during Phase 2, Germany is now triggering an interest rates' upward trend in the European financial markets.

This changed environment in which the Bank of Italy operates is doomed to definitively abolish the margins of monetary policy's autonomy with regard to the flexibility of interest rates. The contraction in the interest differential with Germany, no larger than three points at the end of 1991, matches both the reduced inflation differential and the augmented credibility of the Italian monetary authorities' commitment to exchange rates stability. But the stubborn inflation rate is still almost four points higher than in France, presently the best inflation performer in the EMS. Owing to inflationary expectations, revealed by the lessened reaction of long term interest rates to short term rates' variations, interest expectations are upward moving in the Italian money and financial markets. Therefore, the reduction in interest rates which is needed for boosting the industrial recovery will be postponed until the inflation rate starts falling again.

The Community decision to follow a gradualist approach to EMU does not seem to favour the Italian monetary authorities' commitment to accomplish the convergence process of the economy. The viewpoint according to which the complete harmonization of monetary and fiscal policies by the divergent countries is a precondition to the leap to EMU, is at variance with the credibility gained by the Bank of Italy. However slow the Italian government's shift is to a budget surplus aimed at compensating the T-bills issues financing the huge interests payments, so that the public debt could start going down, the Bank of Italy's reliability cannot be doubted. After the seignorage had been drastically reduced during the eighties, the average life of the public debt has already been lengthened and the abolition of the automatic money-financing of the Treasury will soon be implemented. Moreover, the monetary mechanism will be adjusted to the European standards by means of reform of the reserve requirements imposed on banks and of the taxation on bank deposits.

The main tenet of the gradualist view is that budgetary policies in divergent countries might generate financial instability if a rapid transition to EMU were implemented. Once financial markets completely trust in the exchange rate fixity, governments troubled by huge public debts might be taken by the temptation to put aside expenditure cuts and keep making recourse to borrowing. Public debt issued by different countries, because of the absence of risk premia, would then be considered perfectly substitutable, so that interest rates would be pushed up in the whole area rather than just in the borrowing country. The implicit assumption is that neither a Treaty on EMU forbidding the Eurofed to accumulate national public debts and to bail out governments, or granting the Eurofed full independence in the fixing of the monetary stance, could restrain overborrowing. Instead, the Eurofed would finally be forced to inject more liquidity in order to prevent the credibility of a particular country being jeopardized and financial instability developing. A European central bank entitled with the power to run monetary policy at the Community level while fiscal policy continues to be decided at the national level, would not be effective therefore. The establishment of Eurofed has been postponed to Phase 3 in which – after the passage to irrevocably fixed exchange rates – the common currency will be introduced.[5] However, it has to be reckoned that in the present more symmetric EMS, a source of instability is also represented by the recent evolution experienced by capital markets in countries like Britain, Germany and France. Financial innovations and deregulation processes have brought about higher substitutability between money and the very liquid financial assets created by the non-banking intermediaries, which in turn has augmented the instability of the demand for money function in these countries. Since the M1 correlation with final targets like the GNP is less predictable, central banks have been forced to monitor broader monetary aggregates, the control on which is still much looser (Goodhart, 1989, Ch.IV). Therefore, the control on the domestic component of the monetary base, in spite of sound fiscal policies, has also been undermined in these countries.

Sources of monetary and financial instability are then not only present in the traditional divergent countries but are widely spread inside the EMS. During Phase 2, even the Bundesbank might lose independence with respect to the other EMS countries' central banks, due to its difficult control on the broad monetary aggregate M3 which it has been compelled to choose as intermediate target. In Phase 3, as a consequence of asymmetric velocity changes among national moneys, a European central bank entitled to fix the money growth rate for the whole area might be in trouble when the monetary growth rate for each single country has to be set. Thus, the reason why Germany has endorsed the gradualist approach and opposed a rapid transition to EMU mainly lies in the Bundesbank's willingness to keep full monetary policy independence and enhance the Deutschmark's role as reserve currency (breaking the European dependence on the US dollar) before the ECU will be established as the European common currency in Phase 3.[6]

Therefore, whereas the absence of a common monetary policy and of rigid regulations during Phase 2 meets German interest, the consequent requirement to achieve full convergence as a pre-condition to EMU does not properly serve the interest of the traditional divergent countries. Provided that the present ERM parity grid – in order to preserve financial markets' credibility – will become the irrevocably fixed exchange rates of the EMU, Italian firms have to bear the burden of competitive losses accumulated from the beginning of the last ERM realignment in 1987 (the correction in the lira's central parities which in January 1990 accompanied the passage to the narrow band was in fact very small). The other EMS countries' opposition to allow Germany to curb inflationary tensions by means of a Deutschmark nominal revaluation *vis-à-vis* other currencies of the ERM does in fact waive a possible relief to the Italian manufacturing export sectors. On the other hand, Germany is slowly releasing the excess demand stemming from the unification expansionary trend which could help Italy in reversing the trade account imbalance. In effect, the sequence of events which in the last years enhanced competition in attracting capital flows – the financial liberalization that allowed the Italian operators' portfolios to be reshuffled towards foreign assets, the shrinking of the interest differential with Germany and the German effort to divert capital to Frankfurt in order to finance the excess investment demand – are squeezing the contribution of the capital account to the re-equilibration of the Italian balance of payments. The structural deficit of the current account is then doomed to be left without compensation, thus magnifying the contrast between the fixed exchange rates of the lira and the loss in competitiveness due to the lasting cost differentials. Therefore, the correction in the fundamentals cannot be postponed any longer, as demonstrated by the Bank of Italy's strategy to force wages and prices dynamics to become compatible with the announced restrictive monetary targets and the exchange rate constraint.

It can be observed that this strategy would have been much more enforceable if it could have been framed inside the Eurofed ex-ante policy co-ordination. Similarly, the working of the Bundesbank's monetary stance as the external constraint (which in the eighties helped the Bank of Italy to impose monetary stability internally), full convergence will be less easily obtained in the absence of a fully-fledged European central bank entrusted with the authority to dictate a common monetary policy.

On the other hand, the completion of the European market (for goods, persons, services and capitals) in 1993 will surely put under pressure the overall competitiveness of the Italian industrial system. In the long run the reduction in production unit costs which will arise out of the full abolition of tariff barriers and frontier controls will result in a boost to Community trade (Padoa-Schioppa et al., 1987, pp.196–7). However, in the medium term a loss in employment is expected (Emerson et al., 1988, p.212) and the productivity gap of a large section of the Italian firms will broaden.

Since the de-industrialization problem might arise in Italy once the balance of payments constraint vanishes in the full-fledged EMU, a leap to higher efficiency, productivity rationalization and scale economies is strongly needed by Italian manufacturing sectors. Owing to inefficient resource allocation by public enterprises and low productivity spread throughout public services, a cut in the dimension of the Italian public sector is obviously needed. However, the harmonization of the fiscal stance to tight monetary targets should not bring about the dismissal of any role for 'activist' fiscal policies aimed at promoting productivity growth inside the industrial sector.

Notes

1. The equation is the following:
   $$(i - i^\star) - s^e = (i - i^\star) - FD + (FD - s^e)$$
   where i is the domestic nominal interest rate, the asterisk marks the foreign variable, s is the expected per cent variation in the exchange rate (by application of the 'rational expectation hypothesis', in Table 1.4 the values of the expected change in the exchange rate lira/Deutschmark are expressed by the ex post observed values), and FD is the forward discount (forward premium, in the case of a positive value), which is the difference between the spot and the forward exchange rates. Because of the obvious difficulty in obtaining observed expectations of the spot rate that will prevail at the time that a forward contract matures, the forward discount (or premium) is the best estimate of the expected change in the exchange rate. Its value roughly corresponds to the difference between the domestic ('inshore') interest rate and the 'offshore' interest rate (in our case, the rate of return determined in the Euromarket). Deviations from zero in the first term – the 'covered' interest differential – depend on imperfect financial markets' integration (i.e., on the presence of capital controls which impede arbitrage operations). Deviations from zero in the second term indicate the presence of speculative profit opportunities, so that the forward rate is a biased indicator of the future spot rate. In this case, the forward discount (or premium) does not match the ex post per cent variation in the exchange rate either because the rational expectations hypothesis fails or due to a 'risk premium' on the currency.

2. According to Frankel and MacArthur, the wedge which opened between the Italian and the foreign interest rates can be explained by the need to compensate foreign private investors for the risk of existing or expected controls on capital outflows (see Frankel and MacArthur, 1988, p.1096).

3. The Italian authorities have alternately or jointly resorted to the following administration measures: a tax on the purchase of foreign exchange, the regulation of settlement period for export receipts and import payments, and the requirement for importers to make prior non-interest-bearing deposits at the Bank of Italy as a stipulated percentage of the foreign exchange needed for import payments.

4. The Sargent-Wallace condition for the 'sustainability' of high public debt has been applied to the Italian case by several authors (e.g., see Masera, 1987). The rationale has been pointed out according to which a high premium against the risk of a possible debt's monetization (or even of its consolidation) had to be granted by the monetary authorities, in order to persuade the Italian shareholders to accept in their portfolios an increasing amount of government bonds. Yet, this view does not take into account that the presence of a risk premium cannot bear the burden of explaining the spread between the T-bills and the bank deposit rates which widened up since 1981–82. However small the interest elasticity of the demand for government bonds might have been, this differential which opened up in the Italian money market (as large as the range from 4 to 7 points) is at odds with the near-perfect substitutability between these financial assets.

5. The European Monetary Institution (EMI) – the provisional institution envisaged for Phase 2 in the place of a full-fledged European central bank – will join the Council of Governors of the European System of Central Banks in the monitoring of policy co-ordination by divergent countries. As is well known, the required conditions for the participation in the further steps towards monetary unification consist in the almost complete annulment of inflation and interest rates differentials, and in the drastic correction of public deficits and public debts as percentages of the GNP.

6. The ECU (European currency unit), after having emerged from the mere function of basket of the EMS currencies to the role of financial instrument, would be promoted as

a full-fledged European currency along with the implementation of the integration process between its private and official markets (see Allen, 1989, pp. 28–31).

Bibliography

Allen, P. R. (1983), 'The ECU and monetary management in Europe', in P. De Grauwe, and T. Peeters (eds), *The ECU and European Monetary Integration*, London: Macmillan.

Artis, M. J., and Taylor, M. P. (1989), 'Some issues concerning the long-run credibility of the European Monetary System', in R. MacDonald and M. P. Taylor (eds), *Exchange Rates and Open Economy Macroeconomics*, Oxford: Basil Blackwell.

Bank of Italy, *Annual Report*, various years.

Begg, D. and Wyplosz, C. (1987), 'Why the EMS? Dynamic games and the equilibrium policy regime', in R. C. Bryant and C. Portes (eds), *Global Macroeconomics: Policy Conflict and Cooperation*, London: Macmillan.

Bini-Smaghi, L. and Vona, S. (1989), 'The effects of economic convergence and competitiveness on trade among the EMS countries', in D. R. Hodgman and G. E. Wood (eds), *Macroeconomic Policy and Economic Interdependence*, London: Macmillan.

Canzonieri, M. B. and Henderson, D. W. (1988), 'Is sovereign policymaking bad?' *Carnegie Rochester Conference Series on Public Policy*, vol. 28: 93–140.

Caranza, C. and Fazio, A. (1983), 'Methods of monetary control in Italy: 1974–1983', in D. R. Hodgman (ed.), *The Political Economy of Monetary Policy: National and International Aspects*, Federal Reserve Bank of Boston, Conference Series, 26.

Collins, S. M. (1988), 'Inflation and the European Monetary System', in F. Giavazzi, S. Micossi and M. Miller (eds).

De Cecco, M. (1989), 'The European Monetary System and national interests', in P. Guerrieri and P. C. Padoan (eds).

Emerson, M. *et. al.* (1988), *The Economics of 1992: The EC Commission's Assessment of the Economic Effects of Completing the Internal Market*, Oxford: Oxford University Press.

Farina, F. (1990a), 'La politica monetaria e valutaria della Banca d'Italia e la crescita del debito pubblico', in A. Giannola and U. Marani (eds), *Tassi di interesse e debito pubblico*, Naples, ESI.

Farina, F. (1990b), 'I tassi di cambio SME e l'autonomia della politica monetaria', *Rivista di Politica Economica*, Supplement, vol. 80: 369–393.

Farina, F. (1991), 'From the EMS to the EMU: The Role of Policy Coordination', *Rivista di Politica Economica*, May, Vol. 81: 442–465.

Frankel, J. A. and MacArthur, A. T. (1988), 'Political vs. currency premia in international real interest differentials: a study of forward rates for 24 countries', *European Economic Review*, vol. 32: 1083–1121.

Fratianni M. and Von Hagen J. (1990), 'The European Monetary System Ten Years After', in Meltzer A. H. and Plossers C. (eds), *Carnegie-Rochester Conference Series on Public Policy*, vol. 32.

Giavazzi, F. and Giovannini, A. (1989), *Limiting Exchange Rate Flexibility: The European Monetary System*, Cambridge, Mass.: MIT Press.

Giavazzi, F., Micossi, S. and Miller, M. (eds) (1988), *The European Monetary System*, Cambridge: Cambridge University Press.

Giavazzi, F. and Pagano, M. (1985), 'The Advantage of Tying Ones Hands', *European Economic Review*, vol. 32: 1055–74.

Giavazzi, F. and Spaventa, L. (1989), 'Italy: the real effects of inflation and disinflation', *Economic Policy*, vol. 2: 131–58.

Goodhart, C. A. (1990), *Money, Information and Uncertainty*, London: Macmillan.

Guerrieri, P. and Padoan, P. C. (1989), 'Integration, co-operation and adjustment policies', in P. Guerrieri and P. C. Padoan (eds), *The Political Economy of European Integration*, Hemel Hempstead: Harvester Wheatsheaf.

Hodgman, D. R. and Resek, R. W. (1989), 'Italian monetary and foreign exchange policy', in D. R. Hodgman and G. E. Wood (eds), *Macroeconomic Policy and Economic Interdependence*, London: Macmillan.

Masera, R. (1987), 'Four arguments for fiscal recovery in Italy', in M. Boskin, J. S. Fleming and S. Gorini (eds), *Private Saving and Public Debt*, Oxford: Basil Blackwell.

Mastropasqua, C., Micossi, S. and Rinaldi, R. (1988), 'Interventions, sterilisation and monetary policy in European Monetary System countries, 1979–87', in F. Giavazzi, S. Micossi and M. Miller (eds).

Padoa-Schioppa, T. *et al.* (1987), *Efficiency, Stability and Equity: A Strategy for the Evolution of the Economic System of the European Community*, Oxford: Oxford University Press.

Russo, M. and Tullio, G. (1988), 'Monetary policy coordination within the European Monetary System: is there a rule?' in F. Giavazzi, S. Micossi and M. Miller (eds).

Vona, S. and Bini-Smaghi, L. (1989), 'Economic growth and exchange rates in the European Monetary System: their trade effects in a changing external environment', in F. Giavazzi, S. Micossi and M. Miller (eds).

Chapter 2

Agricultural policy

Elisabetta Croci-Angelini

2.1 Introduction

Though costs and benefits of the Common Agricultural Policy (CAP) have stimulated interest among various circles since the origin of the policy itself, the main debate about their definition and calculation arose between the end of the 1970s and the beginning of the 1980s.

The definition problem included such questions as 'costs and benefits to whom?', the answer to which implies a choice in the aggregation level, which is crucial in order to characterize the results. At that time the most common choice was a disaggregation at the member-state level: this choice will be retained here, too.

The calculation problem has been dealt with by several methods: by referring to sheer budgetary figures, or by means of cost–benefit analysis, again either by the 'traditional' or by the 'new' approach. For various reasons, however, none of these methods has proved completely satisfactory.

Ten years on now since the apex of that debate, the lack of agreement on a single methodology able to assess these costs and benefits has given rise to a serious information problem whereby figures indicating some budgetary flows occurring between the EC and the member countries have too often been used for describing the costs and benefits of the CAP (and sometimes, all the more, of EC membership) to the member countries.

This situation has emerged mainly because, on the one hand, the EC does not publish official figures referring to the most common definition of costs and benefits of the CAP (i.e. at the member-state level), while, on the other hand, all independent estimates have hardly achieved the same charisma as official figures, and their diffusion remains more or less restricted to academic circles and research institutions.

There is, however, a growing demand from the general public to know more about European matters, and in the absence of appropriate official figures the second best choice for the press is between correct unofficial and incorrect official figures.

The result is that the use of incorrect official figures in the vast majority of cases prevails and, in such cases as CAP costs and benefits to Italy, popularizes unverified, and often incorrect, commonplaces which regrettably happen to play a significant role in opinion-making.

This chapter aims to recollect the debate (section 2.2), review and clarify the different methodological positions (sections 2.3 and 2.4), stress the point about the hiatus existing between the kind of figures officially available and their (mis)use (section 2.4), and touch upon the role of information. It also appeals to the EC Commission to perform and publish such studies in some periodical publication series because more transparency in these matters can certainly ease the knowledge of the effects of policies and is likely to improve the policy-making process.

2.2 A brief history of the appraisal of costs and benefits of the CAP

Criticism of the CAP is likely to be as old as the policy itself, but the origin of the official history of the appraisal of costs and benefits of the CAP can be dated back to 1974 when the EC Council of Ministers, concerned with the rapidly growing expenditure under the agricultural fund (FEOGA) invited the EC Commission to present a complete summary of all aids and subsidies in the member-states and to take stock of the CAP, with special reference to the objectives of Article 39 of the Treaty of Rome.

Strictly speaking, this request did not necessarily imply a cost–benefit analysis of the CAP: such analysis examines the balance between costs and benefits and is usually performed before implementing a project. The stock-taking was rather aimed at checking whether or not the policy was attaining the stated objectives (at reasonable costs).

The document released to answer this request (EC Commission, 1975) pointed at regional disparities and budgetary costs as major disadvantages of the CAP. The subject was treated in very aggregate terms at the EC level and did not specify with whom in particular those advantages and disadvantages were to be associated.

The dissatisfaction over the lack of details at the member-state level in that document prompted a sequence of written questions by members of the European Parliament about the total financial flows occurring between the EC and the member-states, and eventually to a reluctant answer by the Commission (Official Journal of the European Communities, C28 31/1/79).

The Commission rightly warned that '... it can be misleading to study the transfers of resources which are incidental to the execution of the budget without examining the true impact of the related costs and benefits' (OJEC, ibid., p. 2).

Nevertheless, the figures presented in the Commission's answer were *de facto* used to calculate member countries' net payments to the common budget and gave immediate rise to a considerable quarrel about net gainers and losers from the CAP and, by extension, from EC membership. If the confusion between the different concepts of costs and benefits of the CAP, and of EC membership did not originate from these events, they may certainly have contributed towards increasing it.

It is apparent that the stock-taking of the CAP and the financial inflows and outflows caused by EC membership to the member-states are, in principle, two rather separate issues. However, since the bulk of the common budget is spent by

FEOGA, agricultural expenditure is often mistakenly associated with the total cost of EC membership and, similarly, it is often wrongly held that the budgetary figures represent the cost of the CAP.

The country's breakdown of financial transfers so cautiously issued by the Commission for the years 1976 and 1977, and later (OJEC, C164 2/7/79, p. 11) also for 1978, referred only to budgetary figures. Recorded transfers had been adjusted for MCAs (as since 1976 they were paid only in the exporting country) and this added difficulty to the interpretation of these figures: see, for instance, 1977 when these adjustments make the Italian and the British positions shift from being net contributors to become net beneficiaries.

Subsequently, and again upon request of the Council of Ministers, the Commission produced another document (EC Commission, 1979) showing the financial transfers likely to materialize when the new system of financing the common budget through 'own resources' would be fully working.

It is rather odd that, though the EC maintains with reason that these figures do not represent the costs and benefits of EC membership for the member countries, nevertheless they are often taken officially into account as reliable proxies of costs and benefits and heavily contribute to opinion- and decision-making. Since 1980 they have played a determinant role in approving UK budgetary rebate, they have served as a basis for new members' accession negotiations, and they are invariably reported by the press.

As for the Italian situation, for example, one may read that 'Since the end of the 1970s Italy had become a net beneficiary in the budget balance, so that the Government assumed an attitude favourable to a certain enlargement of total expenditure. It was felt that any ceiling in this respect would clash with almost all decisions about the CAP' (Petit et al., 1987, p. 77). This quotation is just one among many examples about how easily agricultural and budgetary issues are confused by policy-makers and how deep-rooted their connection is regarded.

It is well known by the profession that many authors pointed out that these figures do not represent the true balance between costs and benefits of the CAP to the member countries, but only that fraction which is recorded in the common budget.

In particular, they overlook the 'invisible transfers', i.e. the income flows due to the price support policy which accrue to EC exporting countries' producers and are paid by EC importing countries' consumers. They are termed 'invisible' as they do not appear in the balance sheets of the common budget and 'transfers' as they represent income transferred within the EC, although for a single member country they represent a net cost or benefit.

Nowadays, the notion that the economic analysis of costs and benefits of the CAP to the member countries should include the 'invisible transfers' is as widely accepted amongst scholars as it falls short of being understood and popularized by the media, with the unhappy result of partial and misleading information at the lay level which can easily be manipulated.

The different concepts and methods will now be clarified by resorting to the aid of the Venn diagram presented in its general form in Figure 2.1. For the general and correct understanding of these diagrams it should be pointed out that they do not try to adhere proportionally to the actual dimension of the variables

Member-states' inflows

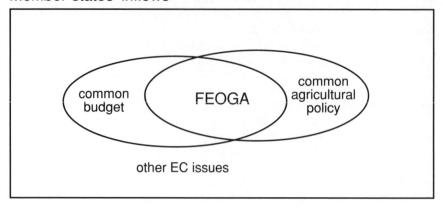

Member-states' outflows

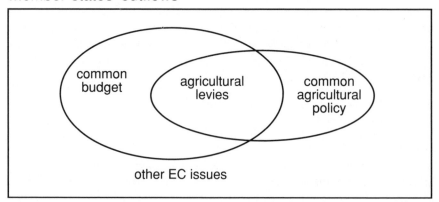

Figure 2.1

under examination. It would not be possible to represent member-states' inflows and outflows by a scale drawing, as each country would require its own diagram. On the contrary, they attempt only to give the idea of the relationship existing between each other, and in particular to illustrate the data presented by the tables that follow.

Figure 2.1 sketches the relation existing between the concepts presented so far:

1. the common budget includes, on the EC expenditure side, the agricultural fund, FEOGA, which has persisted around 70 per cent on total expenditure throughout the 1980s, and, on the EC revenue side, the agricultural levies, which have declined from 13 to 7 per cent on total 'own resources' during the same period;
2. the system of budgetary revenue coming from agricultural levies, and expenditure going through FEOGA, is the backbone of the common agricultural policy, which, however, involves more income transfers other than sheer budgetary revenue and expenditure;

Member-states' inflows

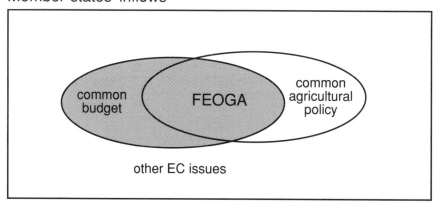

Member-states' outflows

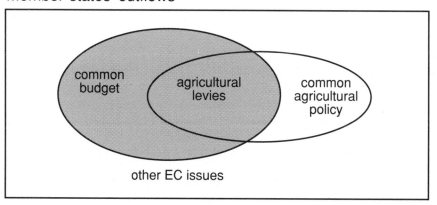

Figure 2.2

3. the common budget and the common agricultural policy overlap so far as FEOGA expenditure and agricultural levies revenue are concerned;
4. many more extra-agricultural policies and issues may be related to the costs and benefits of EC membership, but they do remain outside the scope of this analysis.

2.3 The appraisal of costs and benefits through budgetary figures

2.3.1. Figures related to the entire common budget

The two sides of the balance of inflows and outflows between the member states and the EC, as published by the EC Commission in 1979, are indicated by the shaded areas in Figure 2.2 while Table 2.1 shows the resulting net budgetary transfers for 1976–80.

Table 2.1 *EC budgetary transfers*

Countries	1976	1977	1978	1979	1980
Belgium★	346.2	328.8	350.3	338	538
Denmark	294.0	293.0	381.3	224	283
FRG	-1053.6	-1466.9	-519.8	-1155	-1107
France	58.1	-309.9	-321.0	-322	-120
Ireland	155.1	212.0	320.1	365	436
Italy	247.8	293.6	-304.9	754	871
Luxembourg				251	292
Netherlands	220.8	87.5	57.0	72	359
UK	-89.8	125.8	-407.0	-527	-1552
Total	178.6	-436.1	-444.0	0	0
(1)	21.5	16.7	39.0		
(2)	-299.0	324.3	393.9		
(3)	98.9	95.1	11.1		
Total	0	0	0		

(1) Other currencies
(2) Change in Commission's balances with national treasuries.
(3) Differences on exchange rates.
Source: OJEC, C164 2/7/79, p. 11; COM(79)462, pp. 15–16.
★including Luxembourg in 1976–77–78

It is self-evident that the balance between these two terms cannot stand either for anything reflecting a balance related to the agricultural sector – as the latter is only a subset in the common budget – or for the costs and benefits of EC membership – as this includes a number of other issues at least as important as the common budget itself.

The budgetary figures reported in Table 2.1 are straightforward financial transfers with little other meaning than for general accounting and without any univocal link with the effects of EC policies. Indeed, the economic analysis of costs and benefits of EC membership should focus on EC policies and their effects rather than on budgetary accounts.

Leaving aside the wider issue of costs and benefits of EC membership, which should include the economic and non-economic effects of a very comprehensive range of policies, the following notes will focus only on agricultural matters.

2.3.2. Budgetary figures strictly related to agriculture

When one endeavours to strike a balance between costs and benefits of the CAP to the member-countries through the budgetary figures connected to the agricultural sector, an initial difficulty arises because, in the EC, agricultural expenditure does not have earmarked funds within 'own resources'.

In other words, since all member states' contributions to the common budget are pooled together and then spent according to the obligations of the various funds, there is no separate budget where agricultural revenue and expenditure can

Member-states' inflows

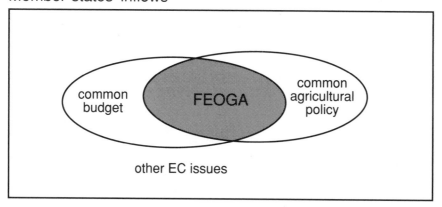

Member-states' outflows

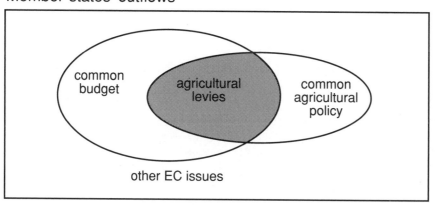

Figure 2.3

be compared. Figure 2.3 shows the approximation to this concept carried out by striking the balance between member countries' outflows towards the common budget through agricultural variable levies and inflows from FEOGA expenditure (shaded areas).

There is, however, an additional difficulty: although in the early times, when the CAP was devised, '... it was generally expected that [import levies] would more than cover agricultural expenditure' (Tracy, 1989, p. 270), the CAP developed in such a way that FEOGA has always needed funds from other sources to bridge the gap between continuously declining revenues from agricultural levies and its steadily growing expenditure.

Since 1980, the value of FEOGA expenditure in absolute terms has always been over six times that of agricultural levies, with a maximum of more than ten times in 1986. Being the agricultural balance to be established between numbers of very different size, it was calculated in relative terms by subtracting each country's

Table 2.2 *Net balance between FEOGA expenditure and agricultural levies (percentage)*

	1980	1981	1982	1983	1984	1985	1986	1987	1988	1989
Belgium	-5.86	-7.31	-8.39	-11.80	-8.28	-8.01	-5.06	-9.04	-5.65	-5.96
Denmark	4.29	2.93	3.03	2.28	2.90	1.75	2.31	2.21	2.29	1.53
FRG	4.24	0.92	-1.23	1.31	-2.80	-1.29	1.30	-0.34	-0.76	-3.42
Greece		0.26	2.08	3.95	3.75	4.66	4.53	4.82	3.83	4.98
Spain							0.15	-1.59	-3.35	-0.51
France	13.06	13.50	10.47	6.60	-1.42	4.12	3.34	6.55	3.72	-1.27
Ireland	4.74	3.45	3.45	3.06	3.89	4.96	4.74	3.59	3.21	4.04
Italy	-6.55	0.79	3.67	-0.18	6.44	-0.62	-4.91	-1.66	-3.58	0.42
Luxembourg	0.10	0.03	0.02	0.02	0.01	0.02	.00	0.00	0.01	0.00
Netherlands	0.15	-1.69	1.10	1.28	2.12	-0.45	1.11	4.69	6.25	5.92
Portugal							-0.68	-0.72	-0.85	-1.29
UK	-14.29	-12.89	-14.25	-6.53	-6.65	-5.18	-6.84	-8.51	-5.18	-4.44
Total EC	0	0	0	0	0	0	0	0	0	0

Source: Author's calculations from ASIC and OJEC data (various years)

percentage share of agricultural levies from its share on FEOGA expenditure. Table 2.2 shows the breakdown of these values for every country and year: a negative value indicates that a country's percentage share of contributions to the common budget in the form of agricultural levies exceeds its share of revenues.

The set of net gainers and losers has changed *vis-à-vis* the previous table. While the United Kingdom always shows negative figures, the Federal Republic of Germany is no more an unambiguous net contributor, and France is always a net gainer (with the exception of 1984 when there was a small difference). Italy is more often recorded among the net contributors than the net gainers. Given the structural character of the sector and in the absence of dramatic policy changes, this cannot be entirely due to the effect of a different reference period.

2.3.3 Budgetary figures notionally related to agriculture

Another more common method of finding the balance between member-countries' inflows and outflows with the EC budget and due to agriculture was first employed by Rollo and Warwick (1979) for 1977 and 1978. They circumvented the obstacle caused by the absence of an agricultural budget by imputing to FEOGA the same share each member-country was paying to the common budget.

Their study showed the United Kingdom, Italy and the Federal Republic of Germany among net contributors both in 1977 and 1978, and their results were fostered by those published by the Cambridge Economic Policy Group (1979) for the same years. Employing a similar method, Thomson (1989) shows a FEOGA balance for Italy in 1986 amounting to a deficit of 100 million Ecu, while France joins

Member-states' inflows

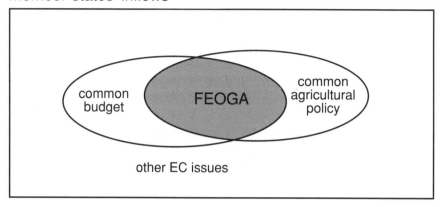

Member-states' outflows

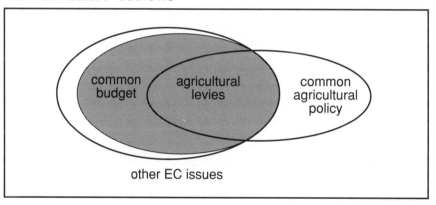

Figure 2.4

the United Kingdom and the Federal Republic in the group of net contributors.

By means of the usual diagram, Figure 2.4 shows how the two sides of the balance change: member-countries' inflows from FEOGA expenditure now are matched by the notional outflows towards the common budget (shaded areas). Table 2.3. is calculated by subtracting from each country's FEOGA receipts a share of total FEOGA receipts proportional to its share on the common budget.

A quick comparative look at the tables presented so far reveals that:

1. the United Kingdom is the only unequivocal net contributor;
2. Denmark and Ireland are always net beneficiaries;
3. for the remaining member countries the situation varies according to the set of data employed: in particular, the French and the Belgian positions change to the opposite *vis-à-vis* the figures published in the EC documents.

As for the Italian position (a net gainer in the EC official data as well as in popular beliefs), it is worth stressing that the more the calculations are specific to

Table 2.3 *Net balance between FEOGA expenditure and equivalent budget revenue*

	1980	1981	1982	1983	1984	1985	1986	1987	1988	1989
Belgium	-144.8	-155.3	-156.2	-284.7	-252.0	-112.6	-15.6	-284.2	-545.6	-562.8
Denmark	384.5	277.4	322.6	350.5	488.2	374.6	554.6	533.6	583.8	448.3
FRG	-978.7	-1235.9	-1368.4	-1488.8	-1935.9	-2281.5	-1814.2	-2352.4	-2981.3	-2966.2
Greece		-9.2	464.2	816.5	741.8	1041.7	1086.4	1134.3	1134.5	1546.3
Spain							-1272.0	-874.9	-61.6	169.1
France	730.6	929.1	414.0	467.2	-94.4	512.6	905.5	1174.7	487.0	-485.5
Ireland	525.5	402.8	469.8	533.1	752.9	1006.5	1054.5	820.5	907.1	1122.3
Italy	414.7	730.1	1028.9	930.0	1567.4	704.2	-87.5	594.6	278.9	775.7
Luxembourg	-2.8	-10.9	-11.9	-19.7	-24.4	-34.1	-42.2	-41.2	-46.9	-41.9
Netherlands	612.8	335.3	562.8	597.3	711.3	602.9	790.2	1238.9	1908.4	2008.1
Portugal							-132.1	-22.6	2.6	59.3
UK	-1541.9	-1263.4	-1725.6	-1901.3	-1954.9	-1814.2	-1027.5	-1921.3	-1667.1	-2072.9
Total EC	0	0	0	0	0	0	0	0	0	0

Source: Author's calculations from ASIC and OJEC data (various years).

the agricultural sector (i.e. balance between FEOGA and agricultural levies), the more a minus sign is found in front of Italian figures.

This is not surprising for, Italy being a net importer of agricultural produce, it is likely to contribute comparatively more than other countries to common budget agricultural levies and receive comparatively less through FEOGA expenditure (except for structural policies).

What is more surprising is that, in the views of the Italian government quoted above, benefiting from the common budget equals benefiting from the CAP. Indeed, these data show that, in terms of sheer budgetary figures, Italy benefits proportionally more from the non-agricultural than from the agricultural part of the common budget. The opposite is true for the Federal Republic of Germany, while for France the results of Table 2.3 reflect those of Table 2.2.

However, it should be stressed that these figures do not tell the entire story of costs and benefits of the CAP to the member-countries. So far only that part of the CAP which overlaps with the common budget has been examined, while the rest of the area, which symbolizes other effects of the policy, remains as yet unexplored.

The following section aims to present a more complete evaluation of the balance between costs and benefits of the CAP to the member – countries. This is not only necessary for policy-makers, but is called for by private as well as public decision-makers and is also of interest to the general public. Therefore it is worth trying to obtain a more accurate picture through a cost–benefit analysis specifically directed at the CAP.

2.4 The appraisal of costs and benefits of the CAP through cost–benefit analysis

Cost-benefit analysis is a popular branch of applied welfare economics. Though its origins can be traced back to the work of Dupuit (1844), only since the early 1960s has it been employed as a basic tool in project evaluation. In some respect policies can be regarded as projects undertaken by the government and therefore explored by cost-benefit analysis.

Reflecting in some way the difficulty of welfare economics in reconciling equity and efficiency issues, cost-benefit analysis, too, may be differentiated into two approaches.

The 'traditional' approach, more directly deriving from 'new welfare econom-ics', is generally associated with the names of Harberger (1974, 1977) and Mishan (1975, 1981) and, in the economic assessment of a project, stresses the efficiency aspects by means of the Marshallian surplus analysis.

The 'new' approach, on the other hand, is not restrained by the application of a strict efficiency criterion but, being more concerned with equity issues, allows other considerations to affect the analysis, mainly through the use of distributional weights. This approach follows the work done by Little and Mirrlees (1968, 1974) for the OECD, where the social profit is evaluated in terms of variations in foreign exchange taken as the numeraire, and the work done for the UNIDO by Dasgupta, Marglin and Sen (1972), where consumption is taken as the numeraire and shadow prices are calculated for foreign exchange, investment and wage rate.

Shadow prices, or, in Tinbergen's terminology, 'accounting prices', which '... reflect the "true value" of a certain product or factor to the country' (Tinbergen, 1956, p. 180), represent a central element in cost-benefit analysis. They differ from market prices when the economy is not in competitive equilibrium (or if the project to be undertaken is likely to affect the structure of relative prices in the economy) and should replace market prices in the economic evaluation of public intervention.

It is then apparent that shadow prices are bound to be somewhat arbitrary, ultimately depending on the government's objective function and constraints. To circumvent this difficulty a common working assumption postulates the existence of a unitary government with a given social welfare function.

However, when the government deciding a project or a policy is a supra-national organization like the EC, whose members are committed to economic integration through the composition of diverging interests, the hypothesis of a unitary government does not strictly hold true. Actual negotiations among mem-ber states take place reflecting geographically relevant preferences. Unlike a single country which is usually identified with a single market for a given product, several markets can be identified. The assessment of shadow prices then becomes really critical because only under very restrictive and unlikely hypotheses would the common objective function be exactly the same as that of each country individually taken, while deviations from it should be considered as costs or benefits to a particular country.

2.4.1 *The traditional approach and the role of shadow prices*

2.4.1.1 World market prices as shadow prices

At about the same time as when the Commission was issuing its official figures, a number of alternative estimates came to light showing that the costs and benefits of the CAP to the member countries should never be confused with the balance between revenue and expenditure in the budget. A lively discussion took place on this subject, predominantly amongst academics, often addressing the issue of costs and benefits of the CAP to the various member-countries and then ending up by focusing on its redistributive effects.

A common assumption of these studies was that known in international trade theory as the 'small country assumption' (Corden, 1974, p.10): the international terms of trade are unaffected by variations of the policy. World market prices were employed as shadow prices in the calculation of the costs and benefits of the policy to each member country.

However, maintaining that the EC, the first major importer and second major exporter on world agricultural markets, can reasonably be considered a small country is hard to swallow. But for the purpose of this analysis, the 'small country assumption' is tantamount to the hypothesis that exactly the same policy would be carried out at the national level. Therefore, it is retained here as a working assumption that is able to highlight the main changes occurring when the same policy is performed at the national and at the supranational level.

By such comparison, this method assesses those inter-country redistributive effects taking place in the EC, and due to the CAP through the rules of financial solidarity, according to which import levies and export restitutions are paid respectively to and from the common budget to the member countries, instead of being administered by the member countries themselves. When these results are summarized into a single net figure expressing the cost or the benefit of the CAP to each member country, the choice of this hypothesis would provide an outcome which points at costs and benefits in terms of inter-country redistribution rather than in pure allocative terms.

Figure 2.5 shows a market space diagram for a customs union C which has been disaggregated into two member-countries A and B. Since a customs union implies no trade barriers within it, and a common barrier against third countries to ensure preferential trade among partners, the common internal price Pc is placed above the world market price Pw. The diagram is divided into four parts: a customs union showing a net deficit for the goods under examination is drawn on the upper part, with the net surplus country on the left, while a customs union showing a surplus situation is represented on the lower part, with the net deficit country on the right side.

The customs union budgetary inflows collected on imports from third countries are indicated by the dark chequered area (a), budgetary outflows paid when the system is reverted into exports are indicated by the shaded area (b), while the dotted (c) and the netted (d) areas respectively indicate a positive and a negative 'would-be' budgetary flow taking place in the absence of the customs union. With

Table 2.4 *Budget and trade transfers at actual world market prices*

Countries	1976* ($USm.)	1977† (EUAm.)	1978† (EUAm.)	1978‡ (£m.)	1978§ (£m.)	1980¶ (EUAm.)
UEBL	-232	-50	-50	156	-259	148
Denmark	-25	800	950	618	324	1377
FRG	-219	-1200	-750	-671	-1740	-1740
France	489	800	850	734	-286	-36
Ireland	–	600	750	475	201	1156
Italy	-1325	-700	-1250	-646	-1541	-933
NL	164	1100	1100	631	206	1946
UK	-1067	-950	-1200	-1123	-1370	-1922

Source: *Blancus, 1978; †Rollo and Warwick, 1979; ‡CEPG, 1979; §Morris, 1980; ¶Buckwell *et al.*, 1982.

reference to the previous sections, the areas indicated with a and b represent the net situation for the EC as a whole and appear in the budgetary accounts, while those indicated with c and d represent the member country's situation and include the 'invisible transfers'.

The diagrams show that the customs union's net budgetary flows are exactly the residual after an algebraic sum of member-countries' invisible transfers is calculated. A self-sufficiency situation in the customs union is shown in Figure 2.6 to clarify this point.

It is apparent that the customs union net budgetary flows – which are the only visible and recorded, and are imputed to the importing country in case of net imports and to the exporting country in case of net exports – conceal substantial would-be budgetary flows of opposite sign which do cancel at the customs union level, but do not cancel at the member-state level.

Table 2.4 shows that Italy is always listed with the net contributors, together with the United Kingdom and the Federal Republic of Germany by those authors who assess costs and benefits of the CAP to the member countries in this way. The results reported in the table refer to the same period, when studies on this subject were flourishing, especially in the United Kingdom. Since that period, interest in the subject has declined both in academic circles – because the method was not particularly controversial – and also among policy-makers, once the dispute on the UK contribution was over and a rebate on net budgetary contribution was allowed to that country. Lack of recent data, however, is especially detrimental to those countries, like Italy, whose position changes from being a net gainer to becoming a net loser when budgetary figures are replaced by figures derived from cost-benefit analysis.

Although this method, once officially accepted, could offer some bargaining power to Italy during the annual price review as well as in other internal agricultural negotiations, it has never been very popular in this country. In general the Italian government's attitude towards the CAP appears more characterized by

Customs Union C: Importing situation

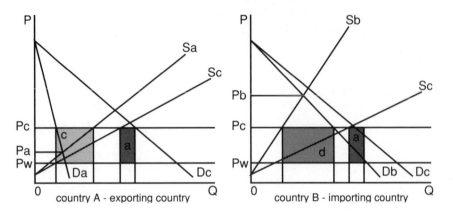

Customs Union C: exporting situation

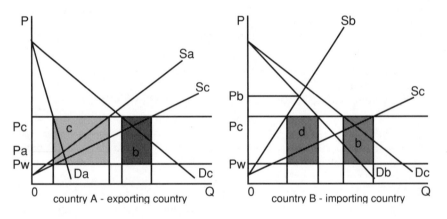

Figure 2.5

trying to play somebody else's game, and perhaps to win some occasional concessions, than by playing an active role in shaping the policy. It is revealing reading
that Marcora '… the only Minister whose political weight was comparable to that
of the Ministers of Foreign Affairs and Finance … was able to persuade the
Community to adopt a series of compensatory measures in favour of Italian
agriculture, and on the financial front Italy moved from the position of a net
contributor to that of a net beneficiary' (Petit *et al.*, 1987, p. 72).

Whether this attitude is intended or incidental may be debatable. As a matter of
fact, though the Italian agricultural sector is not negligible in terms of several
criteria (Tarditi, 1987), when it comes to CAP decision-making Italy often feels
and behaves as a minority partner which is more keen to adjust somehow, rather

Customs Union C: self-sufficiency situation

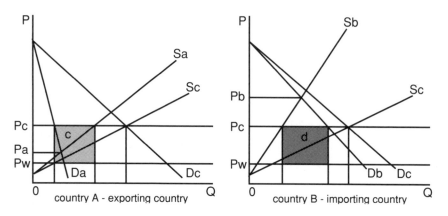

Figure 2.6

than to strive for the defence of its interests.

However, the assumption of pursuing the same policy does not need to be realistic. Its importance resides in singling out for analytical purposes, and therefore being able to evaluate, the inter-country redistributive effects as the difference between the effects of the same policy when it is either nationally or commonly carried out. For this reason it seems more sensible to keep the analysis of the actual situation separate from all subjective judgements about its likelihood and desirability.

2.4.1.2 International shadow prices

The approach presented above has the double merit of being simple to understand and of founding its calculation on actual world market prices as derived from EC import levies and export restitutions. However, the working assumption that each member country would pursue the same policy is quite unrealistic and its useful-ness is limited to the assessment of costs and benefits to the member countries in the past, since that policy has actually materialized. Yet, in order to look into the future effects of a policy, its likelihood matters and therefore the terms of the comparison have to change.

In this respect, it seems sensible to compare the state of affairs with and without the policy under examination. The absence of EC intervention on agricultural markets should then be taken as the natural benchmark for evaluating the costs and benefits of the CAP as it is, while all other policy options should be ranked against this reference system.

For the EC, this is equivalent to using the large country hypothesis: actual world market prices are affected by the absence of that policy and should not be employed as shadow prices (Tarditi and Croci-Angelini, 1982). The correct shadow prices in this case are the world market prices after having allowed for the effect of agricultural trade liberalization (Tarditi et al., 1989). The emphasis of the exercise is now on the allocative effects of the policy, which is supposed to change – and on the redistribution resulting after liberalization has taken place – rather than on its actual and past redistributive effects.

However, this way of assessing the costs and benefits of the CAP has the drawback of being based on shadow prices that need to be estimated, rather than historically observed, and are therefore dependent on hypotheses about some 'scenario' and consequently more difficult to calculate (Parikh et al., 1988).

As it happens, due to data collection, parameter evaluation and similar difficulties, a most accurate methodology might not be able to provide results readily accepted as reliable, especially by the policy-maker.

2.4.2 The new approach and the role of distributional weights

The different ways of assessing costs and benefits presented above are all in the framework of the 'traditional' approach.

However, other costs and benefits of the CAP exist, though not so strictly linked to the market situation as represented by the market space: concern for income distribution, environmental pollution and conservation, as well as a number of other valuable issues, can place the analysis in the 'new' approach.

In the evaluation of costs and benefits of the CAP, the new approach, often called the 'social' approach, has not had the same success as the traditional approach, in terms of copious literature. Some studies may be found where income distribution is taken into account through the use of distributional weights, mainly referring to individual markets (Sarris, 1989), but also pointing at regional imbalances as a consequence of the CAP (Kirschke, 1983). However, these studies have seldom presented the same comprehensive character as well as regionally detailed results as those mentioned under the traditional approach. The requirement of having a distributional judgement explicitly specified into a social welfare function has always proved to be a major obstacle (Tarditi and Croci-Angelini, 1987).

The same kind of problems are experienced when environmental issues are taken into account. Also in this case, the approach of many studies is to examine the consequences of a given project on a given area, while the global effects of the CAP on a member-country's environment – e.g. costs and benefits to Italy of a policy that through intensification tends to encourage the use of fertilizers and pesticides in the Po Valley, thereby contributing to the pollution of the Adriatic coast – are very rarely analysed in detail. With a similar approach, benefits very difficult to quantify and allocate, such as the merits of having developed co-operation among the EC member-countries, having shown some willingness to overcome thorny points – it is argued that 'the first success of the CAP resides in its own existence' – or having ensured over thirty years of peace in Europe, have sometimes been considered, too.

A comprehensive assessment of costs and benefits of the CAP to the member-countries, which includes these effects, is very difficult to accomplish. The kind of externalities and public goods the policy provides (or may provide) and to whom, should be clearly identified and weighted accordingly. Given the high heterogeneity of the studies carried out in this perspective, the discussion of these aspects would require a separate study.

2.5 What choice?

It might seem that this lengthy discussion on the costs and benefits of the CAP and the most correct shadow prices to be used in evaluating them is only relevant for the price support policy.

A number of policies, other than the import levy and export restitution system, have recently been enforced in the EC and there is a feeling that the importance of the so-called pillar of the CAP is declining. Nevertheless, finding the most appropriate set of shadow prices on which to anchor the cost–benefit analysis is a crucial issue because the effects of all CAP instruments should then be evaluated against the same (correct) set of shadow prices.

The choice about which shadow prices should be employed in the evaluation of costs and benefits of the CAP is then somehow linked to the kind of results one is seeking. This is in line, not in contrast, with the aims of cost–benefit analysis and with the definition of costs as opportunity costs. In particular, the analysis should specify: costs and benefits of what (e.g. the actual policy, or which alternative policy) and to whom (e.g. to the EC, to individual member-countries, to domestic producers, consumers, taxpayers, third countries, other groups).

The results presented above are obviously related to each other, though they were obtained from different approaches. However, it is worth adding some qualifications. World market prices are the correct set of shadow prices that enable one to assess actual intra-EC redistribution caused by CAP rules. Taking actual world market prices as a proxy for international shadow prices is likely to lead to inaccuracies in the size of eventual intra-EC transfers, once some degree of trade liberalization has taken place. The higher the degree of trade liberalization and the larger the EC share is on a given market, the greater the tendency to overvalue these transfers.

In contrast, the use of budgetary figures, in the case of economic integration under the rules of the CAP, may also lead to more or less random errors in the sign of values (i.e. gainers can be mistaken for losers and vice versa) unless very strict assumptions are introduced (e.g. intra-EC trade is ruled out).

However, in the unlikely event that no trade of agricultural goods was taking place within the European Community, some appropriate budgetary figures could be employed for assessing the net cost or benefit of the CAP for a given country in case it would individually withdraw from this policy, or it could be taken as a proxy in case the policy were discontinued for all partners. But even these figures would only represent the net transfers between that country and the rest of the world due to protection, but they would not include domestic redistribution so far as the protected good is also domestically produced and/or consumed, and therefore would not help when applying the 'social' cost–benefit analysis.

Though budgetary figures seldom reflect the entire reality in economic terms, their official source gives them an authority which is not easily challenged by less accessible academic work. Since the media often over-evaluate the reliability of budgetary figures, these are more prone to misinterpretation and misuse.

However, it should be underlined that calculations of costs and benefits to the member-countries, based on the 'traditional' approach and using world market prices as historically observed, are by no means less 'real and true' than any budgetary figure. Their official publication by the EC would certainly help prevent CAP decision-making from being thwarted by misinformation.

2.6 Conclusions

In the previous paragraphs it was argued that world market prices are the correct shadow prices for assessing the actual inter-country redistribution which has taken place among the member-countries as a consequence of the CAP in the past, while international shadow prices are more adequate in evaluating the costs and benefits of the policy in the future. Budgetary figures are rough and ready but it should always be clear that they may often represent a misleading evaluation.

In applying cost–benefit analysis one is often warned that shadow prices are always based on assumptions and that this represents a problem in assessing the generality of the results. It should be stressed, however, that it is difficult to avoid arbitrariness in such issues escaping the difficulty involved in the use of shadow prices by employing budgetary figures is itself an arbitrary choice. This arbitrariness, however, applies only to the future: as for the past, world market prices have been observed and are just as objective and reliable as budgetary figures.

In addition, it was shown that the definition of which budgetary figures are most appropriate to answer the question of costs and benefits of the CAP for a member-country is not obvious and, once again, it is the subjective choice that determines the results. Assessing costs and benefits to the member countries on purely budgetary figures is even more surprising if one is aware of the fact that they are not univocal, but are subject to some interpretation, too. Moreover, in the budget co-responsibility levies are treated as negative FEOGA expenditure, MCAs have been moved in and out FEOGA through the years, while schemes under the CAP guidelines and control, but mainly nationally financed (e.g. land set aside), are a good example of benefits in terms of savings in export subsidies without costs for the EC budget.

While in many other respects the Commission's philosophy and attitude has changed in the course of time (e.g. on direct income payments, single countries' schemes, single market fragmentation through dairy quotas, some renationalization like land set-aside programmes), in calculating official figures for the intra-EC redistributive effects of policies (markedly of the CAP) the Commission still shows some excessive caution.

This seems to be a major reason why all qualifications and warnings by the Commission about the (mis)use of budgetary figures have not succeeded in preventing their almost universal employment in opinion-making at the widest level.

Bibliography

Ahrens, H. (1984), 'Effets de la PAC sur les positions budgétaires et commerciales des pays-membres de la Communauté européenne', *Economie Rurale*, vol. 164, Nov./Dec.

Blancus, P. (1978), 'The CAP and the balance of payments of the EEC member countries', *BNL Quarterly Review*, vol. 5.

Buckwell, A., Harvey, D., Thomson, K. and Parton, K. (1982), *The Costs of the Common Agricultural Policy*, London: Croom Helm.

Cambridge Economic Policy Group (1979), 'Policies of the EEC', *Cambridge Economic Policy Review*, vol. 5: 23–30.

Chakravarty, S. (1987), 'Cost–benefit analysis', in J. Eatwell, M. Milgate and P. Newman (eds), *The New Palgrave*, London: Macmillan.

Coleman, D. and Young, T. (1990), 'Overestimating and misinterpreting costs and benefits of agricultural policy', in P. C. van den Noort (ed.), *Costs and Benefits of Agricultural Policies and Projects*, Kiel: Wissenschaftsverlag Vauk.

Corden, W. M. (1974), *Trade Policy and Economic Welfare*, Oxford: Clarendon Press.

Croci-Angelini, E. (1986), 'Welfare and redistributive effects of sectoral economic integration: the Common Agricultural Policy', doctoral thesis, European University Institute, Florence.

Dasgupta, P., Marglin, S. A. and Sen, A. K. (1972), *Guidelines for Project Evaluation*, New York: UNIDO.

Dupuit, J. (1844), *On the Measurement of the Utility of Public Works*, Annales des Ponts et Chausses.

Eatwell, J., Milgate, M. and Newman, P. (eds) (1987), *The New Palgrave*, London: Macmillan.

EC (various issues), *Official Journal of the European Communities*.

EC Commission (various issues), *The Agricultural Situation in the Community*, Brussels.

EC Commission (1975), *Stocktaking of the CAP*, COM(75)100, Brussels.

EC Commission (1979), COM (79)462, Brussels September, 12th.

Harberger, A. C. (1974), *Taxation and Welfare*, Boston: Little Brown.

Harberger (1977), 'On the UNIDO guidelines for project evaluation', in H. Schwartz and R. Berney (eds), *Social and Economic Dimensions of Project Evaluation*, Washington, DC, Inter-American Development Bank.

Hicks, J. R. (1939), 'The foundations of welfare economics', *Economic Journal*, December, 698–712.

Hicks, J. R. (1940) 'The rehabilitation of consumers' surplus', *Review of Economic Studies*, vol.viii, 108–16.

Hicks, J. R. (1946), 'The generalized theory of consumers' surplus', *Review of Economic Studies*, vol.xiii, 68–74.

Kirschke, D. (1983), 'Optimal agricultural prices within the European Community', Discussionsbeiträge no.52 Institut für Agrarpolitik und Marktlehre Universität, Kiel.

Koester, U. (1977), 'The redistributional effects of the common agricultural financial system', *European Review of Agricultural Economics*, vol.4, no.4: 321–47.

Little, I. M. D. and Mirrlees, J. A. (1968), *Manual of Industrial Project Analysis in Developing Countries*, Paris: OECD.

Little, I. M. D. and Mirrlees, J. A. (1974), *Project Appraisal and Planning for Developing Countries*, Paris: OECD.

Mahè, L. P. and Moreddu, C. (1989), 'Analysis of CAP trade policy changes', in S. Tarditi, K. Thomson, P. Pierani and E. Croci-Angelini (eds).

Mishan, E. J. (1975), *Cost–Benefit Analysis*, London: Allen and Unwin.

Mishan, E. J. (1981) *Economic Efficiency and Social Welfare*, London: Allen and Unwin.

Morris, C. N. (1980), 'The Common Agricultural Policy', *Fiscal Studies*, vol.1.

Parikh, K., Fischer, G., Frohberg, K. and Gulbrandsen, O. (1988), *Towards Free Trade in Agriculture*, The Hague: Martinus Nijhoff.

Petit, M., de Benedictis, M., Britton, D., de Groot, M., Heinrichsmeyer, W. and Lechi, F. (1987), *Agricultural Policy Formation in the European Community: The Birth of Milk Quotas and CAP Reform*, Amsterdam: Elsevier.

Ray, A. (1984), *Cost–Benefit Analysis*, Baltimore, Johns Hopkins Press.

Rollo, J. M. C. and Warwick, K. S. (1979), *The CAP and Resources Flows among EEC Member States*, GES Working Paper no.27.

Sarris, A. H. (1989), 'Price policies and international distortions in the wheat market', in S. Tarditi, K. Thomson, P. Pierani and E. Croci-Angelini (eds).

Tarditi, S. (1987), 'The Common Agricultural Policy: the implications for Italian agriculture', *Journal of Agricultural Economics*, vol.xxxviii, no.3.

Tarditi, S. and Croci-Angelini, E. (1982), 'Regional redistributive effects of common price support policies, *European Review of Agricultural Economics*, vol.9, no.3: 255–70.

Tarditi, S. and Croci-Angelini, E. (1987), 'Efficiency and equity components of sector policy analysis and evaluation', in Y. Léon and L. P. Mahé, *Income Disparities among Farm Households and Agricultural Policy*, Kiel: Wissenschaftsverlag Vauk.

Tarditi, S., Thomson, K., Pierani, P. and Croci-Angelini, E. (eds) (1989), *Agricultural Trade Liberalization and the European Community,* Oxford: Clarendon Press.

Thomson, K. J. (1989), 'Budgetary and economic effects of CAP trade liberalization', in S. Tarditi, K. Thomson, P. Pierani and E. Croci-Angelini (eds).

Tinbergen, J. (1956), *Economic Policy: Principles and Design*, Amsterdam: North-Holland.

Tracy, M. (1989), *Government and Agriculture in Western Europe 1880–1988*, London: Harvester Wheatsheaf.

Whitby, M. (ed.)(1979), *The Net Cost and Benefit of EEC Membership*, Centre for European Agricultural Studies, Wye College, Ashford.

Chapter 3

Competition policy

Paolo Cesarini*

3.1 Introduction

The aim of the present survey is to assess, from a legal viewpoint, the impact on Italian interests of the Community competition rules which apply to undertakings. These rules cover two main policy areas: the legal control of anti-competitive behaviour of undertakings on the market (articles 85, 86 and 90 of the EC Treaty) and the legal control of operations of concentration between undertakings (Council Regulation no. 4064/89 of 21 December 1989)[1] In particular, article 85 prohibits trade practices which restrict competition within the common market, although it makes provision, under paragraph 3, for granting exemption to agreements producing certain beneficial effects.

Article 86 prohibits abusive conduct of undertakings holding a dominant position within the common market. Article 90 contains specific provisions concerning competition in the public sector. Moreover, Council Regulation no. 4064/89 (OJ 1989, L 395) has extended the scope of the Commission's jurisdiction by providing for a systematic monitoring of 'all concentrations with a Community dimension' (article 1).

As a preliminary remark, it may be noted that, in each of the above-mentioned policy areas, costs and benefits arising from EC membership depend mainly on two concurrent factors: firstly, the range of powers actually derogated to the Community and the resultant limitation of Member-States' jurisdiction; and secondly, the degree of consistency between Community policy objectives and national interests.

In the first place, it should be observed that, with regard to articles 85 and 86, the Treaty does not prevent, in principle, Member States from enacting and enforcing national rules on competition. In particular, in its *Walt Wilhelm* judgment of 1969 (case 14/68, ECR, 1969: 1), the Court of Justice established that Community and national anti-trust may very well co-exist and receive parallel application since they 'consider cartels from different points of view'. However, in view of the possibility of a conflict between national and Community rules on competition, the Court limited the ambit of Member-States' jurisdiction and declared that

---

*Administrator at the EC Commission (DG IV, Competition). The views expressed are personal.

a parallel application of the national system can only be allowed in so far as it does not prejudice the uniform application throughout the Common Market of the Community rules on cartels and the full effect of the measures adopted in implementation of those rules.

Therefore, according to the Court, whenever it appears possible that a decision of a national authority would be incompatible with a decision adopted, or to be taken, by the Commission, such a conflict 'must be resolved by applying the principle that Community law takes precedence'.

It follows that any discrepancy between the two legal systems is likely to result in a situation whereby national policy objectives would succumb to more general Community interests (for a recent study on the relationship between Community and national antitrust, see Menis, 1990: 79). Therefore, whereas the risk of this type of conflict occurring largely depends on the content of the two respective sets of rules (and the policy objectives thereof), the assessment of costs and benefits of EC membership in this particular field calls for an analytical comparison of national and Community provisions.

Such a premise is valid also, *mutatis mutandi*, in relation to the EC rules applying to concentrations between undertakings. In fact, under Regulation 4064/89, concentrations having a Community dimension are subject solely to the Community's jurisdiction. In other words, Regulation 4064/89 replaces the principle of the parallel applicability of national and Community antitrust with a principle of 'mutual exclusivity', which implies that Member-States can no longer exert their jurisdiction over cases subject to the control of the Commission. As a result of such limitation of national jurisdiction, it can be assumed that the decisions adopted by the Commission under Regulation 4064/89 are more likely to clash with national interests in those cases where the Community policy relies upon principles which depart from the principles enshrined in the domestic legislation.

In the second place, as regards the Italian legal system it should be kept in mind that Italy has been the last among the Member-States of the Community to have enacted national anti-trust provisions. In fact, an organic body of domestic rules on competition has entered into force in Italy, for the first time, in October 1990 (law no. 287, *Gazzetta ufficiale della Repubblica italiana*, 13 October 1990:3). Therefore, national policy objectives relating to governmental supervision of competition are still less clearly defined in Italy, than in other member-states with stronger anti-trust traditions. Under these circumstances, the identification of the relevant national interests involved in this field requires examination, on the one hand, of the historical background of law no. 287 and, on the other, the main political options underlying the aforesaid law (section 3.2 below). In section 3.5 below, national policy objectives will be then compared with the relevant aspects of the EC antitrust policy with a view to a final cost and benefits appraisal. In such context, a distinction will be made between the rules applying to anti-competitive behaviour and rules governing the control of concentrations.

3.2 National Policy Objectives

3.2.1 Historical background

As is generally admitted, the prolonged lack of a domestic competition law in Italy has stemmed from a deep-rooted 'public intervention' approach to the problems raised by industrial development (Petriccione, 1989:379). In fact, it should not be forgotten that, at the time when the Italian Civil Code was conceived, the dominant ideology regarded certain forms of anti-competitive co-operation between undertakings as inherent to the corporative economic system in force during the period between the two world wars. The transition to democracy involved the abolition of the corporative system and led to the adoption of a concept of economic justice whereby the safeguard of the free access to, and the individual exploitation of, market opportunities, was constitutionally linked to the need of protecting the social function of labour and of economic activities (article 41 of the Constitution). The recognition of such a principle gave the State a new role to play within the process of industrial development. Such a role took on different forms, ranging from public control on prices to governmental regulation of specific sectors where market operation appeared to be closely connected with more general economic interests (e.g. insurance, banking and public services).

As some authors have observed (Lupi, 1988: 1374), such a situation led to the conviction whereby sectorial regulations and State ownership of undertakings operating in politically sensitive sectors, on the one hand, and the progressive dismantlement of State barriers within the framework of the EC Treaty, on the other, were to be regarded as the most appropriate means to safeguard market conditions in Italy. As a result, Italian political and economic culture has shown, until recently, a lack of appreciation for anti-trust legislation. An historical review of the various legislative proposals put forward during the 1950s and 1960s would confirm this impression.

However, the situation has evolved considerably during the past few years. The economic process towards fuller international integration, particularly in the perspective of the unification of the European markets by 1993, have shed new light on anti-trust issues. Two points may be mentioned in this respect. Firstly, the past decade has seen Italian industry undergoing a far-reaching process of structural rationalisation and technological innovation designed to create economies of scale, in accordance with the new dimension of markets. At the same time, market strategies have been extensively re-adjusted according to the changing patterns of international competition. The result has been a rapid increase in the number of structural operations and intensified co-operation between industrial groups at the national and transnational level. Secondly, growing criticism has focused upon the traditional models of the regulated economy. It has been stressed, in particular, that those sectors which for a long time have been sheltered from competitive pressure, such as State monopolies, have gradually become unable to keep pace with the process of technological and managerial innovation. Furthermore, the bureaucratic machinery governing the operation of public undertakings has been increasingly regarded as an obstacle to the improvement of their efficiency and competitiveness. Recent experiences of deregulation, notably in the car manufacturing, textile and food sectors can be interpreted as a first attempt, though limited in scope, to cope with the drawbacks of this traditional approach.

At the legislative level, such developments gave rise, in 1987, to two parallel initiatives by the Ministry of Industry and the Senate, which led to a comprehensive review of the issue. These preliminary works resulted in two bills (*Senato della Repubblica, X, Doc. no. 1012 and no. 1240*) which were submitted to the Senate in May and July 1988, respectively. The final draft was adopted by the Senate and transmitted for approval to the Lower Chamber in March 1989 (*Camera dei Deputati, X, Doc. no. 3755*). After a long and harsh debate on certain specific questions such as the relationship between industry and financial institutions and the provision applying to operations of concentration, the Parliament adopted the 'Norme per tutela della concorrenza e del mercato' (law no. 287) on 10 October 1990.

A detailed analysis of law no. 287 would be beyond the scope of the present survey. Therefore, in the following paragraphs, textual references to specific provisions will be made only insofar as they are necessary to identify the main national policy objectives underlying the new legislation. Accordingly, a distinction will be made between rules relating to the control of anti-competitive behaviour (section 3.3) and those concerning the legal control of concentrations (section 3.4).

3.3 National control of anti-competitive behaviour

3.3.1 Economic efficiency within the national market

The studies carried out in 1987 and 1988 by the 10th Standing Committee of the Senate (*Internazionalizzazione delle imprese e concentrazioni industriali*) and by the Special Committee appointed by the Ministry of Industry (*Studio della concorrenza nel sistema economico italiano*) relied on the assumption whereby, in a free market system the economic efficiency of markets presupposes the control of individual or collective behaviour of undertakings, which could impede or distort effective competition. Therefore, the emphasis was put on the backwardness of the Italian legislation in the field of antitrust. In addition, beyond their respective peculiarities, the two final reports explicitly recognised the positive role displayed by EC competition policy in promoting economic efficiency at the Community level and underlined the need for domestic rules on competition on the basis of two main arguments. Firstly, articles 85 and 86 of the Treaty of Rome apply only to agreements, concerted practices or abuses of a dominant position 'which may affect trade between Member States' and do not therefore cover operations producing their anticompetitive effects solely within the national territory. Secondly the establishment of a domestic anti-trust authority could allow more effective co-operation and policy co-ordination between the national administration and the Commission.

Law no. 287 stems from such premises. Its purported aim is, on the one hand, to provide for a legal framework complementing EC anti-trust legislation in relation to cases involving no effect on trade between member-states; and on the other, to ensure consistency between national and Community policy objectives in order to avoid possible conflicts with the Commission's decisions. Two remarks can be made in this connection.

Firstly, as regards the scope of the Italian law, article 1 provides, in principle, for exclusive Community control of situations involving an effect on intra-Community trade, thus limiting the national authority's jurisdiction to situations falling outside the reach of articles 85 and 86. It should be stressed that such a system has no equivalent in the legislation of other member-states, which generally abide by the principle of the 'parallel applicability' of national and Community rules on competition (subject however to the conditions set out in the *Walt Wilhelm* judgment and with the exception of cases of concentration coming within the scope of Regulation 4064/89. Secondly, the basic substantive provisions of law no. 287 applying to individual or collective behaviour of undertakings (articles 2 to 4) follow *mutatis mutandi* the text of Articles 85 and 86 of the EC Treaty. They provide in particular, both for the nullity of agreements, concerted practices and decisions of associations 'which have as their object or effect the prevention, restriction or distortion of competition within the national market' (article 2) and for the prohibition of abuses of a dominant position carried out by 'one or more undertakings within the national market or a substantial part of it' (article 3). Furthermore, as provided for in article 85(3) of the EC Treaty, article 4 sets forth the conditions under which certain restrictive agreements falling under the prohibition of article 2 could benefit from an exemption: agreements which contribute to improving production or distribution, or to promoting technical or economic progress may qualify for such an exemption provided that they do not lead to unnecessary restrictions on competition and that they allow consumers a share of the resulting benefits.

However, despite its close linkage with EC competition rules, the Italian law presents certain peculiarities as regards *the scope of possible derogations* to the prohibition set forth in article 2. Such peculiarities will be briefly outlined in the two following paragraphs.

3.3.2 *International competitiveness of the national industry*

First of all, it may be observed that, unlike article 85(3), article 4 provides explicitly that an exemption may be granted in relation to agreements 'which contribute to improving the offer on the market, having regard to the need to enhance the international competitiveness of the undertakings concerned.'

In view of the subject-matter of the present survey, we will omit here to comment on the apparent contradiction existing between this rule (which supposes that the agreements under examination may have an effect on intra-Community trade) and article 1 of law no. 287 (which would exclude in such cases the exercise of domestic jurisdiction). We will confine our analysis instead to the policy objective underlying the rule. In this respect, the opinion has been expressed that the Italian industrial system would still be characterised by structural and regional imbalances which may require, at the industrial level, rationalisation and co-operation strategies, with a view to a better exploitation of production capacities and financial resources. Moreover, it has been observed that the achievement of such objectives might involve a certain degree of concertation between undertakings, which, though reprehensible under strict anti-trust standards, could be regarded as legitimate in so far as it contributes to enhancing the international competitiveness of the industry. It should be added, also, that both the legislative proposals originally submitted to the Senate by Senator Rossi on behalf of the Independent Left-wing Parliamentary Group (*Senato della Repubblica, X, Doc. no. 1012*) and, respectively, by the Government (*Senato della Repubblica, X, Doc. no. 1240*), bore witness to this concern. In fact, despite their different inspiration, both of them acknowledged 'the role of certain cooperative behaviours and agreements in promoting economic efficiency' (*Ibid. Doc. no. 1240:4*).

This raises the question whether such an approach, as reflected in article 4 of the Italian law, could be regarded as compatible with Community policy standards. In section c.2 below, we will try to show to what extent, and on the basis of which criteria, the Commission has accepted, under article 85(3), a wide range of industrial co-operation agreements and practices likely to promote the international competitiveness of European industry.

3.3.3 Sectoral economic objectives

While the Italian economic system is still characterized by a large public sector and by a variety of sectorial regulations, the recent debate in the Parliament has highlighted a widespread concern for the shortcomings of such a system and emphasised the need to introduce fresh competition within regulated economic areas. Such concern is reflected in article 8(1) of law no. 287, which provides that competition rules should apply to all undertakings, whether public or private, and by article 21 which sets out special procedures for an ongoing review of laws or administrative regulations likely to distort competition. Nevertheless, certain derogations are explicitly provided for in respect of specially 'sensitive' sectors.

Firstly, article 8(2) of the Italian law provides that 'the undertakings entrusted with the operation of services of general economic interest' shall *not* be subject to the anti-trust provisions 'in so far as the particular tasks assigned to them are concerned'. This provision, which reverses the legal presumption in article 90(2) of the EC treaty, has been interpreted as a residual safeguard of the position of public services in Italy (Lupi, 1988:1409). In this context, the telecommunications sector seems indeed to enjoy privileged status in that as even potential competition by 'in-house' parallel networks is expressly forbidden (article 9).

Secondly, with regard to the financial sector, article 20 of the Italian law provides for a specific derogation in respect of agreements or practices which, although limiting competition among financial institutions, may be regarded as positive 'on the ground of the stability of the monetary system.' While it may be premature to draw conclusions on this matter, in the absence of concrete examples of implementation of this rule, it may nevertheless be useful to recall that the need to reconcile anti-trust with monetary policy objectives had been repeatedly invoked within the framework of the debate which preceded the adoption of law no. 287. In this respect it has been observed for instance that 'competitive practices, susceptible of provoking instability, should be regarded as undesirable and be subject to some form of control' (*Studio della concorrenza nel sistema economico italiano, 1988*). As a result, it cannot be excluded that certain anti-competitive practices, such as inter-bank agreements on interest rates, could be appraised, in the future, more permissively under national standards than under the EC rules.

3.4 National merger control

This issue has been at the heart of a difficult debate in the Parliament and concerns three different sets of rules: firstly, the rules governing the administrative control of operations of concentrations; secondly, the rules defining the limits within which industrial and trading companies may acquire interests in financial institutions; and thirdly, the rules applying to the media sector.

3.4.1 National dimension and international competitiveness

Articles 5 to 7 and 16 to 19 of the Italian law deal with the first aspect. In particular, article 6 defines the operations of concentration which are to be regarded as restrictive of competition and, hence, prohibited. These concentrations are those leading to 'the creation or the strengthening of a dominant position on the national market as a result of which competition is substantially and durably restricted or eliminated'. Furthermore article 6 specifies that such a situation must be eliminated by taking into account different economic factors such as the market position of the parties, the freedom of choice of suppliers and users, the structure of the markets concerned and barriers to entry. However, besides these factors, which are directly drawn from article 2 of Council Regulation 4064/89, article 6 of the Italian law contains an additional criterion, i.e. 'the competitive situation of the national industry'.

For a proper understanding of this provision, it may be useful to refer to the preparatory works from which it appears that, from the beginning of the parliamentary debate, one of the main sources of concern was represented by the need to take account of certain structural weakness of the national industrial system. In particular, it was argued that

the average dimension of undertakings has been consistently lower in Italy, during the past decade, than in the majority of European countries ... The levels of concentration in the manufacturing sector are still comparatively low, while the high levels of the imports bear witness to the openness of the Italian market to international competition (*Studio della concorrenza nel sistema economico italiano, 1988*)

As a result, a certain doctrine has emphasised the need to follow an approach centred more on the control of the individual *behaviour on the market* than on the *structure of markets*, and aimed at prohibiting monopoly profits or other abusive conducts rather than preventing concentrative operations. Traces of such concern could be found in the Draft law adopted by the Senate on March 1989. The draft provisions thereof specified in fact that concentrations leading to the creation of a dominant position on the market could be authorized, should they 'concern one or more economic sectors in respect of which the CIPE (Inter-ministry Committee for Economic Planning), following a proposal of the Ministry of Industry, shall declare, in the interest of the national economy, the opportunity to encourage a higher degree of concentration, with a view to enhancing the international competitiveness of undertakings'.

Although the final text of article 6 no longer contains such a specific provision, it nevertheless appears to mitigate the principle of the prohibition of concentrations creating dominant positions with the need to take account of the competitive situation of the national industry, a criteria whose implementation may very well result in decisions inspired more by industrial policy objectives than by strict antitrust considerations.

The foregoing remarks seem therefore to suggest that, in the mind of the legislator, the ultimate objective of article 6 of law no. 287 is to prevent negative changes in the competitive structure of the national market without, however, prejudicing *the international competitiveness of the domestic industry*.

An indirect confirmation of this can be found in article 25, which vests the Government with the power to determine 'general guidelines on the basis of which, in exceptional circumstances, the Authority may authorize in the interest of the national economy ... concentrations which would normally be prohibited under article 6'. In this connection, it should also be noted that article 25(2) seems to strengthen the 'defensive' rationale of the norm in that as it subordinates the authorization of concentrations involving foreign companies to the requirement that the State where the said companies are established applies equivalent standards in respect of, and does not implement discriminatory measures against, Italian companies.

3.4.2 Cases of concentration in the financial sector

In addition to these general remarks concerning the principles applicable to all operations of concentration, it should be noted that law no. 287 provides for specific sectorial rules governing *the relationship between industry and financial institutions*. In particular, article 27 introduces a control procedure in relation to transactions whereby non-financial undertakings acquire interests in financial institutions. The system adopted provides for an authorization mechanism in relation to acquisitions exceeding a certain capital threshold (5 per cent) and prohibits, *de jure*, operations leading to either the control of the bank targeted, or the acquisition of at least 15 per cent of its capital. In this context, antitrust criteria have been coupled with stricter standards in view of a specific policy objective, i.e. *the independence of the financial sector*.

3.4.3 Cases of concentration in the media sector

For a complete outline of the national rules applying to concentrations, reference should also be made to the regime applicable to the *media sector*. Special regulations apply in fact to concentrations within the radio and television broadcasting sector (law no. 223 of 6 August 1990) and the newspaper publishing sector (law no. 416 of 5 August 1981, as amended by law no. 137 of 30 April 1983 and by law no. 67 of 25 February 1987), and an *ad hoc* authority is vested with the responsibility of controlling transactions affecting the structure of these markets. The peculiarity of the above-mentioned regulations is that the legal appraisal of an operation of concentration relies here on a notion of 'dominant position' whose scope is defined on the basis of certain absolute thresholds which have no equivalent under article 6 of law no. 287 and result in a rather strict regime. The relative severity of this regime is justified by an autonomous policy objective which, ultimately, outweighs anti-trust standards, i.e. *the protection of the plurality of sources of information*

3.5 Community objectives: a cost and benefits analysis

The various policy objectives briefly described in the previous section will now be compared with the EC competition policy objectives, on a cost and benefits basis.

3.5.1 Competition and integration of national markets

When approaching European anti-trust, one should be aware of the interdependence between the general objectives of the Treaty and the more specific rules enshrined in articles 85 and 86. The constitutional aim of the Community system is defined in article 2 as the promotion of a 'harmonious development of economic activities, a continuous and balanced expansion, an increase in stability, an accelerated raising of the standard of living and closer relations between the States belonging to it'. While similar objectives are inherent to virtually all democratic economies, what distinguishes the Community system is the means for their achievement. To this end, the Treaty of Rome provides for the establishment of a barrier free internal market and 'the institution of a system ensuring that competition in the common market is not distorted' (article 3.f).

Therefore, contrary to US anti-trust, EC competition policy has a specific role to play within the European integration process. More precisely, its ultimate objective is twofold.

Firstly, as a complement to the Treaty provisions on free movement of goods, services, persons and capitals, Community anti-trust aims at ensuring that, once governmental barriers between Member-States have been removed, private economic operators do not erect new obstacles through restrictive agreements or abuses of dominant positions which may restore national divisions in trade within the Community. In accordance with such an objective, articles 85 and 86 apply only in respect of behaviour which may affect trade between member-states. The integrative function of the European competition law has repeatedly been affirmed by the Court of Justice since its 1966 judgment in the *Grundig-Consten* case (56 and 58/64, ECR, 1966: 299).

Secondly, in accordance with the assumption that free market efficiency depends, critically, on the competitive interaction of economic agents in the marketplace, EC anti-trust is designed to create an environment which encourages and guarantees competition as a stimulus to economic activities. Accordingly, the Commission has been vested with the task to secure uniform application of Articles 85 and 86 in the common market. In particular, specific investigatory and decision-making powers have been conferred on the Commission by Council Regulation 17/62 of 6 February 1962 (OJ L13, 1962) with a view to ensuring an effective detection and repression of anti-competitive agreements, concerted practices or abuses of dominant position throughout the common market.

From a costs and benefits viewpoint, there is no doubt that in so far as EC anti-trust provisions contribute to promoting economic efficiency by controlling abuses of market power, the Community system has given Italy, for about three decades, a fundamental advantage, i.e. to provide, in the absence of a domestic system, the legal basis and administrative machinery for the control of anti-competitive practices and, therefore, the protection of consumers' interests and the economic freedom of third parties.

Nevertheless, certain authors have argued that the co-existence, within EC anti-trust law, of heterogeneous policy objectives, such as economic efficiency and market integration, would lead in certain cases to dis-economies. In line with the theories developed by the Chicago School during the past decade, it has been stressed in particular that the severity shown by the Community in respect of territorial restraints within exclusive or selective distribution or patent and know-how licensing agreements, although understandable from a market integration viewpoint, would not be fully justifiable on the basis of purely economic criteria. Similarly, the notion of 'abuse' and its enforcement under article 86 would fail, in certain cases, to take account of commercial realities: for example, the fact that a dominant undertaking maintains price differentials between national markets (see case 27/76, *United Brands v. Commission*, ECR, 1978: 207) would receive less severe treatment under US anti-trust law than under article 86 (for these critics, see generally Hawk, 1989: 6).

A detailed review of such arguments would be beyond the scope of the present survey. In fact, our purpose is to determine the extent to which EC policy objectives in the field of competition may hinder or foster national interests. In this perspective, it should be observed that, although the inclusion of market integration as a policy objective of the EC anti-trust may outweigh, in a limited number of cases, certain short-term gains of productivity, such a disadvantage may be largely compensated, in other cases, by macro-economic advantages following the establishment of a single European market and the consequent expansion of business opportunities: the scope for such a compensation will be further investigated in other studies within the present volume, specifically devoted to EC internal market policy.

Apart from such a general remark, the integration of national markets as a specific objective of the EC anti-trust policy may entail at least two consequences which, in the case of Italy, have some bearing on the assessment of the costs and benefits of its membership of the EC. On the one hand, the close link between anti-trust policy and the integration of national markets has resulted in a relaxation of the anti-trust regime in relation to certain forms of industrial co-operation. On the other hand, it has led the Commission progressively to extend the application of competition rules to economic sectors subject, in most member-states, to governmental regulations limiting competition and preserving divisions between national markets (e.g. public services and financial sectors). These two aspects will now be examined in greater detail.

3.5.2 International competitiveness in the European market

As has been seen certain forms of industrial cooperation designed to enhance the international competitiveness of the industry are generally regarded in Italy, as beneficial for the national economic system as a whole and likely to benefit from an exemption under article 4 of the Italian law.

Turning now to EC competition policy, a glance at the Commission's practice shows that considerations of general economic policy, such as the enhancement of the international competitiveness of European industry, have played an increasingly important role in the application of article 85(3). It might be useful, in this connection, to quote the following statement made by the Commission in its 13th Report on Competition Policy.

The decisions the Commission took hence reflected a continuing determination to enforce rigorously the competition rules, but also the desire to encourage industrial restructuring, to improve the competitiveness of European industry, to promote research and development and innovation, and to accelerate the progress towards a single Community market, (...) Competition policy also contributes to improving the allocation of resources and raising the competitiveness of Community industry, and thanks to this greater competitiveness, secured largely by encouragement of research and development, to enabling the Community at length to overcome the economic problems now facing it and in particular to combat structural unemployment. (1983:11)

A few examples will help to understand the nature of the *EC* policy objectives and assess their possible impact on national interests.

Firstly, it is worth recalling briefly the Commission's practice in the field of *industrial restructuring agreements*. In this respect, the decision *Eni/Montedison* of 1986 (OJ 1987, L5/13) is particularly interesting, as it comes within the process of rationalization of the Italian petrochemical industry. This case concerned a major restructuring operation which formed part of the Chemical Plan devised by the Government in order to cope with the structural overcapacities affecting the sector. In the Commission's appraisal, the operation brought about several restrictions of competition: sharing of markets through a *de facto* specialisation and no-competition clauses; restriction of output through a mutually agreed reduction of capacities; co-ordination of respective behaviours on those markets where the parties continued to be actual or potential competitors. Nevertheless, the Commission expressly took into account the objective of the restructuring of an industry suffering from structural overcapacities and decided to grant an exception under article 85(3). It was observed, in particular, that the agreements enabled the parties to rationalize more quickly and rapidly than would otherwise have been the case. Furthermore, the benefits of the rationalization would have passed to the consumer, since the degree of competition on the relevant market, though diminished, was still at an acceptable level.

The decision *ENI/Montedison* developed a doctrine which had already been tested, in part, in the cases *Synthetic Fibres* (OJ 1984, L207/17) and *BPCL/ICI* (OJ 1984, L212/1) and which has been confirmed, *inter alia*, in the decision *Enichem/ ICI* of 1987 (OJ 1988, L50/18).

Secondly, reference can be made to the Commission's approach to *research and development* agreements. In this respect, it has been observed that

although innovative efforts should be regarded as a normal part of the entrepreneurial spirit of individual undertakings, it cannot be denied that, in many cases, the synergy arising out of the cooperation is necessary because it enables the partners to share the financial risks involved and to bring together a wider range of intellectual resources, thus promoting the transfer of technology. (*14th Report on Competition Policy*, 1984: 38)

In accordance with such premises, the Commission's Regulation no. 418/85. provides for a block-exemption of agreements concerning both joint R & D activities and joint exploitation of the results arising from that R & D. This notion of 'joint exploitation', which covers joint manufacturing and licensing to third parties, but *not* joint distribution or selling, illustrates well the particular balance between anti-trust and industrial criteria which is at the heart of Regulation 418/ 85. In some cases, however, individual exemptions have been granted in respect of R & D agreements which included restrictions going beyond the limits set out in Regulation 418/85 (see, for instance, the Commission's decisions *BBC/Brown Boweri*, OJ 1988, L301/11; *Continental/Michelin*, OJ 1988, L305/33; *Alcatel Espace/ ANT*, OJ 1990, L32/15). A concrete example can also be found in the decision *Olivetti/Cannon* of 1988 (OJ 1988, L52/51) which concerned the creation of a joint venture designed to enable the parties to update their technologies in a more efficient manner.

Thirdly, the objective itself of market integration has led the Commission to accept certain horizontal restrictions in consideration, *inter alia*, of the need to promote across-the-border co-operation and a more competitive European industry. For example, exemptions have been granted in respect of certain joint manufacturing and distribution agreements (see, as regards the Italian automobile sector, the decisions *Iveco/Rockwell* in OJ 1983, L224/19 and *Iveco/Ford* in OJ 1988, L230/39), joint exploitation of complementary technologies (*Optical fibers,* OJ 1986, L236/30) or industrial specialisation (see generally the Commission Regulation no. 417/85, in OJ 1985, L 53/23).

From a costs and benefits viewpoint, the foregoing remarks suggest that there exists a substantial similarity between the policy criteria underlying the application of article 85(3) of the EC Treaty and the cases of derogation covered by article 4 of the Italian law. In general terms, it could be observed that both sets of rules aim at ensuring a balanced application of anti-trust with a view to protecting of competitive markets and, at the same time, safeguarding entrepreneurial decisions designed to foster industrial development and international competitiveness. It follows that, in such a specific matter, any possible conflict between the Italian and the Community systems should represent a marginal risk.

3.5.3 Community competition policy within special sectors

One of the most significant features of the Commission's recent practice is the tendency to extend the application of the EC competition rules to economic sectors which initially had not been given priority but which have begun to require attention in view of a fuller integration of national markets. Anti-trust enforcement has been thus extended into the services sector, particularly telecommunications and air transport, as well as banking and insurance.

As regards the insurance sector, the Commission first took a formal stand in its decisions *Verband der Sachversicheren* (OJ 1985, L35/20) and *Nuovo Cegam* (OJ 1985, L99/29) which concerned, respectively, certain agreements concluded among a German association of property insurers and an Italian association of industrial insurers. In these cases, the Commission carefully weighed the benefits of free competition against more general economic interests (solvency of insurance companies, limitation of the financial risks involved with the operation of insurance services, etc.). After the ruling of the Court of Justice in the *Fire Insurance case* (45/85, ECR, 1987: 405), the Commission confirmed its position in the decision *Concordato incendio* (OJ 1990, L15/25).

In the banking sector, the Commission has recently exempted a number of agreements concluded within national banking associations in Belgium, Ireland, the Netherlands and Italy and designed to rationalize financial operations, although these exemptions were granted only after certain restrictive practices in respect of commissions charged to customers were abandoned (see, in particular, *Associazione bancaria italiana*, (OJ 1987, L43/51). Until now the Commission has not taken a formal stand on the delicate problem of interbank agreements on interest rates, although in a press release of November 1989 it was pointed out that 'such agreements restrict competition as do price cartels' (IP/89/869) and should therefore be avoided or abandoned.

Finally with regard to the telecommunications and air transport sectors, it should be recalled that in 1989 the Commission adopted a directive based on article 90 of the EC Treaty requiring member-states to establish a system of free competition in the Community market for telecommunications terminal equipment (Directive 88/301, in OJ 1988, L131/73 and case C-202/88, *French Republic and Others v. Commission*, of 19 March 1991). Furthermore, after adopting a number of legislative measures empowering the Commission to enact block-exemption regulations within the air transport sector (Regulation no. 2671/88, 2672/88, 2673/88, OJ 1988, L239), the Council is at present discussing a package of further measures designed to bring to completion the liberalisation of the air transport sector by 1993.

In general, the impact that the above-mentioned developments may have on national policy objectives depends on the degree of regulation or liberalization within each member-state. In Italy, as already noted, the trend emerging from the recent parliamentary debate, confirms to a large extent the traditional prerogatives of the State in directing market operations within certain areas of services. Thus, it cannot be excluded that, in some cases, Community policy objectives could conflict with national interests. In the case *Italian Republic v. Commission* of 1985 (case 41/83, ECR, 1985: 873), for instance, the broad interpretation of article 90(2) advanced by Italy in respect of a statutory monopoly for telecommunications was rejected by the Court of Justice which confirmed the applicability of article 86 to all types of conduct serving business purposes and not strictly related to the official functions entrusted to State enterprises.

In addition, as regards the financial sector, the Commission's policy has until now been based on a just equilibrium between EC anti-trust principles and national priorities of monetary policy (see the *Second Report on Competition Policy*, 1973: 63). Nevertheless, the question is open as to whether a possible extension of Community anti-trust provisions to, for instance, interbank agreements on interest rates, would not impinge upon the exception provided for in article 20 of the Italian law.

Altogether, the observations made under 3.5.1, 3.5.2 and 3.5.3 above may suggest that, insofar as Articles 85 and 86 are concerned, the risk of conflict between national interests and EC anti-trust policy objectives is, indeed, limited to certain specific areas of services, while the similarity existing between national and Community general principles bears witness to the will of the Italian legislature to comply with the Community system. Furthermore, as regards the advantages of the latter system, it should not be forgotten that, in a context of close economic interdependence, a national anti-trust authority could hardly carry out investigations and enforce decisions with regard to certain international cartels without risking to create jurisdictional conflicts with other national authorities. On the contrary, Regulation 17/62 overcomes such an obstacle by establishing procedures under which the Commission, acting in liaison with the competent authorities of the member-states, may take the requisite measures in respect of both fact-finding and enforcement of decisions, throughout the common market.

3.6 Community merger control

As has been said, the system introduced by Regulation 4064/89 confers on the Commission the exclusive competence to take decisions in respect of concentrations having a Community dimension. In particular, article 21(2) specifies that 'no member-state shall apply its national legislation on competition to any concentration that has a Community dimension'. The latter notion is defined by the combination of three criteria: (i) the aggregate world-wide turnover of all undertakings concerned, which must be more than 5 billion ECU; (ii) the aggregate EC-wide turnover of each of at least two of them, which must be more than 250 million ECU; and (iii) the condition that none of the parties derive more than two-thirds of their Community business in one and the same member-state.

In so far as all concentrations having a Community dimension are, pursuant to Regulation 4064/89, removed from member-states' jurisdiction, it may well happen that decisions taken by the Commission in respect of such operations do not always reflect the same economic policy options of the member-states concerned. In this connection, as far as Italy is concerned, it is worth recalling that the Italian general rules applying to national concentrations are aimed at reconciling two fundamental policy objectives: the safeguard of a sound competitive environment, and the need to allow further structural development of the national industry.

3.6.1 Prevention of market dominance and 'European' dimension of undertakings

Turning now to the substantive rules of Regulation 4064/89, it should be observed that the basic principles governing the legal assessment of Community-wide operations of concentration do not differ from those enshrined in the Italian law. In fact, under article 2 of the Regulation, 'a concentration which creates or strengthens a dominant position as a result of which effective competition would be significantly impeded in the common market or in a substantial part of it shall be declared incompatible with the common market.' Furthermore, as in the Italian law, article 2 sets out a comprehensive list of factors which must be taken into account. These include the structure of the markets concerned, actual and potential competition (both from inside and outside the Community), the market position of the parties, freedom of choice of suppliers and users, barriers to entry, the interests of the consumers and technical and economic progress. However, certain differences between the two legal systems may be pointed out.

The first difference concerns the role that *industrial policy considerations* may play, respectively, under the EC rules and national standards. In particular, the emphasis placed by article 6 of the Italian law on factors relating to the 'competitive situation of the national industry' have not a direct equivalent within the text of the Regulation. This does not mean that the Community rules neglect the need to take account of the different levels of industrial development throughout the common market as well as certain sectorial realities. In fact, in the Preamble to Regulation 4064/89, it is stated that the Commission must place its appraisal within the framework of the general principles of the Treaty 'including that of strengthening the Community's economic and social cohesion, referred to in article 130a'. However, the Italian system may allow a more flexible market analysis in view of national economic policy objectives. In this respect, it can be observed that during the first year of implementation of Regulation 4064/89, such difference has resulted in a conflict of interests in one concrete case involving the Italian aerospace sector (case *Aerospatiale-Alenia/de Haviland* of 2 October 1991, to be published).

The second difference relates to the *reciprocity* standard which, under article 25 of the Italian law, subordinates the governmental authorization of 'national' concentrations involving foreign companies. In this respect, it should be noted that the implementation of such a standard is incompatible with the obligations which Italy has contracted in the framework of the EC Treaty, and namely with article 7 thereof. In fact, under the EC system, member-states cannot invoke the principle of reciprocity in respect of other member-states. (As regards the incompatibility with Community law of national provisions on reciprocity, see the judgment of the Court of Justice of 15 October 1986, *Commission v. Italian Republic*, case 168/ 85, ECR, 1986: 2945). It should be added that Community law provides for a specific remedy, which outweighs such limitation of national jurisdiction: under article 170 of the Treaty, member-states are in fact allowed to make an appeal to the Court of Justice, should one of their companies be the victim of any discrimination by other member-states.

From a costs and benefits viewpoint, it should be added that, notwithstanding the possibility of a conflict (in the framework of which Community interests would take precedence over national economic policy objectives), the EC system provides, in all circumstances, two important 'benefits', i.e. a higher degree of legal security for undertakings and a limitation of the risk of jurisdictional conflicts between different national authorities. In fact, it should be kept in mind, firstly, that national merger control, given the growing number of cross-border operations of concentration in Europe, could give rise to legal uncertainty in so far as a set of parallel procedures carried out by different anti-trust authorities could lead to diverging decisions with respect to the same operation. Secondly, in a context of economic interdependence, even mergers taking place outside the national boundaries may affect competition within the territory of the State and lead to extraterritorial enforcement of domestic provisions. This could result in jurisdictional conflicts among different national bodies. In view of such a risk, for instance, the Dutch government renounced enacting provisions on the control of concentrations, *inter alia*, on the ground that, owing to the high level of international integration of its economy, the risk of jurisdictional conflicts would outweigh any advantage of a national control.

3.6.2 Financial sector and national public interests

As has been seen above, the Italian legislation contains special provisions concerning acquisitions of interests in financial institutions by non-financial undertakings. In particular, article 27 of law no. 287 sets out strict criteria designed to ensure the independence of the financial sector.

Regulation 4064/89, on the contrary, does not prevent undertakings operating in non-financial sectors from acquiring control of financial institutions. In such a case, in fact, the operation would not create a dominant position on a specific market. As a result, operations having a Community dimension would be authorized by the Commission whereas 'smaller' operations subject to the national legislation would be subject to stricter criteria and, eventually, prohibited. This incongruency stems from the fact that the independence of the financial sector does not come within the policy objectives recognized by Regulation 4064/89. In case of conflict, the sole remedy open to Italy would be the special procedure set forth in article 21(3) of the Regulation, which entitles the Commission both to recognise a national public interest not expressly covered by the Regulation as compatible with the Community law and to authorize the member-state concerned to take appropriate measures in order to protect such 'legitimate interest'.

3.6.3 Community-wide concentrations and plurality of media

Regulation 4064/89 applies also in respect of concentrations having a Community dimension within the media sector. However, while the Commission is vested with the sole responsibility to appraise the compatibility of such concentrations with the common market, member-states are not, in this framework, deprived of the possibility to exert certain competences.

For our purposes, it should be stressed that under article 21 of Regulation 4064/89, member-states may take appropriate measures to protect legitimate interests other than those taken into consideration by the said Regulation, in so far as they are compatible with Community law. In particular, the same provision specifies that 'plurality of media' can be regarded as a legitimate interest which fulfils such a condition. Therefore, Community law does not prevent Italy from taking, under law no. 287, appropriate measures in order to prohibit Community-wide concentrations which, pursuant to national standards, would be regarded as prejudicial to the plurality of sources of information.

3.7 Conclusions

For a period spanning over three decades, EC anti-trust provisions have been the sole legal instrument designed to preserve competitive international trade within Italy. Therefore, on account of the 'benefits', there is no doubt that the Community system has effectively contributed, in the absence of domestic law, to the protection of competition and economic efficiency in Italy. It should be added in this connection that, although articles 85 and 86 of the EC Treaty apply only to behaviour 'which may affect trade among member states', the broad interpretation given by the Court of Justice to this notion has enabled the Commission to supervise a large range of market operations liable to affect the national market.

Following the adoption of law no. 287, in October 1990, the foregoing assessment of cost and benefits of Community anti-trust legislation has taken account of two factors: firstly, the fact that article 1 of the Italian law limits, by way of principle, the exercise of national jurisdiction over cases which do not fall under article 85 and 86 of the EC Treaty: and secondly, the fact that the basic substantial principles enshrined in law no. 287 are, to a large extent, drawn from the Community rules on competition.

With regard to national jurisdiction, the political choice made by the Italian parliament within the context of article 1 bears witness to its will to minimize the scope of any possible conflict with the Community decision-making process. While the Court of Justice has confirmed the applicability of national legislation on competition in parallel with articles 85 and 86, the Italian Parliament has voluntarily opted for a system which excludes, in principle, national jurisdiction in respect of behaviour affecting trade among member-states. In this regard, it has been observed that the Italian option is unique, if compared to the various anti-trust systems in force in other member-states. From a cost and benefits viewpoint, the aforesaid option may imply the advantage to valorize the *subsidiarity* existing between national and Community anti-trust legislation. At the same time, the evaluation made by the national authority with respect to the circumstances allowing the exercise of its jurisdiction (i.e. a behaviour which does not affect trade among member-states), could diverge, in concrete cases, from that made by the Commission. In such cases, however, Italian law appears to allow pragmatic solutions, having regard in particular to article 1(4), under which the interpretation of the national substantive rules 'shall be made in accordance with the principles of Community law on competition'.

In so far as the substantive content of Community and national rules is concerned, a distinction has been made, in the foregoing analysis, between rules applicable to (i) anti-competitive behaviour and (ii) the control of concentrations.

With regard to the first aspect, it has been observed that a certain divergence between national policy objectives and EC practice may eventually subsist in relation to special sectors which, particularly in Italy, have been traditionally subject to the regulatory intervention of the State. In fact, while the Italian rules relating to the financial sector and certain areas of services allow a relaxation of anti-trust criteria on the basis of general economic policy objectives, the Commission's recent practice shows instead a stricter application of anti-trust standards in relation to such sectors. However, it has also been observed, that the risk of this type of conflict arising is rather marginal. In fact, having regard to the general principles, articles 2 to 4 of the Italian law and articles 85 and 86 of the EC Treaty appear, indeed, to reflect essentially similar approaches. In particular, the policy objective relating to 'the need to enhance the international competitiveness of the national industry', as contained in article 4 of the Italian law, appears to be compatible with the well-established practice of the Commission and a number of block-exemption regulations. In both legal systems, the ultimate aim is to reconcile the objective of ensuring that competition is not distorted with certain industrial policy criteria. Moreover, it should be added that Council Regulation no. 17/62 vests the Commission with investigatory and decision-making powers designed to allow effective detection and repression of cartels: such powers, if operated solely by national authorities, would not only be less effective from the point of view of fact-finding and collation of evidence, but could also create the risk of extra-territorial enforcement of national anti-trust provisions and result, eventually, in jurisdictional conflicts.

The second policy area examined concerns the control of concentrations between undertakings. In this area, a case of inconsistency between national provisions and EC rules has been examined in connection with article 25 of the Italian law, in so far as this provision allows the national authority to prohibit acquisitions operated by foreign undertakings whose State of origin does not apply reciprocity standards in respect of Italian companies. It has been seen in particular that the EC system, and namely article 7 of the Treaty, prevents a member-state from using its anti-trust legislation in order to retaliate against discrimination carried out against its undertakings. However, it has also been observed that, in such a case, the Treaty makes provision for a specific remedy (i.e. the procedure set out in article 170) in order to obtain the redressment of possible discriminations suffered by national companies within the common market. In addition, certain sectorial policy objectives expressly recognized under Italian legislation (e.g. independence of the financial sector) are not directly contemplated by Council Regulation 4064/89. Finally, industrial policy criteria may play a greater role under the national system than in the context of EC provisions. Against these potential discrepancies, however, it has also been noted that the Community system of mergers control has two important advantages, in so far as it offers a higher degree of legal security to all undertakings operating within the common market and, at the same time, reduces the risk of jurisdictional conflict between member-states.

Notes

1. The present survey will be dealing only with the anti-trust system provided for in the EC Treaty.

Bibliography

Associazione fra le società italiane per azioni (1989), *Relazione presentata all'Assemblea del 23 giugno 1989*, Rome. 1989.

Bellamy and Child (1987), *Common Market Law of Competition*, London, Sweet & Maxwell.

Bernini G. (1991), *Un secolo di filosofia antitrust,* Bologna, CLUEB.

Bork R. H., (1978), *The Antitrust Paradox*, New York, Basic Books, Inc.

Confindustria (1988), *Libertà del mercato e tutela della concorrenza*, Roma.

Donativi V. (1990), *Introduzione alla disciplina antitrust nel sistema legislativo italiano,* Milano, Giuffrè.

Esch B. Van der (1985), Some Aspects of 'Extra-territorial' Infringement of EEC Competition Rules, Fordham Corporate Law Institute, New York, p. 285.

Hawk B. G. (1989), La révolution antitrust américaine: une leçon pour la Communauté économique européene?, Revue trimestrielle de droit européene, Vol. I, p. 6.

Hornsby S. (1988), National and community control of concentrations in a single market: should member states be allowed to impose stricter standards?', European Law Review, Vol. 13, p. 295.

Lupi G. (1988), 'La tutela della concorrenza in Italia: le iniziative parlamentari nella decima legislatura', Rivista di polica economica, Vol. XII, p. 1373.

Menis C. (1990), Les Rapports entre le droit communautaire et la nouvelle loi italienne relative à la protection de la concurrence', Economia delle Scelte pubbliche, Vol. 2/3, p. 79.

Moavero Milanesi E. (1989), 'Concorrenza e concentrazioni fra imprese', Diritto comunitario' e degli scambi internazionali, Vol. 3, p. 499.

Petriccione R. M. (1987), 'Competition law in Italy: a consultative document', European Law Review, Vol. 12, p. 379.

Shenefield J. H. and Neale A. (1985), 'Jurisdictional conflicts arising from antitrust enforcement', Antitrust Law Journal, Vol. 54, p. 751.

Slot P. J. and Van der Woude M. (1989), (eds.), *Exploiting the Internal Market: Co-operation and Competition Toward 1992*, Deventer, Kluwer.

Stockmann K. (1985), Foreign Application of European Antitrust Laws, Fordham Corporate Law Institute, New York, p. 251.

Chapter 4

Environmental policy

Andrea Bianchi

4.1 Introduction

The cost–benefit assessment of EC membership for member-states with regard to environmental policy is no easy task. Many areas of environmental law could be considered and all the different legal tools that have been employed to deal with environmental issues merit an in-depth evaluation. Given the general character of this series, however, we will first focus on the main features of EC environmental law, especially since the adoption of the Single European Act (SEA) which came into force in 1987, thereby giving environmental policy an autonomous legal basis (see Title VII devoted to the Environment: article 130R–T). We will then consider the Italian legislative framework in the domain of environmental protection.

A survey of EC environmental law is helpful in several respects. First of all, one can ask whether a Community environmental policy existed before the SEA was enacted. Secondly, by examining relevant provisions of the SEA and the case-law of the European Court of Justice (ECJ), we can begin to make a tentative assessment of advantages and disadvantages of EC membership for member-states in terms of legislative and external relations competence.

In addition, a short history of developments that have occurred in Italy in the field of environmental protection may provide useful hints as to the effects of Community environmental measures on the Italian legal system.

Knowledge of the relevant legal aspects of both systems and of the various tools used to ensure good environmental and living conditions will enable us to evaluate the real impact of EC legislation upon domestic law and to verify what are the costs and benefits, in terms of legislative techniques and concrete results, that Italy respectively has to bear or to gain out of its EC membership.

Given the deliberate choice not to take into account quantitative data bearing upon budgetary matters related to the implementation of different environmental policies, which would better fit the idea of a cost–benefit approach from the traditional standpoint of economic analysis, the following evaluation will be mainly based upon the testing of the consistency of national and Community policies with the common goals set forth in the domain of environmental protection, such as, for example, the preservation, protection and improvement of the quality of the environment (Ripa di Meana, 1989).

Due regard will also be paid to comparing the stringency of environmental

standards adopted by Italy and by the EC, to evaluating their scope of application
and effectiveness, and to assessing the overall coherence and comprehensiveness of
the legal framework set up by both legal systems to cope with environmental
issues. The institutional co-operation on a European scale, although fundamental
in dealing effectively with some of these issues, should not, however, cause us to
overlook the importance for member-states of continuing to co-operate with third
parties (non-EC states) in an effort to provide a solution to regional problems that
do not constitute a concern for the EC as a whole (for example, pollution of the
Mediterranean Sea, bilateral arrangements with Yugoslavia for the preservation of
the Adriatic Sea, and bilateral agreements on transboundary pollution with countries such as Austria and Switzerland).

The basic assumption of this chapter is that the quality of environmental
protection and the improvement of environmental conditions, being the shared
objectives of both national and Community environmental policies, will also be the
criteria used to evaluate such costs and benefits. The priority thus assigned to the
above-mentioned values will consequently prevent us from taking into account, in
the following assessment, general positive and negative effects on trade and economic development resulting for Italy from the laxity or stringency of environmental protection measures taken at the Community level.

Finally, consideration will be devoted to determining whether the competing
objectives of economic integration and growth on the one hand and environmental protection on the other can be rendered consistent within the context of the
European Communities.

4.2 The legal framework for environmental protection in the EC Treaty: costs and benefits for member-states in general

When the Rome Treaties establishing the European Economic Communities
were drafted in 1957 no specific rule was provided for environmental protection.
The main concern and the long-term goal for the drafters was the achievement of
a common market within a limited geographic area, although a certain regard to
social aspects of the economic integration process was to be taken into account.
Among the general rules set forth in the first articles of the Rome Treaty it is
worth mentioning article 2 which includes, as one of the goals to be pursued by
the Community, the promotion of 'a harmonious development of economic
activities, a continuous and balanced expansion, an increase in stability, an accelerated raising of the standard of living and closer relations between the States
belonging to it'.

4.2.1 The first fifteen years of European environmental policy

In fact the expansive interpretation of article 2 has been for some fifteen years the
legal basis invoked to justify the adoption by the Community of environmental
action plans.[1] In the absence of *ad hoc* provisions in the constitutive treaty, article 2

allowed for a modern interpretation of economic growth, which cannot be seen as an end in itself, but rather should represent the final outcome of a complex socio-economic process that must include, *inter alia*, the improvement in living standards and quality of life as well as environmental protection.

If the protection of the environment could be seen as one of the objectives to be pursued by the European Communities, then the legal instruments commonly used by the Community to implement its policies in various fields would be also available. Although the very first measure indirectly aimed at protecting the environment was probably directive 67/548 on the classification, packaging and labelling of dangerous substances (OJ no. L196, 27/6/1967:1), the earliest attempt at providing a comprehensive and organic action in the field of environmental protection has to be traced to the early 1970s when the Commission prepared, following a specific mandate given to it at the Paris Summit of 1972, the first Environmental Action Programme (EAP) (subsequently endorsed by the Council by way of a Declaration; reproduced in OJ no. C112, 20/12/1973). The structure of the Action Programme consisted of two parts: the first one containing general principles and objectives of a Community environmental policy; the second providing detailed specific measures to be adopted with a view to protecting the environment and improving the quality of life. Since then three other EAP have been adopted in 1977 (OJ no. C139, 13/6/1977:1), 1983 (OJ no. C305, 17/2/1983:2) and 1987 (OJ, no.C70,18/3/1987:3).

Looking carefully at the content of the four EC Environmental Action Programmes it is easy to discern the fundamental principles upon which the Community Environmental Policy still relies. They include the principle of preventing pollution at source; the principle of integration, according to which considerations of environmental protection should be adequately taken into account in planning any activity likely to have an impact on the environment; the polluter pays principle; the differentiation of Community action having regard to regional differences; the promotion of co-operation at various levels – locally, nationally and internationally – and the harmonization of national programmes and legislation, research and training, etc, (Plenivaux, 1984).

With regard to the practical measures necessary to implement environmental policy, some general remarks can be made. First of all, the overwhelming majority of measures in the field of environmental protection have been taken by means of directives. The legal bases, in the absence of specific provisions in the Rome treaty, have been either article 100, concerning the approximation of member-states' national legislation, (whenever the establishment or functioning of the common market could be impaired by the existence of different environmental regulations), or article 235, which allows the Council, subject to some procedural conditions, to act whenever necessary to fulfil one of the goals set forth in the Rome Treaty (in this case article 2; Vaughan, 1986, pp. 752f.).

A second observation concerns the areas of intervention by the Community. The directives adopted in the field of environmental protection refer to the quality of surface waters and of waters for human consumption, air quality standards, waste, chemicals, noise, the discharge of dangerous substances into the environment, nuclear safety, etc. In other words, the Community has adopted a sectorial approach, legislating upon specific areas within a framework of general principles, and leaving aside for national regulation other subjects closely interconnected with environmental issues. Nevertheless the amount of Community measures in existence remains impressive and certainly has made a remarkable impact on member-states' legal systems.

Assessing the development of the Community's action over the years, one can see that at the beginning the EC legislative technique was mainly aimed at reacting to critical environmental conditions already existing. So the focus was on the reparation or limitation of damage rather than on prevention. This trend slowly shifted to a fully preventive approach the apex of which can be considered to be the Fourth Action Programme of 1987. Another innovative aspect of EC policy in the 1980s has been the endorsement of the integration principle, subsequently stated in the SEA as well. The principle, whose fundamental legal tool is obviously the environmental impact assessment procedure, provides that environmental considerations should be taken into account in the early stages of decision-making that will have a bearing on Community policies. It goes without saying that the effective implementation of such a principle in connection with other Community policies would have positive and far-reaching consequences in the domain of environmental protection.

A final remark concerns the implementation and enforcement action undertaken by competent national organs. As is well known, the Commission has the task of monitoring member–states' compliance and execution of obligations stemming from Community primary and secondary law. In fact, the effective implementation of EC environmental legislation, considered of primary importance for the Community and a priority under the Fourth Action Programme (Koppen, 1988, pp. 24ff.), has over the years been a very difficult task to perform (Kräemer, 1988). A series of infringement procedures has been set up before the European Court of Justice by the Commission against defaulting member-states who have not implemented environmental directives in good time and others are still pending. The resort to the infringement procedure, however, is a sort of *ultima ratio* for the Commission. Indeed, the practical difficulties in implementing environmental directives as a result of the heterogeneous legislative and administrative systems of the member-states should push the Commission to pursue closer co-operation with national officials in order to achieve an effective implementation of such directives.

4.2.2 The emergence of environmental policy as a Community policy before the SEA: the relevant ECJ case-law

It is a widely shared view in legal scholarship that environmental policy, due to the absence of specific rules in the Rome Treaty, was made part of the EC constitutional framework only after the adoption of the SEA (Roelants du Vivier and Hannequart, 1988, p. 225). In fact this opinion is supported by consistent technical arguments. Since the SEA represents a series of amendments to the Rome Treaty, all ratified by member-states, it is only in 1987 when the SEA came into force that we can recognize environmental policy as having formal constitutional status as a Community policy.

But this argument is not entirely convincing. In our view the Community environmental policy formed an integral part of primary EC law, both in practical and legal terms, before the SEA. This is so because the subsequent practice of the states parties to the EC Treaty, a relevant factor to be taken into account in order to interpret correctly the scope of application of the constitutive treaty (see article 31(3)(b) of the 1969 Vienna Convention on the law of treaties, VIII ILM (1969):679ff.), had already demonstrated the acceptance of environmental policy as an official Community policy in several respects. First of all, all directives touching upon environmental issues, being taken at the level of the Council where government representatives take decisions, already presuppose an agreement among the member-states *vis-à-vis* the competence of the EC to take legislative action in this field. It is worth mentioning that the legal form of the four EAPs has ranged from a declaration of the Council and of the member-states' representatives meeting in Council (first programme), through a resolution of the Council and of the member-states' representatives meeting in Council (second and third programmes), to a Resolution of the Council endorsing the fourth action programme (Koppen,1988, p. 4). Disregarding any speculation concerning the legal value of these various instruments, it is reasonable to conclude that member-states had already recognized the validity and legitimacy of EC environmental policy well before the SEA.

Another argument which can be used to support the thesis that environmental policy came within the scope of EC powers prior to the SEA is that the ECJ in several judgments considered the validity and legitimacy of EC environmental policy in a series of cases decided in the 1980s. The issue was raised as a preliminary one in various instances, the majority of which were brought under the infringement procedure as envisaged in article 169 of the EC Treaty.

Of particular interest are two cases where Italy appeared as defendant for not having implemented two environmental directives within a reasonable period: the Council directive 73/404 on the approximation of the laws of the member-states on detergents (OJ no. L347, 17/12/1973) and Council directive 75/716 on the approximation of the laws of member-states on the sulphur content of certain liquid fuels (OJ no. L307, 27/11/1975). The Commission brought an action *ex* article 169 against Italy who had refused to comply with the abovementioned directives (ECR, 1980: 1105). The Italian government indirectly contended that the EC legislative competence on environmental matters was 'on the fringe of Community powers' and that the relevant directives were to be interpreted as an international agreement. Italy, however, did not expressly contest such a competence since it would have been in sharp contrast with the undertakings jointly accepted at the Paris Summit where member-states had clearly shown their willingness to start a Community environmental policy (Bianchi and Cordini, 1983, p. 50).

The Court rejected the argument stating that the directives were clearly Community measures and not international agreements. Furthermore, both directives were aimed at setting up product requirements, directly instrumental to prevent distortions of the Common Market and therefore correctly founded upon article 100. The ECJ went on to say that the directives were perfectly admissible in implementing measures of both the 1969 General Programme on the elimination of technical barriers to trade and of the first Environment Action programme.

In this case the relevance of environmental standards for the maintenance of fair competition within the EC and for the avoidance of distortions in intra-Community trade was a decisive factor in environmental directives being held legitimate and validly founded upon article 100 (ECR, 1980: 1106).

The Court considered again the legitimacy of environmental directives in a series of six cases brought by the Commission against Belgium under article 169 (Cases 68/81–73/81, ECR, 1981,: 157ff.). Belgium did not question the legitimacy of the six environmental directives it had failed to implement in good time within its legal system, but simply contended that the delay was due to internal administrative reforms. In line with its long-established case-law, the Court rejected the Belgian argument asserting that a member-state cannot plead as a defence its internal legislation or practice to justify its failure to comply with Community obligations. But what is worth mentioning here is that the Court in several *obiter dicta* stretched the admissible legal basis of environmental directives from article 100 so as to encompass also article 235. The action taken by the Council was deemed necessary by the Court to achieve some of the objectives set forth in the constitutive treaty, namely article 2, listing among the Community's goals the achievement of a 'harmonious development of economic activities' and the Preamble where the Contracting Parties to the Rome Treaty affirm as an essential objective 'the constant improvement of the living and working conditions of their people'.

Looking carefully at the six judgments, one can extrapolate two significant *dicta* of the Court where the shift from a merely economic approach to environmental protection to an express consideration of the environment as a value worthy of legal protection within the Community appears quite clearly. The first passage is found in case 71/81. Here the Court describes the directive as one of the

Community measures based on article 100 and 235 of the Treaty, which, as part of the Community policy on the protection of the environment aims on the one hand to abolish disparities between the laws of Member States which may, in particular by creating unequal conditions of competition, have a direct effect upon the functioning of the Common Market and, on the other hand, to achieve by means of more extensive Community rules *certain objectives laid down by the Treaty*. (ECR, 1982: 175; emphasis added)

What such objectives were, the Court made clear in case 72/81 when it expressly mentioned as one of the aims to be achieved by the Community '... the protection of the environment and the improvement of the quality of life' (ECR, 1982: 189).

The slow but constant process of recognition of a Community environmental policy, witnessed by the case-law of the ECJ, reached its peak in case 240/83 when the Court, while considering a preliminary ruling under article 177 by the *Tribunal de Grande Instance de Creteil* (France), without quoting articles 100 and 235, presented the Community environmental policy as one of the fundamental tasks to be performed by Community organs. In this case, an organisation vested with the task of defending the interests of burners of waste oils contested the validity of Directive 75/439/EEC on the disposal of waste oils in light of the freedom of trade, competition and commerce envisaged in the Rome Treaty. The ECJ, asserting that the principles in question could be limited when other general interests of the Community were at stake, affirmed that environmental policy '... is one of the Community's *essential objectives*' (ECR, 1985: 549; emphasis added) thus giving a final word on the legitimacy of a Community environmental policy and 'constitutionalizing' the long-disputed principle of environmental protection as one of the fundamental goals of the EC.

The concept of environmental protection as one of the mandatory requirements of Community law which may limit the application of other general principles contained in the Treaty of Rome was more recently restated in case 302/86 (*Commission* v. *Denmark*) which will be considered below.

4.2.3 *The Single European Act: achievements, shortcomings, unclear rules*

As we have tried to demonstrate above, the process of bringing environmental policy within the scope of EC competence was achieved before the SEA was adopted. What the SEA has actually done is to spell out in detail the specific content of the Community environmental policy. The drafters of the SEA, however, have often failed to create a precise thread of clear legal rules. In fact some of the provisions relevant to environmental protection are liable to concurrent if not conflicting interpretation and represent, in the present absence of *ad hoc* rulings by the ECJ, a major interpretive challenge for every scholar.

4.2.3.1 Objectives and principles

It is surprising that the environmental policy, to which an entire and independent chapter was devoted in the SEA (Title VII: Environment, article 130R–T), is the Community's best-spelt-out policy. In spite of the absence of a definition of 'environment' – which can be nevertheless traced in the Commission's practice as 'all the elements which form, in the complexity of their interrelations, the framework, the milieu and conditions of human and social life' (Roelants du Vivier and Hannequart, 1988, p. 226) – the Community objectives are identified as the preservation, protection and improvement of the environment, as the contribution towards the protection of human health, and finally as a prudent and rational utilization of national resources. As to the principles on which such a policy should be based, the principle of preventive action is stressed, a concept already emphasized from the second action programme on, along with the principle of pollution control at source involving, *inter alia*, a piece of legislation based on emission standards rather than one founded on the regulation of immissions in the environmental milieu, and the heavily debated 'polluter pays principle'. In particular this latter principle, already endorsed by the OECD (Recommendation C(74)223, 14 November 1974, reprinted in OECD and the Environment, 1986: 26, and

Recommendation C(89)88, 7 July 1988, reprinted in XXVIII ILM (1989): 1320ff.
See for comments: McCaffrey, 1975; Smets,1982) and by the EEC Council
(Recommendation on the Application of the Polluter Pays Principle, 7 November
1974, reprinted at XV ILM, 1975: 138. See also Meli, 1989), may be subjected to
harsh criticism. Actually the 'polluter pays principle' may turn out to be an
instrument by which polluters are somehow allowed to pollute as long as they
provide reparation for the damage caused. Therefore, if not interpreted in close
connection with the principle of prevention, the 'polluter pays principle' can
hardly be considered consistent with an effective preventive strategy of environmental protection.

Certainly the most innovative and far-reaching provision in the list of the
Community's principles of action is the so-called principle of integration, according to which any policy carried out by the Community should take into account,
in the planning phase, the possible effects on the environment that such a policy
may have. It will be interesting to see how the Commission (which has the burden
of proof) will implement this fundamental principle (EIU,1989: 30), whose basic
instrument in the execution phase is, as we have already mentioned, the environmental impact procedure.

4.2.3.2 Allocation of competence

The first obscure area confronting the interpreter is that related to the allocation of
competence between the Community and the member-states. In fact, a clear
understanding of what the Community can do, under what circumstances and in
which particular areas, will also be a decisive factor for member-states when
assessing costs and benefits arising from EC membership. Article 130R(4) provides
that the Community '... shall take action ... to the extent that the objectives
referred to in paragraph 1 *can be attained better at Community level* than at the level of
the individual Member States' (emphasis added).

The first question one is tempted to raise is how can one objectively say that a
certain action taken at Community level is preferable to national legislation?
Furthermore, who is to decide that?

To this question article 130S can provide an answer by asserting that it is the
Council that will decide which action the Community has to take, after having
possibly received an evaluation from the Commission charged with the task of
proposing relevant rules and therefore responsible for proving the major effectiveness of Community action. This evaluation must be based on available scientific
and technical data, on environmental conditions in the various regions of the
Community, on the potential costs and benefits of action or of lack of action, and
on the economic and social development of the Community as a whole and the
balanced development of its regions (article 130R (3)(i–iv)).

Having identified the competent organ responsible for indicating which measures are to be taken at Community level does not mean that the other issues
underlying the problem are solved. For example, what if some states do not share
the majority's view that environmental measures are to be taken by the Community? In the absence of general consensus, no measure will be taken since unanim-

ity is required according to article 130S. Therefore only measures capable of obtaining general approval – probably the least stringent – will be passed by the Council. Furthermore, if the Commission, proposing action in a certain field, is opposed by certain member-states who take the stance that the Community has no competence in that area, may the Commission bring an action against those states before the ECJ on the grounds that by impeding the adoption of environmental measures by the Council they violate the Treaty? Or, in the opposite case, may a member-state such as Italy initiate proceedings against the Community for failure to act when it is convinced that the Community's organs should have acted in a particular area of environmental protection but refused to do so? Finally, how can the Commission reasonably prove that certain environmental matters are better handled at Community level than at the level of the individual member-states?

All the concerns briefly sketched out above are shared by legal scholars (Krämer, 1987) and all rest on the very unfortunate formulation of article 130R(4); 'what's better?', is actually a question that only affords a *post factum* answer. All evaluations made before the actual implementation of a certain measure can at best be described as pure speculation.

On the other hand, one cannot be satisfied with a solution that is based on the assumption that article 130R is more 'a political guidance … rather than a legal norm' precisely defining the spheres of competence (Krämer, 1987: 665). As a formal amendment to an international treaty, the SEA has to be literally interpreted in its context and in light of its object and purpose (article 31 of the 1969 Vienna Convention on the Law of Treaties) so that, however obscure or vague its provisions may be, a sound legal interpretation will ultimately be suggested. So the Council will decide on a case-by-case basis which measures are to be taken at EC level. It will be up to the Commission to demonstrate that, according to a previous assessment founded on the factors listed in article 130R(3), such measures can attain the objectives pursued by the directive (or regulation or decision since the SEA does not specify which particular legal instrument has to be used in the field of the environment) better than individual measures taken by member-states. Like all binding acts adopted by the Community, such measures are amenable to judicial review by the ECJ, which may consider the validity and legitimacy of any such measure. Of course, it is unlikely that a state will initiate proceedings against the Community after having agreed within the Council to enact a certain measure. In case of decisions taken by majority, however, this is a likely prospect. Furthermore, the question of validity and legitimacy may well arise before a domestic court so that the ECJ may be seized with a preliminary ruling.

4.2.3.3 More stringent national measures

In order to evaluate the costs and benefits for member-states of EC membership in terms of allocation of competence and of transfer of sovereign rights, especially as far as legislative powers in the area of environmental protection are concerned, it is fundamental to verify whether or not member-states retain the power of enacting more stringent national measures. The answer is certainly in the affirmative if relevant Community measures are taken pursuant to article 130S. In that case, according to article 130T, member-states are not prevented 'from maintaining or introducing more stringent protective measures compatible with this Treaty' (i.e. *not* amounting to trade barriers or to major obstacles to inter-state trade within the Community).

The potentially wide measure of discretion enjoyed by states in introducing more stringent national measures involves the evaluation of relevant limits to state action. To what extent are states free to impose more restrictive laws and regulations within their territory? A recent case decided by the ECJ, though not strictly referring to the scope of application of article 130 since the SEA was not yet in force, can nevertheless shed some light on this point. The case at issue, *Re Disposable Beer Cans* (case 302/86, (*EC Commission United Kingdom intervening* v. *Denmark*, ECR (1988): 4607), presented a situation where Denmark had introduced by regulation a return system for beer and soft drinks containers so that these latter could be recycled. Therefore the measure was clearly aimed at environmental protection. The Commission contended, however, that the way the system functioned caused quantitative restrictions on imports and consequently it was to be regarded as a measure having effects equivalent to import restrictions prohibited by article 30 of the EC Treaty. The defence of the Danish government was that the measures were aimed at environmental protection, a mandatory requirement of EC law (another argument to support the view that environmental policy had already been constitutionalized before the entry into force of the SEA), and as such could be considered an admissible limit to the operation of article 30.

The Court agreed with this argument but decided against Denmark in so far as the Danish measures did not satisfy the principle of proportionality. In other words, if the deposit-and-return system for empty containers could be seen as perfectly admissible and proportionate to the aim of protecting the environment, the restriction provided for in the regulation of the quantity of products which could be marketed by importers was disproportionate to the objective pursued and therefore it amounted to a violation of article 30.

Under the rationale of the *Re Disposable Beer Cans* case, therefore, which could be applied *mutatis mutandis* correctly to interpret the scope of application of article 130T, states are free to introduce more stringent measures as long as they are proportionate to the objective of environmental protection and do not result in undue constraints on intra-Community trade. The assessment of the proportionality requirement is to be made by the Commission and it is subject to judicial review by the ECJ.

The answer to the same question of the admissibility of the introduction of more stringent national measures, however, would be totally different if the Community protective measures had been taken under a different rule, that is article 100A, the other legitimate legal basis available for environmental protection measures. This remark paves the way to introduce one of the most controversial issues to be faced in this domain.

4.2.3.4 The interrelation between article 130R–T and Article 100A

With a view to 'progressively establishing the internal market over a period expiring on 31 December 1992' (article 8A), article 100A(1) provides that the Council shall, 'acting by qualified majority on a proposal from the Commission in co-operation with the European Parliament and with the Economic and Social Committee, adopt the measures for the approximation of the provisions laid down by law, regulation or administrative action in Member States which have as their object the establishment and functioning of the internal market'. The Commission while proposing action according to article 100A(1) in the field, *inter alia*, of environmental protection '... will take as a base a high level of protection'.

So here we have another possible legal basis for adopting environmental protection measures. Whenever an action, instrumental in the establishment and functioning of the internal market and having a bearing also on environmental protection, is needed the Commission may propose to the Council highly protective measures and the Council is to take a decision by qualified majority acting in concert with the European Parliament, according to the procedure envisaged in article 149 which gives the Assembly more extensive powers than in the past. Therefore all measures such as product requirements in terms of environmental standards are likely to fall under article 100A rather than under article 130R–T.

If a directive or regulation is taken under article 100A, member-states are allowed to apply more stringent national measures in connection with environmental protection subject to notification to the Commission which must verify whether or not such measures amount to arbitrary discrimination or to disguised restriction on intra-Community trade (article 100A(4-5)). The stress posed by the provision on the application of national measures leads the interpreter to deny the admissibility of member-states introducing new environmental measures after the introduction of the SEA. This interpretation seems all the more correct in light of the Danish interpretative declaration attached to the SEA whereby the Danish government declares that it interprets article 100A(4) as allowing member-states to apply national provisions in case measures adopted under article 100A do not safeguard higher environmental requirements laid down by domestic law. If the above-mentioned article allowed *per se* the application of national measures after 1992 or the introduction of any such measure at any time, it would have been meaningless for the Danish government to produce that interpretative statement.

It has to be borne in mind that Denmark, the Federal Republic of Germany and the Netherlands (Jans, 1989), since they have environmental laws and regulations often stricter than Community measures, have strongly resisted all attempts to transfer to the EC too broad a legislative competence *vis-à-vis* environmental protection without adequately safeguarding their national measures.

If the approximation of laws process mentioned in article 100A(1)is not completed in due time (before 1993) the Council, according to article 100B, may decide that all the provisions in force in a member-state must be recognized as equivalent to those in force in another member-state.

Now that the legislative framework of relevant EC primary law has been described in detail, we can attempt to expound the many interpretative questions left open by the drafters of the SEA.

First of all, it is quite clear that adopting a measure under article 130S or under article 100A makes a great difference in several respects. The decision-making procedure is different: under article 130 the Council usually takes unanimous decisions after consultation with the European Parliament, while under article 100 the voting procedure is that of a qualified majority and the involvement of the European Parliament is more intrusive due to the application of article 149.

Furthermore, while under article 130 states are granted the opportunity of introducing more stringent national measures, such a possibility does not exist – unless the harmonization measures include a safeguard clause authorizing member-states to take provisional measures subject to a Community control procedure (article 100A(5)) – under article 100A (*contra* Kromarek, 1986, p. 12), whose major task is to ensure the establishment and proper functioning of the internal market. In this latter case the Commission has to meet a qualitative requirement since the SEA provides that the proposed measures will have as their basis in the field of the environment a 'high level of protection'.

4.2.3.5 The choice of the proper legal basis

The decisive issue, therefore, is to assess whether a certain Community measure is to be adopted under article 130S or whether it should have article 100A as its legal basis. The borderline between measures exclusively aimed at environmental protection and those also having effects on the free circulation of goods and services (thus impairing the proper functioning of the Common Market) is indeed a very tenuous one (De Ruyt, 1987, p. 218). If we take the common example of the directive on emission standards for motor vehicles, it is difficult to determine which particular aspect, whether environmental protection from exhaust emission or the free circulation of goods, which may be impaired by having different environmental requirements or standards, prevails.

One could suggest, for instance, that all measures on product requirements fall under article 100A, while all other measures expressly aimed at the protection and preservation of the environment (preservation of species, disposal of waste, landscape protection, etc.) be adopted under article 130. For example, Council directive 89/458/EEC of 18 July 1989 amending, with regard to European emission standards for cars below 1.4 litres, directive 70/220/EEC on the approximation of the laws of the member-states relating to measures to be taken against air pollution by emissions from motor vehicles (OJ no. L 226, 08/03/1989:1) was adopted by the Council under article 100A since it was directly concerned with product (in this particular case cars) requirements. On the other hand, Council directive 88/609/EEC of 24 November 1988 on the limitation of emissions of certain pollutants into the air from large combustion plants (OJ, no. L336, 12/07/1989:1), having no apparent impact on the completion of the internal market, was adopted under article 130S.

Scrutinizing the practice of both Commission and Council since the adoption of the SEA, the interpreter is confronted with a persistent effort by the Commission to propose the majority of measures, mostly directives, likely to have impact on the environment under article 100A because of the effects they are also likely to have on completion of the internal market (Hancker, 1989, pp. 501ff.). By contrast, the Council has often altered the legal basis of the same directives and has adopted them under article 130. Some outstanding examples of this trend may be seen in two recent directives: the first one, directive 90/219/EEC on the contained use of genetically modified micro-organisms (OJ, no. L117, 05/08/90:1), adopted by the Council on 23 April 1990, and the second one, directive 89/428/ EEC, adopted by the Council on 21 June 1989, on procedures for harmonizing programmes for the reduction and eventual elimination of pollution caused by waste from the titanium dioxide industry (OJ, no. 201, 07/14/89:56). Both directives were adopted under article 130S, although originally the Commission had proposed their adoption pursuant to article 100A (see SI (89) 489:3).

The opposite stance taken by the Commission and by the Council is not at all surprising in light of the differences – in terms of both the decision-making procedure and of the wider measure of discretion on the part of member-states under article 100A for adopting more stringent measures – existing between the two legal bases. The Commission, mainly concerned with the task of ensuring a high level of environmental protection and effective action, and backed up by the European Parliament whose intervention is required by article 100A in a more substantive form than under article 130S, prefers to limit states' powers to enact different national measures both because of the risk of less effective environmental protection strategies and of the existence of several different environmental regulations that might well represent a major hindrance to the completion of the internal market and seriously threaten the freedom and fairness of intra-Community trade.

The recent debate that took place during the 1345th session of the Council on the Environment (SI (89) 654/2) supports the above view. In the course of the discussion concerning the directive on waste proposed by the Commission (COM(88)391-SYN 145), amending directive 74/442/EEC, and before an overwhelming majority of the Council voted to adopt article 130S as the proper legal basis, C. Ripa di Meana, the European Commissioner for the Environment, strenuously defended article 100A as the only legitimate basis for the directive at issue, stating that it was 'la seule base susceptible de garantir le résultat recherché. Le 130(S) ne ferait qu'encourager l'adoption de mesures nationales plus sévères et différentes les unes des autres, donc la désharmonisation' (SI (89) 654/2:15).

Given the present contrast in position between the Commission and the Parliament on the one hand and the Council on the other concerning the exact scope of application of articles 130S and 100A, and in the absence so far of an interpretative ruling by the ECJ, what can we say about the proper legal basis for a measure adopted by the Community with respect to environmental protection?

Taking into account some recent precedents of the Court related to the proper choice by the Council of a legal basis for the directive or other measure enacted (see case 68/86 UK v. Council (1986) ECR: 855; case 131/86 UK v. Council (1986) ECR: 905; case 45/86 Commission v. Council (1987), ECR: 1493), one can assert that: (a) according to the first paragraph of article 173 of the EC Treaty and to the relevant case-law of the ECJ, any member-state may bring an action for annulment in order to challenge the legality of any Council directive without making the exercise of that right conditional on proof of an interest in bringing proceedings (Case 45/86, *op. cit.*,1493); (b) the proper legal basis for a measure enacted by Community organs must be evaluated in light of its specific content and declared objectives; and finally (c) 'the determination of the appropriate legal basis for a measure does not depend on the discretion of the Community legislature but must be based on objective factors which are amenable to judicial review' (case 131/86, *op. cit.*, 933).

From the above remarks it follows that in order to evaluate whether a certain directive has to be taken under article 130S or article 100A regard must be taken of the objectives and specific content of the measure at issue. So if the primary purpose of a certain directive is the protection of the environment (for example, measures to ensure acceptable levels of pollution of water courses, measures to control forests pollution, etc.), then the only legitimate basis would be article 130S along with all the consequences such a choice entails. If, on the other hand, a directive is mainly aimed at fixing product requirements, however linked to environmental standards they might be, then article 100A should be used since the measure would certainly affect the internal market and the free circulation of goods.

In such grey areas as measures related to plant and equipment environmental standards, the balancing test carried out by the Community may lead either to article 130S on the grounds that the fundamental goal pursued is that of environmental protection, or to article 100A on the basis of the possible consequences, in terms of location of production sites due to lower or higher costs of complying with environmental requirements, that different national standards may bring about. So far, however, the Council seems to have preferred the first option (see Directive 88/609/EEC on the limitation of emissions of certain pollutants into the air from large combustion plants (OJ no. L336, 12/07/88:1).

In any case, member-states have at their disposal the instrument provided for in article 173 of the Treaty and may at any time bring an action before the ECJ when they perceive that the legal basis used by the Community is not legitimate. The principle of judicial review of all binding acts enacted by the Community will sooner or later result in a ruling by the Court on the interpretation of the scope of application of the provisions applicable to environmental protection.

Such clarification would be of the utmost importance when identifying with a reasonable degree of certainty what competence and autonomy remained with the member-states after the enactment of the SEA. In fact, until this determination is made thoroughly, it would not be possible to assess for each member-state the actual cost and benefit of EC membership. For the time being it suffices to point out the ambiguities of EC law and to look at the practice of EC organs as they have developed so far.

4.2.3.6 External relations

In order to evaluate the costs and benefits of EC membership for member-states a final remark is needed with regard to external relations in the field of environmental protection. In fact, member-states' sovereign rights are likely to be limited by the extent to which the Community has the right independently and exclusively to conclude international agreements in this area. Once again the provisions laid down by the SEA turn out to be quite obscure; nor are they free of ambiguities, so that some legal scholars have described the subject of environmental external relations as 'a political context with legal boundaries' (Nollkaemper, 1987, p. 91). Article 130R(5) sets forward a general principle of co-operation between the Community and member-states 'within their respective spheres of competence' and, after having restated the possibility of the Community negotiating and concluding agreements with third parties in accordance with article 228, it finally concludes that the above provisions 'shall be without prejudice to Member States' competence to negotiate in international bodies and to conclude international agreements'. So far, the wording is clear enough to allow a literal interpretation of the relevant provisions: the Community and member-states are requested to co-operate and both retain the power to negotiate and conclude international agreements. Some doubts arise, however, when one realizes that in the Declaration of the Final Act of the Intergovernmental Conference where the SEA was adopted the parties agreed that the provisions of article 130R(5) are not prejudicial to the case-law of the ECJ as it was expressed in the famous *ERTA* case of 1971 (ECR 1971:263), where the theory of 'parallel powers' was asserted for the first time. According to this theory, once the Community has enacted binding acts in a given area it *ipso facto* also assumes the powers to conclude international agreements in that same area. These powers are such as to exclude an independent action by member-states if such an initiative may affect Community rules.

The theory of 'parallel powers', further developed in the jurisprudence of the Court in the *Kramer* case (ECR, 1976: 1279) and in *Opinion 1/76* (ECR, 1977: 741), has been extended so far as not to require the prior enactment of legislation by the Community in order to acquire external powers but simply to state that the actual exercise of external relations is necessary to reach Community objectives. Obviously the crucial issue is to assess in which case Community powers are exclusive and do not allow states to act individually. Some authors (Mastellone,1981, pp. 110–11), prior to the enactment of the SEA, suggested the radical view that in all areas covered by Community directives the Community has acquired exclusive rights. This view cannot be accepted, mainly because it does not correspond to practice. So more subtle interpretative solutions are to be pursued.

How can we solve the apparent inconsistency between article 130R and the Declaration of the Final Act? Since the object of this chapter is to evaluate the advantages and disadvantages of Italy's participation in the Community as far as environmental policy is concerned, the basic question to be answered is whether or not a member-state, such as Italy in this case, retains its sovereign powers to negotiate and conclude international agreements even on subjects where European legislation has already occurred. In practice, it is reasonable to answer that the basic principle of Community law in this particular field is that of co-operation. When there is consensus among the member-states over the participation of the Community to a convention no problem arises. However, in the case of no agreement between member-states as to whether or not to participate in an environmental convention provided that consultations have been undertaken within the Community, member-states are not prevented from acting by themselves, especially when community legislation covering the subject-matter of the convention has been enacted under article 130, that is when minimum-standard directives are at stake. The possibility of adopting more stringent measures should in principle allow states to participate in international agreements, with the effect of imposing on the parties more stringent obligations in so far as these obligations are compatible with the Treaty, in other words if they do not have adverse consequences for intra-Community trade. In fact whenever such obligations individually undertaken by member-states are to affect Community rules, especially those protecting the freedom of circulation of goods, or those referred to areas covered by extensive Community rules, states' residual powers are to be restrictively interpreted, although they probably cannot be excluded (Nollkaemper, 1987, p. 91).

In fact with regard to environmental protection, the exclusive external powers doctrine, as it has been developed over the years by the ECJ, is not fully consistent with the principle of co-operation envisaged in the SEA, which is a much more flexible instrument when it comes to ensuring environmental co-operation. As long as Community rules are not negatively affected by international obligations that are individually undertaken, member-states should enjoy a reasonable degree of freedom to enter international treaties in their individual capacities. This is all the more so when one realizes that some environmental issues are a concern only for some states and not for others, or are likely to have a bearing only on some specific geographical areas within the Community. The awareness of the need to promote international environmental co-operation might have been a reason for the drafters of the SEA to refer only to the *ERTA* case in the Final Declaration and not to the subsequent, more far-reaching case-law of the Court in the domain of external relations.

Against this background it is therefore fair to say that member-states are not, at present, unduly constrained by the EC as far as their treaty-making power is concerned. The principle of co-operation set forth in the SEA seems to be prevailing over the former case-law of the ECJ, whose jurisprudence, recalled in the Declaration attached to the Final Act of the Conference on the SEA, does not seem, for the time being, to be jeopardizing the still wide latitude of discretion that member-states enjoy in this domain, provided that the principle of co-operation, which may occasionally take the form of prior consultation at Community level, is duly respected.

The flexibility of such an arrangement, which can be judged as a benefit for all member-states, allows for a much more active and effective external environmental policy, as is shown by recent practice (Nollkaemper, 1987) – and all the more so in all those domains where EC action would not be quite as effective. Italy in particular can take advantage of such a proviso to continue fostering co-operation with neighbouring states that are not members of the EC in order to cope with regional issues (pollution of the Mediterranean and Adriatic Sea) and transfrontier pollution with bordering countries such as Switzerland and Austria.

4.3 Environmental law in Italy

Environmental law in Italy has only recently emerged as an autonomous set of rules. The following introductory observations will try to place its development in a historical perspective so that our assessment of costs and benefits may take into consideration the different scope and degree of intensity of environmental governance in Italy in different periods of recent history.

4.3.1 Environmental law in Italy until the mid-1980s

The lack of an organic legislative strategy on environmental protection which seems to characterize the Italian legal system is certainly the outcome of a troublesome process that has its origins at the beginning of the century when theories concerning medical and social health were embodied in several pieces of legislation: general sanitary regulations, public health laws, administrative rules, etc. (Greco, 1988, pp. 311ff.).

A first attempt at an autonomous approach to environmental issues can be traced to law 615 on atmospheric pollution of 13 July 1966 (LII *Le leggi* (1966): 1406) and law 319 on the protection of water from pollution, enacted ten years later on 10 May 1976 (LXII *Le leggi* (1976): 1313). Both laws provided for a series of specific prohibitions outside a general and coherent framework of principles and objectives. Furthermore, the many permissible derogations and loopholes provided for in the original text and those subsequently enacted rendered the dogmatic approach inspiring both laws all the more meaningless.

It is certainly safe to say that the basic feature of the Italian legal system as far as environmental protection is concerned has been for a long time a remarkable fragmentation and lack of co-ordination among a set of relevant rules scattered throughout our law (Onida, 1986).

The environment was not itself worthy of legal protection and its preservation and protection were covered, except for some laws specifically dealing with the protection of landscape in certain areas, by laws and regulations whose major focus was on other matters such as public health, urban planning, transport, etc. This overlap of interests and procedures caused delays and shortcomings and, above all, prevented Italy from developing a comprehensive legislative scheme for environmental protection. Thus legislative policy was based on sectorial plans; no organic law setting out principles and general objectives existed, nor was there much apparent interest among competent authorities and public opinion to have one.

The other factor that affected the development of an Italian environmental policy negatively in this period was a procedural one, that is the extreme fragmentation of competence between different ministries (health, public works, admiralty, etc.), on the one hand, and between the central state and the various decentralized centres of state authority (Regions, Provinces and Municipalities), on the other (Urbani, 1986; Greco, 1988, pp. 165 ff.).

The shift towards the establishment and progressive development of an environmental policy in Italy can be attributed to two main reasons: the growing awareness of public opinion that the environment is a shared resource worthy of being legally protected; and the development by the EC of an environmental policy which represented a remarkable push towards the autonomous development of an organic set of rules.

If the more active role played by environmental leagues and associations accelerated the process of developing environmental law as it stands today (Benedizione, 1988, pp. 69ff.), the decisive push has certainly to be attributed to EC law.

For some fifteen years the implementation in the Italian legal system of EC environmental directives has been a troublesome process indeed. Italy has for the most part reacted to EC directives with delay and non-completion. This trend is clearly shown in a recent comprehensive study (Capria, 1988) on the state of implementation in Italy of environmental directives.

Some main reasons for the delays and inconsistencies in the process of execution of such directives can be indicated in the many technical and bureaucratic hindrances of the Italian legal and administrative system, especially in the field of environmental protection, where many overlaps of interests and procedures occur; in the lack of co-ordination among the various administrative branches involved in the process of implementation; in the practice too often adopted by Italian authorities of implementing environmental directives by means of a new law or regulation even when such an integrative legislative activity was not required by the directive; and, finally, in the delegation by Parliament of the legislative competence to enact relevant rules for implementing the directives to the government which has often presented its bills with undue delay (Capria, 1988, p. 38).

This quite discouraging scenario, however, which caused some authors to speak of a sort of 'addiction to illegality' (Tizzano, 1989, p. 314) in relation to the Italian EC directives implementation practice, has recently changed to a considerable extent by way of a manifold legislation strategy touching upon environmental protection and the process of implementation of Community law into our legal system.

4.3.2 Recent changes in the strategy of legislative action 1986–89

On 8 July 1986 the Italian Parliament passed law no. 349 (LXXII *Le leggi* (1986): 1411) establishing the Ministry of the Environment (Labriola, 1988; Postiglione, 1986). This is certainly a turning point in our legal system as far as environmental protection is concerned because, first of all, it was the first time that Italian legislation had achieved the goal of establishing national principles concerning environmental protection and, second, because it created a single administrative centre responsible for the establishment, management and implementation of a national environmental policy, thus overcoming the haphazard practice of intervention with *ad hoc* measures.

Law 349/1986 proclaimed the environment as a 'fundamental interest of the community' and as such worthy of legal protection (a position expressly endorsed also by the Italian Constitutional Court in judgments no.151–152–153/1986 (FI,

1986, I, 2689–90) and subsequently confirmed in two later judgments no. 210/1987 (FI, 1988, I, 329) and 641/1987 (FI, 1988, I, 1057)).

The legislative framework laid down by law 349, in spite of some shortcomings (above all, no definition of environment is provided), sets forth a comprehensive scheme of rules touching upon preventive action, information, sanctioning measures and co-ordination with the other branches of the state administration.

It is worth mentioning that the majority of relevant rules are fully consistent, in principle, with the established trend of Community law and with recent developments in international practice. Needless to say, this reflects the influence of EC law on the development of Italian environmental law.

Among the most innovative prescriptions of law no. 349 is the citizens' right to be informed on the state of the environment with information to be made available at public offices; the citizens' and environmental leagues' right to notify the state of events causing or likely to cause environmental damage (the state will be held responsible if it fails to act, following such notification) and the right for ecologists' organizations to intervene in trials and administrative proceedings concerning environmental damage and to start an action before the Regional Administrative Tribunal or the Council of State to have illegitimate acts declared null and void.

Any environmental damage is considered as unlawful damage to the state and whoever causes such damage is to restore it to the status quo ante, or to repair it if such restoration is not possible. A fault-based system of responsibility is thus established and besides administrative action there is the possibility of resorting to the ordinary judicial system (Cocco, 1986).

The Ministry of the Environment has the overall responsibility of preventing pollution, preserving nature, protecting the environment and rendering public opinion sensitive to environmental issues by way of constant and precise information. Moreover, the Ministry is also given the task of ensuring 'promotion, preservation and restoration of environmental conditions in conformity with the fundamental interests of the Community and with the quality of life'.

In order to achieve these goals the Ministry may also adopt urgent protective and conservative measures. It has exclusive competence with regard to water pollution and the management of waste, while it has joint competence, along with the Ministry of Health, in other areas such as atmospheric pollution, noise, radiation, etc. (Postiglione, 1986).

From the above remarks it is reasonable to conclude that Italy shares the EC objectives in the field of environmental protection. The strategy for action does not seem to diverge either; a mixed blend of preventive and sanctioning measures has been adopted. On the other hand, it is worth noting that law no. 349 has had a difficult start and it is not able to display fully its intended effects. The several interpretative ambiguities in the wording of the law which resulted in several rulings by the Constitutional Court, along with the endemically slow pace of Italian bureaucracy to adapt to structural legislative changes, has rendered the implementation of law 349 a challenge. One cannot deny, however, that, in spite of some harsh criticism (Rescigno, 1988), it represents the first attempt by the Italian government to establish and manage a coherent strategy of action for ensuring environmental protection in line with the international obligations undertaken by Italy.

In order to speed up and better ensure the timely implementation of EC directives into its domestic legal system, Italy has recently passed a law explicitly dealing with the procedures needed to implement Community obligations: law no. 86 adopted on 9 March 1989 (*Le leggi* (1989), I: 545ff.). This legislation represents the final outcome of a series of attempts to improve the process of implementation of EC secondary law in the Italian legal system. The law aims, *inter alia*, to provide effective mechanisms of implementation for EC binding acts. Remarkable innovations are also contained in the law regarding the appropriate information to be given to Parliament by the government on the development of EC law and its state of implementation, as well as the relation between the state and the Regions in the participation and execution of EC law. This goal is pursued by means of a bill, presented each year by the government, containing all necessary provisions to comply with Community measures (the so-called 'Community law'). This new legal tool should in principle ensure an organic, continuous and timely implementation of relevant Community acts, although much of its success will depend on the prompt presentation of the bill and on the subsequent conversion into law by Parliament.

The 'Community law', presented on a yearly basis, will guarantee the execution of obligations stemming from EC law either by directly prescribing the necessary rules, by conferring a legislative delegation to the government, or by authorizing the latter to enact *ad hoc* regulations. The choice of the means will depend, of course, on the nature of the measure needed for providing adequate implementation.

One of the most interesting aspects, already underlined by legal doctrine (Gaja, 1989, p. 64; Tizzano, 1989, pp. 319–20), is that the government, if duly authorized by Parliament, may also intervene by means of regulation in those areas previously covered by law (this is not possible, however, for areas exclusively reserved to be regulated by law). This 'deregulation' carries with it the risk of governmental abuse of power, especially at the expense of the autonomous powers of the Regions; nevertheless this legislation has the inherent merit of being a serious attempt to depart from the existing approach to the problem.

The use of delegation is not a new instrument for Italian authorities. It has been used for many years along with the practice of applying directly, by means of a single legislative instrument, the force of law to directives not yet implemented. The most pertinent example in this respect was law 183/1987 (LXXIII *Le leggi* (1987): 1082) by which about one hundred directives were executed in the Italian legal system.

It is then reasonable to conclude that law 86/1989 supports an optimistic view of the future as far as the timely implementation of EC directives is concerned and has to be considered a remarkable step forward in the process of keeping pace with Community legislation.

4.3.3 The participation of the regions in the implementation of EC environmental directives

One of the distinguishing features of the Italian constitutional system is the decentralization of power through regionalism. The country contains twenty Regions. Special forms and conditions of autonomy are conferred by constitutional laws, on five of them due to their particular position and status. The others are given legislative powers in some particular subjects (agriculture, urban development, health, tourism, etc.) within the limits fixed by state laws and provided that the laws enacted by them do not run counter to the national interest or the interest of the other Regions (article 117 of the Italian Constitution).

Whether or not the Regions can participate in the implementation of EC directives in matters covered by their legislative competence has been a very controversial issue over the years (for the implementation of environmental directives, see Mengozzi, 1988). On the one hand, one could argue that the state as a whole is internationally responsible for the execution of international obligations and so it alone can delegate such an implementation to the Regions. This argument was put forward by the Constitutional Court in judgment 142/1972 (LV RDI (1972): 722), when it ruled that the delegation was in the end the only conceivable means of ensuring the substitution of the state to the Regions in case they failed to act in due time.

This solution, however, did not sufficiently recognize the primary legislative competence of the Regions, constitutionally guaranteed. So eventually, as a result of some legislative changes (see, in particular, article 6 of DPR no. 616/1977 (LXII *Le leggi* (1977): 1775) and article 11 of law no. 183/1987), and the case-law of the Italian Constitutional Court since judgment 81/1979 (FI, 1980, I:18), it was asserted that the state and the Regions have a concurrent legislative competence as far as the implementation of EC secondary law is concerned.

As to the implementation of directives not previously covered by national law or not reserved to be regulated by law, the Regions may implement them by way of administrative measures (article 11 of law 183/1987). According to article 13 of law 183/1987, the five Regions having a special statute may immediately implement EC directives in areas of their exclusive competence, provided that they eventually adjust to state laws subsequently enacted, while the other Regions can only act, by way of legislation, after the adoption by the state of a measure of implementation of the directive, fixing 'peremptory principles' and specific and detailed rules applicable only in so far as the Regions fail to legislate in due course.

The two basic principles governing the relation between the state and the Regions, that is the competence of the state to fix 'peremptory norms' in a framework law and the principle of subrogation in case the Regions fail to act, have not been changed by law 86/1989 which only spells out in detail the formal procedures to be followed by the state to make up for the Regions in case of their inactivity. This solution, which is indeed a guarantee of the exercise of regional autonomies, has been suggested by recent case-law. In particular, in its judgment no. 830/1988 (GC, 1989, I:3983), the Italian Constitutional Court held unlawful a decree of the Ministry of the Environment implementing a directive, since no warning had been given to the interested Regions, which were in principle competent to act, nor were they consulted before the adoption of the decree. Therefore, by spelling out the formalities and procedures to be carried out in case of substitution of the state for the Regions, law no. 86/1989 has given more specific content to the principle of 'loyal co-operation' considered by the Constitutional Court (see, among the latest ones, judgment 88/302: FI, 1988, I, 1017; 1412; 1789) to be the guiding principle in the field of state–regions relations, especially as far as the principle of substitution (i.e. the principle whereby the state is entitled to act when the Regions have failed to do so) is concerned (Salerno, 1989, p. 66).

Finally, it is worth noting that in order to involve the Regions more deeply in the formation and implementation of EC law, law 83/1989 has imposed on the Prime Minister the obligation to convene at least twice a year the Permanent State–Regions Conference, a body established by article 12 no. 5(b)(1) of law 400/1988 (LXXIV Le leggi (1988): 1892), concerning the reform of the Prime Minister's powers and composed of the Presidents of all the Regions, which has to be consulted on the general policy of the state as far as the formation and execution of Community law is concerned.

4.4 Impact of EC policy on Italian environmental policy: a tentative cost–benefit analysis

Turning now to the analysis of the impact on Italian environmental law of EC policy, we realize that our task has been facilitated by the general survey of the main features and legislative trends of both legal systems. Indeed, some of the benefits and costs have already been assessed, in very general terms, in the course of the above study on the EC legal framework when we distinguished between the Community's and member-states' competence in the field of environmental protection.

It should be clear, however, that such an analysis may have to be modified over time. Legislative strategies are likely to change over the years and environmental protection goals may vary as well. Furthermore, as we made it clear from the beginning, our attempt at formulating a cost–benefit analysis only concerns the potential effectiveness and efficacy of legal measures taken both at Community and national level in order to strengthen the legal regime of environmental protection.

4.4.1 EC law as a catalyst

In tracing the parallel development of environmental policy within the European Communities and in the Italian legal system, a decisive factor appears to be the close interrelationship between Community action and national responses. At varying speeds and with different degrees of success, Italy has always followed the developments occurring at Community level. It is indeed quite safe to say that Italian environmental policy was actually initiated by Community environmental directives.

Community measures have always been a catalyst for the development of environmental policy in Italy. In the first phase of Community action, when environmental policy began to emerge by means of an extensive interpretation of the Rome Treaty, it took some time for Italy to adjust to the new development. The lack of any organic legislative action scheme in this area caused delays and inconsistencies in the implementation of Community measures. The fragmentation of competence within the different branches of the state administration, the overlap of interests and procedures together with the absence of an autonomous conception of the environment as something worthy of legal protection, were the main reasons for the Italian difficulties of adapting to EC law without some delay.

These data can be interpreted from a number of standpoints. If, on the one hand, one considers EC membership as a net benefit for the development of environmental policy in Italy, on the other hand, it cannot be denied that the strong influence and impact of EC law on a system that had not yet deployed any legislative action in this field induced an unconditional acceptance of the legislative strategy adopted by Community organs. So the sectorial approach of Community measures (water, soil, air pollution, etc.) may have to some extent prevented the earlier development of an organic legislation. The occasional interventions of the Community, therefore, might well have constituted a cost in this respect. There is no concrete evidence to support this assumption, but we deem this argument to be quite reasonable especially in light of the close dependence of Italian policy on EC law. Indeed the vast majority of national measures over the past twenty-five years represent nothing but measures implementing EC directives and international treaties.

This speculation will most likely lose momentum when we apply it to the present legal framework of EC primary law, since the adoption of the SEA, and to the recent Italian law establishing the Ministry of the Environment and setting out national principles of environmental protection. Now environmental protection has been declared a fundamental policy for both legal systems and the principles inspiring such policy have been embodied in legal instruments. The basic principles are not at great variance and the fundamental strategy adopted to achieve the conservation of the environment and the improvement of living conditions is that of preventive action. The endorsement by Italian law of such a principle, however obvious it may sound, is in fact a major shift in our environmental policy. The first laws and regulations touching upon the protection of the environment were sanction-oriented. Proscribed conducts and different prohibitions were listed and sanctions took care of their breach. The EC manifold strategy, starting with the Third Community Action Programme, seemed fully to endorse the principle of preventive action. This once again gave stimulus to the Italian system to follow suit.

By the same token one can also explain the transition from the abstract and dogmatic approach, inspiring the first phase of environmental legislation in Italy, to the piecemeal approach based on the enactment of scientific, flexible standards and updated technical rules, followed in later Italian practice and legislation. There is no doubt that this shift is due to the influence of the EC model just as other international legal instruments rely on the use of flexible legal tools, capable of being easily adapted to scientific and technical processes, as the most appropriate legislative technique to ensure environmental protection.

In general terms, therefore, one can conclude that the impact of EC legislation on the Italian environmental policy has always been a stimulating factor for Italian environmental policy to develop. This is so because the lack of a previous general legal framework relating to the environment rendered the Italian legal system particularly receptive to the influence of EC environmental policy.

The fact that the implementation process of EC environmental directives has been for a long time a very troublesome and cumbersome task for Italian authorities to carry out is, in this context, immaterial. What is significant here is that, in general terms, Italy's absence of an organic legislative strategy or philosophy in this area has facilitated a rather passive reception of the solutions given at EC level. As we have tried to demonstrate above, this has produced 'pros and cons'. One can safely say, for instance, that, were it not for EC environmental directives, the development of Italian environmental law would have been much slower and probably more deficient. At the same time it is not completely wrong to state that, especially in the first fifteen years of Community environmental policy, the sectorial interventions suggested and most of the times imposed by the EC might well have prevented the autonomous development of a more coherent and systematic Italian policy.

The consequences of this impact are not negligible when we take into account that as a result of the latest case-law of the Italian Constitutional Court (judgment 170/1984 in: GC, 1984, I: 1098)), which finally conformed with the jurisprudence of the ECJ (Case 106/77, ECR, 1978: 629ff.), Community law is given priority with respect to internal rules having the same rank in the hierarchy of sources. Therefore, once they are implemented, EC environmental directives are to prevail over any prior or subsequent internal rule conflicting with it. As for the direct applicability of environmental directives in the absence of any implementing measure, no case-law, to our knowledge, exists. One could speculate, however, that according to the jurisprudence of the ECJ, especially case 152/84, no provision contained in the directive could be directly invoked by a private subject in his or her relationship with other private parties but only in so far as the litigation concerns the state, which is the only addressee, from the legal standpoint, of the obligations imposed by EC directives (Capelli, 1987, p. 38).

The last general comment concerns the effect of the growing public sensitivity to environmental issues on the development of Italian legislation. Here it is quite difficult to assess how much the EC has contributed in shaping Italian public opinion towards environmental issues. It is certainly true of the implementation of some EC directives like directive 85/337 on the environmental impact assessment (OJ no. L 175, 5/7/1985: 40), which expressly mentions the right of the individual to be informed about projects likely to have environmental effects and further enhances the principle of participation and consultation with ecologists and environmental leagues in the decision-making phase of any measure concerning the environment, and directive 82/501 concerning the risks of serious accidents resulting from industrial activities (OJ no. L 230, 5/8/1982: 1). In this latter case, according to the Presidential decree no. 175/1988 (LXXIV Le leggi (1988): 1137), implementing the directive, local authorities are to provide the public with a set of information ranging from preventive measures to risk assessment and intended measures to be taken in case of emergency (Amendola, 1989; Cenerini, 1989; Di Lecce, 1988; Culotta, 1989).

The two EC directives, however, are the expression of a general trend in the international community to recognize individually and collectively the right to information with respect to environmental hazards (*Forum*, 1990, pp. 60ff.; Koppen and Ladauer, 1989). Furthermore, the activism of certain non-governmental organizations, engaged in the protection of the environment, has promoted worldwide information on the main environmental threats challenging the earth, thus contributing to the formation of a strong environmental movement across the planet.

Therefore, although it is more difficult in this context to identify the contribution of European action towards the development of this environmental sensitivity, it seems nevertheless acceptable to acknowledge that such an action can be counted as a benefit anyway.

In spite of the above rather optimistic assessment, one must recognize that Community legislative models are not always the best and most effective means to achieve environmental protection goals. This conclusion will hopefully emerge from the following analysis.

4.4.2 The environmental impact assessment procedure

The environmental impact assessment procedure is the process by which potentially significant adverse effects of certain actions on the environment are duly assessed by competent state organs and taken into account in the decision-making process leading to the acceptance or refusal of certain projects (Lee and Wood, 1988, pp. 12-13).

Although many industrial and economic activities present a very high risk rendering it almost impossible to exclude the possibility of ecological damage or even disaster, notwithstanding strict technical measures, the study and subsequent evaluation of the impact of certain projects on environmental conditions may represent, if undertaken before any decision is taken, a very good preventive tool for ensuring an adequate assessment on the advisability and safety of a certain project.

The EC in 1985, after some twelve years of negotiations, enacted directive 85/337 on the Environmental Impact Assessment (EIA) imposing on member-states an obligation to introduce into their legal systems the EIA procedure as provided in the directive, notwithstanding the possibility envisaged in article 13 of adopting a more stringent model.

By means of law 349/1986, Italy, while postponing the final legal settlement of the EIA to a later time, introduced a provisional legal regime for the EIA procedure and by two decrees of the Prime Minister, decree no. 377 of 10 August 1988 (GU 31 August 1988, no. 204: 6) and the decree of 27 December 1988 (GU 5 January 1989, no. 4: 17), provided the necessary regulations and technical rules to implement the procedure.

It is not the task of this chapter to analyse in detail the specific content of the EC directive (Sapienza, 1988; Cutrera, 1987; Greco, 1989, pp. 211ff.) and of the Italian law (Greco, 1988, pp. 495ff.; Greco, 1989, pp. 245ff.). What is worth mentioning is that the EC directive on the EIA procedure is inspired by the French law no. 76 of 10 July 1976. This law represents a restricted version of what can be considered the forerunner of current EIA procedures: the National Environment Policy Act introduced in the United States in 1970. The difference between the two legislative enactments lies in the scope of application: while the French law only applies to single projects, whether private or public (Borgonovo, 1987; Greco, 1989, pp. 129ff.), the American law covers all governmental decisions likely to have an impact on the environment; consequently an environmental impact statement should in principle accompany all actions taken by the federal government or by its agencies (Greco, 1989, pp. 45ff., 98ff.). Despite this lofty goal we know that over the years the ambitious American legislation has almost failed to achieve the goal for which it was intended, as a result of the excessive bureaucratization of the procedure and to the many derogations subsequently enacted (Kennedy, 1988). But what we are concerned with here is the assessment of a legislative model. The potential application of the US law is, in principle, much wider and in itself represents a more effective preventive measure for environmental protection goals. The French law, on the other hand, excluding from its scope of application laws and regulations likely to produce environmental changes and urban planning as well, is undoubtedly a less far-reaching legal tool.

EC directive 337/85 fully endorsed the French approach and listed in two Annexes projects to be subjected to the EIA and projects that may be submitted to it 'where their characteristics so require'. Italian legislation has followed the European model and implementation of the directive in the Italian legal system has closely followed the provisions set forth in directive 337/85.

What is significant here is that Italy had to enact, in the time limits fixed by the EC, internal measures to implement a directive which provided for a basic environmental protection instrument: the EIA procedure. In order effectively to apply such an important measure, which 'cuts across the single environmental media (e.g. air, water, soil regulation), which has always characterised the activities of most environmental agencies and professional bodies in the environmental field' (Lee and Wood, 1988, p. 14), Italy should have already possessed an adequate legislative framework to ensure the implementation of such a complex procedure. Indeed, the EIA procedure presupposes integrated forms of co-operation between the different branches of the administration and a flexible approach to the separation of competence principle. Italy, whose environmental legislation – as we have tried to demonstrate – has been for a long time characterized by an extreme fragmentation of competence and by rather loose co-ordination among different administrative bodies, was not ready at a time of transition, when a remarkable effort to develop more effectively a comprehensive legislative strategy in the field of environmental policy was being made, to adjust accordingly to the EC directive at issue.

Furthermore, directive 337/85 is only a restricted version of the EIA procedure. Therefore, by adapting to this legislative model, Italy has missed, for the time being, the opportunity of developing an autonomous and perhaps stricter law. It is true that according to article 13 of the Directive, Italy could enact a harsher regulation. However, faced with current difficulties in developing an environmental policy, having no pre-existing EIA regulation and considering the time factor, it would have been almost impossible to produce a piece of legislation more advanced than the one offered as a model by the EC.

Now that Italy has implemented directive 337/85, closely following the suggested prescriptions on the works to be submitted to the EIA and thus accepting a very limited solution as far as the scope of application of the EIA procedure is concerned, the following evaluation can be made. At first sight one is tempted to say that the existence of a law aimed at environmental protection is better than no regulation at all. In this case, however, since Italy lacks the many requirements necessary to apply the EIA procedure effectively (information on the state of the environment networks, monitoring systems, adequate structures to gather, elaborate and verify relevant data, etc.), it seems more correct not to consider Community action as a benefit.

We can only wish that in future, when a specific law on the EIA is adopted in its final form, Italy will opt for a stricter and more extensive legislative framework, thus taking the lead in the current international trend towards the general acceptance of EIA as an effective environmental protection technique (Wirth, 1989, pp. 84–7).

4.5 Strains and contradictions between environmental protection goals and integration imperatives

Having scrutinized the costs and benefits of EC membership in the present state of development of EC and Italian legislation, it is necessary to venture into an analysis of the scenarios likely to occur in the near future. The crucial question is whether economic integration imperatives as they have been set forth in the SEA may negatively affect the achievement of environmental policy goals (EIU, 1990, p. 36). The first foreseeable effect of the achievement of the internal market, for example, is likely to be a steady increase in road traffic with all the detrimental effects it may have on the atmosphere (IEEP, 1988, p. 32). The fact that both environmental protection and the removal of trade barriers and completion of the internal market are mandatory requirements of Community law makes the balancing of these two values a difficult task indeed. Solutions once again cannot be given once and for all, but need to be proposed on a case-by-case basis.

4.5.1 Environmental policy v. economic integration: a dichotomy or two sides of the same coin?

In the economic literature the identification of incentives and disincentives to European integration in environmental policy has already been the object of accurate analysis (see for all Rehbinder and Stewart, 1985, pp. 1–13). From a legal standpoint, however, some of the conclusions reached by means of economic analysis can be further evaluated and weighed.

It is a common assumption, for example, that among the advantages of integration one can also count the removal of trade barriers with respect to products. For example, if all states, as far as product requirements are concerned, have their environmental standards approximated and harmonized, costs to meet such requirements will be almost equal for all states and so free competition can be ensured. Now the legal question is the following: is it legally admissible in the present framework of EC law that states maintain different environmental standards so as to impair the free circulation of products to their own advantage?

From what we found in the analysis of relevant provisions of the SEA, it is reasonable to conclude that member-states are free to introduce more stringent standards when implementing measures taken under article 130S, and may, up to 1993, apply more stringent measures in areas covered by directives adopted under article 100A. It is true that product requirements measures, in so far as they are likely to affect the completion of the internal market, should be adopted under article 100A, but, given the present trend of the Council to change, most of the time, the legal basis of proposed measures from article 100A to article 130S, one cannot exclude the possibility that this may also happen in this area. Furthermore, one should not forget that, according to article 100B, at the end of the period expiring at the end of 1992 the Council may decide that the provisions in force in one member-state must be recognized as equivalent to those applied by another member-state, a precaution lest some of the national laws, regulation and administrative provisions which fall under article 100A (as is the case for environmental measures) have not been harmonized.

Therefore, it is a perfectly conceivable scenario whereby states maintain different product requirements in relation to environmental protection. It goes without saying that states constrained by the imperatives of economic growth and expansion in foreign markets, which are obviously less inclined to adopt stringent environmental controls, will enjoy considerable advantages in terms of competition with respect to states that have to bear the high costs of meeting strict environmental standards. Nor can we at present speculate whether states having stricter controls may successfully challenge the introduction into their markets of goods produced in other member-states at comparatively lower costs as a result of less stringent environmental requirements. Under a *Cassis de Dijon* rationale (ECR, 1979: 649ff.), member-states cannot impose restrictions on imports on the grounds that national product requirements are not duly met. On the other hand, in light of the more recent judgment of the ECJ on the *Re Disposable Beer Cans* (ECR 1988: 4607), we could speculate that more stringent measures aimed at environmental protection are admissible in so far as they are proportional to their goals and do not amount to a violation of article 30 of the EC Treaty.

The crucial question would then be the following: under what conditions is the principle of proportionality met? It should be clear that this assessment is to be made by the Commission and in the last instance by the ECJ. In light of the *Danish Containers* case, however, it seems that the free circulation of goods principle is to be deemed to prevail most of the time over environmental goals unless the latter have only but very slight and negligible effects on intra-Community trade.

The conclusion from the above remarks is that states having less stringent environmental standard requirements for their products are likely to be better off with respect to other member-states. This is all the more so with regard to plant and equipment requirements where the free circulation of goods is not at stake. In this case states having less stringent standards will attract industries and entrepreneurs because of the lower costs to be borne in order to meet environmental standards. A major consequence of this might be a remarkable flow of capital and labour in the direction of such states. In the long term, 'competition among States to attract or retain industry may encourage laxity in controls everywhere' (Rehbinder and Stewart, 1985, p. 4).

The conflict of interests between states more interested in environmental protection and those more concerned with economic growth is likely to have a bearing on future Community action. It is reasonable to assume that as a result of the compromise which has to be reached at Community level in order to pass a certain environmental measure, the setting of standards will be reached at low levels whenever unanimity is required. The opposition of states not interested in introducing strict environmental standards may very well lead to a 'lowest common denominator' level of environmental protection. In particular this is likely to happen in the field of industrial process regulation. Instead, when a decision is taken on the basis of a majority, as is the case for harmonization measures taken under article 100A, a higher level of stringency can be achieved.

The pattern of future developments would certainly appear to be strongly influenced by economic reasoning. In fact there are other factors to be taken into account which modify this scenario to a large extent, namely the strong pressure exerted on governments by public opinion, which is increasingly inclined to support environmental actions even to the detriment of national economic interests, and the need for a common stance on environmental issues having a regional or even universal application.

This latter aspect needs to be explored further. If the rather pessimistic view that Community action may not always result in a high level of environmental protection as far as certain areas such as industrial process requirements are concerned is justified by the present legal framework, it is nevertheless true that production requirements are but one aspect of a manifold environmental policy. There are many problems that are better dealt with at Community level and that all states have an interest in solving because they affect all of them as well as every other member of the international community, namely atmospheric pollution, depletion of the ozone layer, pollution of common areas such as the oceans, etc. In all such cases of transboundary environmental spillovers within the Community, member-states, in the absence of mutual co-operation within the framework of the EC, 'would face an international prisoner's dilemma, in which all are worse off by pursuit of the interests of each' (Gatsios and Seabright, 1989, p. 40). Moreover, at the level of international negotiations, an integrated environmental policy may represent an advantage in terms of bargaining power.

Furthermore, a centralized network capable of gathering, elaborating and exchanging environmental information may offer economies of scale which should easily overcome national resentment at centralized decision-making. It is probably along such a line of reasoning that member-states have recently agreed to establish by regulation 90/1210 (OJ no. L120, 11/5/1990: 1) a European Environment Agency together with a European information and observation network which, in co-operation with national authorities, should be able to furnish objective and reliable data on the state of the environment and provide technical and scientific support for member-states.

As long as the Community, in carrying out its action, takes into account the differences existing among member-states with regard to geographical, ecological and industrial factors, allowing the national authorities to handle issues only affecting national matters such as land-use planning, noise pollution, etc., a common and increasingly integrated environmental policy will always represent, in principle, an effective means of ensuring adequate levels of environmental protection with due respect to economic integration imperatives. For all those states like Italy that are in the process of developing an autonomous environmental policy, the advantages of EC membership are still preferable to the situation that would exist without the EC. Nor is this scenario likely to be greatly modified in the short term.

As to the dilemma of whether or not environmental goals are consistent with economic integration imperatives, the answer lies in the hands of the Community itself. Much will depend on the wisdom of Community organs which are to decide, whenever they are called upon to balance up the two concurrent values, which one is to prevail in the particular circumstances of the case. We may only hope that the Community takes into account the view, currently prevailing in the international community, that no modern conception of economic growth and development can be divorced from an environmentally sound policy.

4.5.2 Environmental protection and the need for a multilateral strategy

As a tentative conclusion of this study concerning the costs and benefits for Italy of EC membership in the field of environmental policy, we could say that the basic finding is that Community action has most of the time resulted in a net benefit for Italy. This thesis is supported by the close relation existing between the development of Community action and the subsequent effort undertaken by the Italian legal system to adapt and adjust to such developments.

Taking into account the structure of the EC, however, we should not forget that the Community may simply provide the impulse for action, while the effective implementation of environmental measures rests upon member-states, the only subjects possessing enforcement mechanisms to ensure the observance of such measures (Haigh, 1987).

This observation upon the interdependence of the two legal systems paves the way to a further, more compelling argument, namely the need for a multilateral strategy of action to be endorsed by states and international organizations as well as the need to ensure, by means of all legal instruments made available (national laws and regulations, binding or merely recommendatory acts of international bodies, international treaties and even customary law rules),[2] an effective protection of the environment on a global scale.

The scientific community has clearly demonstrated that environmental conditions have remarkably worsened and already represent a concrete threat for all mankind in a mid-term perspective. Furthermore, the majority of such environmental problems cannot be dealt with nationally: the greenhouse effect, acid rain, desertification, atmosphere pollution, damage to the ozone layer, etc. In order to cope effectively with these different environmental threats it is certainly true that only international co-operation can guarantee a reasonable degree of protection.[3]

The unity and indivisibility of the environment requires joint and individual action. Thus all sources of regulation, provided that they are aimed at preserving and improving environmental conditions, are to be understood as closely interrelated and mutually beneficial.

The complex interrelation among different sources of legal regulation can be assessed in many areas. With regard to transboundary air pollution – which is certainly one of the most concrete examples one can mention to support the thesis of the necessity of worldwide international co-operation – the transnational character of the environmental threat has induced Western European states to develop a complex thread of legal obligations, ranging from *ad hoc* national measures to EC measures and international treaties (Bothe, 1986; Ercman, 1986; von Weizsäcker and Juras, 1990).

With regard to preventive measures aimed at protecting the ozone layer, the EC has played a very active role by imposing reductions on the production of chlorofluorocarbons and halons (regulation 3328/1988, OJ no. L297, 10/31/1988: 1) stricter than those provided for in the Montreal Protocol to the Vienna Convention on the protection of the ozone layer (XXVI ILM (1987): 1516ff., 1541ff.). Here once again we see the close interrelation between international law, community law and national laws and regulations which are to implement and eventually enforce in internal legal systems obligations undertaken at supranational and international levels.

Another example of this integrated action is the transboundary movement of toxic and noxious waste. The worldwide phenomenon of exports of such waste from industrialized countries to Third World countries is well known. The threat posed to the environment as a whole by this dangerous traffic caused the EC to include in its directive 631/84 on the surveillance and control of dangerous waste transfrontier shipments within the Community (OJ no. L326, 31/12/1984: 40) a specific provision concerning the export of waste to non-EC countries. For the protection of human health and the environment states were obliged to adopt all necessary measures to ensure the surveillance and control of shipments of hazardous waste involving the inward or outward flow of such substances in and out of the Community. This obligation of diligence was subsequently spelled out in detail by Italian law which set up a complex network of provisions with the aim that the export of such waste outside the Community, as well as meeting certain criteria, should in principle be prohibited, and in any case always require the written consent of the importing state. The relevant regulations, adopted in the aftermath of some diplomatic incidents stemming from certain illegal shipments of toxic waste to Third World countries in which Italian vessels were involved (see Scovazzi, 1988), represent, from a legislative technique standpoint, a very good means of ensuring the transparency of all transactions and are inspired by the need to guarantee a high level of environmental protection. In May 1989, under the auspices of UNEP, the Basel Convention on the control of transboundary movements of hazardous waste and their disposal was concluded (XXVIII ILM (1989): 649ff.). The Convention endorses many of the principles already expressed in EC and Italian law and creates a network of obligations which would, if universally accepted, greatly contribute towards solving the problem which is the object of regulation.

The example of the transboundary movement of toxic waste is good evidence for supporting the view that the interrelationship between national, supranational and international action is fundamental to the achievement of environmental protection goals.

Indeed, the preservation of nature and the protection of the environment demand a multilateral strategy and everyone should be committed to pursuing these goals in the knowledge that we have not only a moral but also a legal obligation to provide acceptable living conditions for both present and future generations (D'Amato, 1990, pp. 190ff.; Brown Weiss 1990, pp. 198ff.; Gundling, 1990, pp. 207ff.). The research for this article was carried out in 1990. Therefore, any later developments at national and Community level after 1990 have not been taken into account.

Abbreviations

DPR   Decree of the President of the Italian Republic
FI   Foro Italiano
GC   Giurisprudenza Costituzionale
ECR   European Court Reports
ILM   International Legal Materials
OJ   Official Journal of the EC
RDI   Rivista di diritto internazionale

Notes

1. Following the developments that occurred in Stockholm during the UN Conference on the Environment (XI ILM, 1972: 1416-21), the close link between economic growth and the need to preserve acceptable environmental conditions soon became the new challenge for the Community. This skill of extending EC primary law to new policies had already been tested in other areas (industrial policy, regional policy, energy policy, consumers' policy, etc., Lauria, 1988, pp. 79ff.; Pennacchini et al., 1983/4). Furthermore, the EC realized that uncontrolled national environmental measures could easily lead to disguised barriers, thus impairing the freedom of commerce among member-states. This is why at the 1972 Paris Summit the quest for a Community Environmental Action Programme was no longer a matter of dispute. The first programme for environmental protection was endorsed by the Commission shortly after (OJ no. C112, 20/12/1973: 1).
2. Legal scholars are still divided as to the recognition of the existence of general principles limiting State sovereignty in the domain of environmental protection (Kiss, 1989, pp.

58ff., 93ff.; Conforti, 1987, pp. 200ff.). The old-fashioned approach of classical international law to the principle of sovereignty, however, is subject to a steady and constant process of erosion by the new developments occurring especially in the field of environmental and human rights protection. Evidence of this can be seen in the incredible amount of norms - independently of their formal legal force - which have recently emerged in what is already called the international law of the environment (Kiss, 1989; Forum, 1990), and which touch upon the once indisputable dogma of the freedom of any state to act within its domestic jurisdiction with no limitations, except those long-established rules concerning the treatment of aliens.

3. Another significant reason for the rapid development of international environmental law is that in recent times states, at both national and international levels, have started to consider the environment as a shared resource worthy of legal protection.

Bibliography

Amendola, G. (1989), 'Prime impressioni sul D. P. R. n. 175, 17 maggio 1988', *Rivista giuridica dell' ambiente,* vol. IV: 247-52.

Benedizione, N. (1988), 'Rappresentanza di interessi, rappresentanza politica e tutela dell' ambiente', in N. Greco (ed.), *Il difficile governo dell' ambiente,* Rome: Edistudio, pp. 69-100.

Bianchi, P. and Cordini, G. (1983), *Comunita' europea e preotezione dell' ambiente,* Padua: Cedam.

Borgonovo, D. (1987), 'Gli "etudes d'impact" in Francia: un possibile modello per la via italiana?', *Rivista giuridica dell' ambiente,* vol. II: 25-32.

Bothe, M. (1986), 'Developments and problems of co-operation with regard to transboundary air pollution in Western Europe', in C. Flinterman, B. Kwiatowska and J. G. Lammers (eds), *Transboundary Air Pollution,* Dordrecht: Nijhoff, 117-29.

Brown Weiss, E. (1990), 'Our rights and obligations to future generations to preserve the global environment, *American Journal of International Law,* vol. 84: 198-207.

Capria, A. (1988), *Direttive ambientali CEE. Stato di attuazione in Italia,* Milan: Giuffré.

Cenerini, A. (1989), 'Il decreto di attuazione 17 maggio 1988 n. 175', *Rivista giuridica dell' ambiente,* vol. III: 67-70.

Cocco, G. (1986), 'Tutela dell' ambiente e danno ambientale: riflessioni sull' articolo 18 della legge 8 luglio 1986 n. 349', *Rivista giuridica dell' ambiente,* vol. I: 485-96.

Conforti, B. (1987), *Diritto internazionale,* Naples: Editoriale Scientifica.

Culotta, A. (1989), 'L' attuazione del D. P. R. 175/88 e la realta' industriale italiana', *Rivista giuridica dell' ambiente,* vol. IV: 247-52.

Cutrera, A. (1987), 'La direttiva 85/337/CEE sulla valutazione di impatto ambientale', *Rivista giuridica dell' ambiente,* vol. II: 499-521.

D'Amato, A. (1990), 'Do we owe a duty to future generations to preserve the global environment?', *American Journal of International Law,* vol. 84: 190-8

De Ruyt, J. (1987), *L'Acte Unique Européen,* Brussels: Université de Bruxelles.

Di Lecce, M. (1988), 'Prime osservazioni sul recepimento della direttiva 82/501', *Rivista giuridica dell' ambiente,* vol. III: 70-6.

EIU (Economist Intelligence Unit) (1989), 'European trends N. 2/1989', *Environment Report,* London, pp. 30-6.

EIU (Economist Intelligence Unit) (1990), 'European trends N. 1/1990', *Environment Report,* London, pp. 35-40.

Ercman, S. (1986), 'Activities of the Council of Europe and the European Economic communities related to transboundary air pollution', in Flinterman, Kwiatowska and Lammers (eds), *Transboundary Air Pollution,* Dordrecht: Nijhoff, *op. cit.,* pp. 131-40.

Forum sul diritto internazionale dell' ambiente, Siena 17-21 aprile 1990 (1990-1) Documento introduttivo preparato dal Governo Italiano, in *Vita Italiana. Istituzioni e Comunicazione*, vol. IV (special issue).

Gaja, G. (1989), 'Sulla delegificazione per attuare direttive comunitarie', *Rivista di diritto internazionale*, vol. LXXII: 64.

Gatsios, K. and Seabright, P. (1989/2) 'Regulation in the European Community', *Oxford Review of Economic Policy*, vol 5: 37-59.

Greco, N. (ed.), *Il difficile governo dell' ambiente*, Rome: Edistudio.

Greco, N. (1989), *Processi decisionali e tutela preventiva dell' ambiente*, Milan: Angeli.

Gundling, L. (1990), 'Our responsibility to future generations', *American Journal of International Law*, vol. 84: 207-12.

Haigh, N. (1987), 'Assessing EC environmental policy', *European Environment Review*, vol. 2: 38-41.

Hancker, L. (1989), 'Energy and the environment: striking a balance?', *Common Market Law Review*, vol. 26 no. 3: 475-512.

IEEP (Institute for European Environmental Policy) (1988), *Annual Report 1988*, Bonn, London, Paris, Brussels: IEEP.

Jans, J. (1989), 'Legal problems concerning the implementation of EEC environmental directives regarding dangerous substances and the Netherlands Chemical Substances Act, *Leiden Journal of International Law*, vol. I: 35-47.

Kennedy, W. K. (1988), 'What can Europe learn from 15 years of EIA in North America?', *European Environment Review*, vol. 2: 17-19.

Kiss, C. A. (1989), *Droit international de l' environnement*, Paris: Pedone.

Koppen, I. J. (1988), 'The European Community's environmental policy from the Summit in Paris, 1972, to the Single European Act,' *EUI Working Paper no. 88/328*, Badia Fiesolana, San Domenico (FI), European University Institute.

Koppen, I. J. and Ladauer, K. H. (1989), *Environmental Rights*, Bodia Fiesolana, San Domenico di Fiesole (FI), European University Institute.

Krämer, L. (1987), 'The Single European Act and environmental protection: reflections on several new provisions in community law', *Common Market Law Review*, vol. 4: 659ff.

Krämer, L. (1988), 'Du contrôle de l'application des directives communautaires en matière d'environnement', *Revue du Marché Commun*, vol. 313: 22-8.

Kromarek, P. (1986), 'The Single European Act and the environment', *European Environment Review*, vol. I: 10-12.

Labriola, S. (1988), 'Il ministero dell' ambiente', in N. Greco (ed.), *Il difficile governo dell' ambiente*, Rome: Edistudio: pp. 215-87.

Lauria, F. (1988), *Manuale di diritto delle Comunita' Europee*, Turin: UTET.

Lee, N. and Wood, C. (1988), 'Implementing the EC directive on EIA', *European Environment Review*, vol. 2: 12-17.

McCaffrey, S. (1975), 'The O. E. C. D. principles concerning transfrontier pollution', *Environmental Law and Policy* Vol 5: 1ff.

Mastellone, C. (1981), 'The external relations of the EEC in the field of environmental protection', *International and Comparative Law Quarterly*, vol. 30: 104-17.

Mengozzi, P. (1988), 'L'élaboration et l'application des directives européennes en matière d'environnement: la situation en Italie', *Rivista di diritto comunitario e degli scambi internazionali*, vol. 4: 631-44.

Mieli, M. (1989), 'Le origini del principio "Chi Inquina Paga" e il suo accoglimento da parte della comunità Europea', *Rivista Giuridica dell' ambiente*, vol. IV, no. 2: 217-246.

Nollkaemper, A. (1987), 'The European Community and international environmental cooperation: legal aspects of external Community powers', *Legal Issues of European Integration*, vol. 2: 55-91.

Onida, V. (1986), 'La ripartizione delle competenze per l'ambiente nella pubblica amministrazione', *Rivista giuridica dell' ambiente*, vol. I: 9-17.

Pennacchini, E., Monaco, R., Ferrari Bravo, L. and Puglisi, S. (1983/4), *Manuale di diritto comunitario, vols I-II*, Turin: UTET, vol. I: pp. 422ff.; 88f.; vol. II: pp 631ff.; 663ff; 701ff.; 735ff.; 775ff.

Plenivaux, C. (1984), 'La politica ambientale', in: Pennacchini *et al., Manuale di diritto comunitario, vol. II*, Turin: UTET: pp. 701ff.

Postiglione, A. (1986), 'Una svolta per il diritto all' ambiente: la legge 8 luglio 1986', *Rivista giuridica dell' ambiente*, vol. I: 251-62.

Rehbinder, E. and Stewart, R. (1985), *Environmental Protection Policy*, Berlin, New York: Walter de Gruyter.

Rescigno, G. U. (1988), 'Istituzione del Ministero dell' ambiente e progettazione legislativa', in N. Greco, (ed.) *Il difficile governo dell'ambiente*, Rome: Edistudio, pp. 207-13.

Ripa di Meana, C. (1989), 'Ecologia e tutela ambientale nell' ambito della CEE', *Il diritto dell' economia*, vol. 2: 387-98.

Roelants du Vivier, F. and Hannequart, J. P. (1988), 'Une nouvelle stratégie européenne pour l'environnement dans le cadre de l'Acte Unique, *Revue du Marché Commun*, vol. 316: 225-31.

Salerno, F. (1989), 'Quale "leale cooperazione" tra Stato e Regioni per l'attuazione dei regolamenti comunitari?', *Rivista di diritto internazionale*, vol. LXXII, no. 1: 65-7.

Sapienza, G. 'Environmental Impact Assessment in the European Community', *European Environment Review*, vol. 2: 8-12.

Scovazzi, T. (1988), 'I rifiuti che, partiti dall' Italia, tornarono in Italia', *Rivista giuridica dell' ambiente*, vol. III, no. 2: 341-7.

Smets, H. (1982), 'Legal principles adopted by the O.E.C.D. Council', *Environmental Policy and Law* vol. 12: 110ff.

Tizzano, A. (1989), 'Note introduttive alla legge "La Pergola"', *Il Foro Italiano*, vol. IV: 314ff.

Urbani, P. (1986), 'I problemi della tutela ambientale tra Stato, Regioni e Corte Costituzionale: leggi e decreti nell' imposizione di vincoli paesaggistici', *Rivista giuridica dell' ambiente*, vol. I: 41-60.

Vandermeersch, D. (1987), 'The S. E. A. and environmental policy of the European Economic Community, *European Law Review*, vol. 12: 407ff.

Vaughan, D. (1986), *Law of the European Community*, London: Butterworths, vol. I: pp. 749-827 (para. 8. 01-8. 90).

WCED (World Commission on Environment and Development: Expert Group on Environmental Law) (1987), *Environmental Protection and Sustainable Development: Legal Principles and Recommendations*, London, Dordrecht, Boston, Graham & Trotman/Martinus Nijhoff.

Weizsäcker, E. U. von and Juras, A. (1990), 'La politique européenne de l'environnement', *Cadmos. Institut Universitaire d'Etudes Européennes*, vol. 13, no. 49: 33-46.

Wirth, D. A. (1989), 'International Technology Transfer and Environmental Impact Assessment, in G. Handl and R. Lutz, *Transferring Hazardous Technologies and Substances: The International Legal Challenge*, Dordrecht, Boston: Graham & Trotman/Martinus Nijhoff Publishers, pp. 83-105.

Chapter 5

Fiscal policy

Carlo Garbarino

5.1 Introduction

The main task of the present study is the assessment of the impact on the Italian legal system of the EC process of tax integration.

This impact analysis will be restricted to legislation approved by the institutional bodies of the EC already applicable or being implemented into the member-states and will not extend to proposed legislation that is pending at various stages of the Community law-making process or to EC policies.

This chapter will describe the modifications already introduced – or about to be introduced – into the Italian tax system, and their benefits or costs. The impact-analysis adopted consists of a preliminary description of the EC process of tax integration (section 2) and a description of existing Italian tax rules to be modified by EC rules (section 3). Section 3 focuses only on those rules concerning transnational transactions and section 4 deals with the impact of EC legislation on those rules. The analysis will be applied to three separate sectors of taxation:

1. corporate taxes (sections 5.3.1 and 5.4 1);
2. value added tax (VAT) (sections 5.3 2 and 5.4 2);
3. excises and other charges (sections 5.3 3 and 5.4 3).

This chapter is not concerned with the quantitative assessment of benefits and costs, but with the interpretation and application of new rules within the Italian tax system, and from this a legal analysis is developed. From this perspective, benefits are the positive effects arising from the implementation of EC rules, such as better co-ordination of statutes and regulations, clearer language of rules, elimination of lacunae or resolution of conflicts of rules, easier application of rules, elimination of unfair tax treatments (horizontal and vertical equity), better co-ordination of domestic rules with harmonized EC rules or with other member-states' rules.

Also considered a benefit in the area of transnational taxation is the elimination of fiscal barriers to the free flow of goods, persons and capital (international tax neutrality).

In this chapter, costs are considered as the administrative costs of modifications to the domestic tax systems and the short-term loss of advantage for domestic *vis-à-vis* foreign enterprises. These are costs only from a short-term perspective of national interest, while it is assumed that, from a European and international perspective the benefits are higher than costs in the long run.

5.2 An outline of EC tax integration

Before setting out on an analysis of the impact of EC rules and policies on the Italian domestic tax system, four preliminary notions must be pointed out.

First, it is necessary to distinguish the areas where the EC has intervened in the process of tax integration among business entities during the last decades. Those sectors are the corporate taxes (including capital taxes), value added taxes, excises and other internal charges.

Second, it is necessary to distinguish between the concepts of tax harmonization, tax co-ordination and tax competition. Tax harmonization is the process whereby the tax systems of the member-states are (partly) modified to conform to a common pattern established by EC rules. Tax co-ordination is the process whereby member-states structure freely their tax policies, without intervention through domestic rules and with the freedom of movement of goods, persons and capitals within the EC single market. By tax competition is meant a situation whereby member-states freely structure their tax policies and where they may create distortion with regard to the free flow of goods, persons and capitals within the EC.

In the area of corporate taxes, the EC, after an initial harmonization approach (which proved unsuccessful) has recently adopted a co-ordination approach: (a) by establishing common rules for the elimination of distortion to transnational investments (elimination of withholding taxes on dividends paid to non-residents, exemption of dividends received from parent companies, tax neutrality for transnational mergers); (b) by creating a flexible, multilateral system of dispute resolution for arm's-length transactions of multinationals (treaty on correlative adjustments); (c) by promoting common rules for the determination of tax base (a proposal for a directive has been presented to the Council); (d) by adjusting tax rates of excise duties better to co-ordinate member-state legislation; (e) by eliminating other domestic discriminatory charges both to exports and to imports.

With regard to VAT, the EC, after the completion of the process of harmonization of value added taxes in accordance with the pattern set out by various directives, is now refining the common VAT by shifting to a system of exemption in the import countries.

Third, it is necessary to distinguish between an overall impact analysis of EC tax rules and a specific impact analysis in a single country (Italy). While in general it is possible to assess the costs and benefits for the Community of the tax integration process (partly harmonization, partly co-ordination, partly competition), with regard to Italy the analysis must focus on the effect on rules dealing with transnational transactions (see section 5.3).

Finally, from a strictly legal standpoint, EC directives are considered as self-executing in Italy, but usually they need implementing legislation and administrative regulations to be applied effectively. For this reason a new body of EC domestic-transnational rules is being developed, adapting EC rules to the specifics of the domestic Italian tax system.

5.3 Tax treatment of transnational transactions in Italy

This section relates to direct and indirect taxation of transnational business activities (hereinafter 'transnational transactions'). Transnational transactions are those activities which take place in more than one country, either because a resident of Italy carries out activities abroad, or because a non-resident effects transactions in Italy. Transnational transactions have a link with more than one country (they are not purely domestic) and therefore more than one country can assert its tax jurisdiction.

The impact analysis developed in section 5.4 will focus on those activities carried out by Italian residents abroad and by non-residents in Italy. Those activities can be carried out: (a) by way of income-creating activities abroad not connected with a permanent establishment ('isolated transactions'), such as the rendering of services or the export–import of goods; (b) by establishing a branch abroad (i.e. a 'permanent establishment'); (c) by incorporating one or more subsidiaries ('controlled companies' or 'base companies'). The transnational activities can also be carried out by a group of companies located in various member-states ('multinationals'). The impact of EC tax rules and directives affects multinationals of Italian origin as well as multinationals that only have affiliates located in Italy. Those transnational business activities are subject to different sets of rules which interact: Italian tax rules, tax treaties, EC rules.

The domestic tax rules regarding transnational income are overridden by tax treaties, which give the power to tax to the source country and avoid double taxation on a bilateral basis.

EC rules modify domestic and treaty rules, thereby creating a partially harmonized European tax system, which substitutes parts of the bilateral system of tax integration existing in Europe. Thus this chapter focuses on the modifications to the domestic and treaty rules in Italy dealing with transnational income.

While for Italian companies with branches abroad (and vice versa) it is relatively simple to assess the impact of EC rules because those rules modify the rules of countries of residence which tax the income of residents arising from branches abroad, for the multinationals that analysis is more complex because it relates to the impact on the various domestic tax legislation of the companies belonging to the same group. This impact can be assessed by singling out specific intercompany transactions (payment of dividends, interests, royalties and transfer pricing) and determining the modifications of their tax treatments.

5.3.1 Corporate taxes

5.3.1.1 Taxation of resident companies

General comments. A company is considered resident in Italy for tax purposes if it is incorporated in Italy, if its legal or administrative headquarters are in Italy, or if its principal activities are carried on in Italy. Resident companies are subject to a 46.2 per cent combined tax rate (IRPEG and ILOR). IRPEG (*'imposta sul reddito delle persone giuridiche'*) is a corporation tax applied at a rate of 36 per cent, while ILOR is an additional tax on income arising from capital and business activities applied at

16.2 per cent and deductible from IRPEG.

The Italian corporate tax burden is one of the highest amongst EC member-countries and is partially compensated for by tax credit. Since there is no proposal for harmonizing tax rates, this situation will change if Italy lowers its rates to attract foreign investment, in a process of tax competition with other member-states which might offer lower rates.

There are no EC proposals or rules to abolish the tax credit system and it is unlikely that Italian rules in this area will change in the short – medium term.

Permanent establishment. The profits of an enterprise resident in Italy which carries out business abroad through a permanent establishment situated therein may be taxed in the other state but only so much of them as are attributable to that permanent establishment ('attributable profits'). These are the profits which a resident enterprise might be expected to make if the permanent establishment were a distinct and separate enterprise engaged in the same or similar activities under the same or similar conditions and dealing wholly independently with the enterprise of which it is a permanent establishment. Also in this respect no major change will intervene at the EC level. Proposal for harmonization of rules for determining the tax base may clarify this issue.

Under Italian tax law, in determining the profits of a permanent establishment, expenses that are attributable to the activities of the permanent establishment are deductible, including a reasonable allocation of executive and general administrative expenses, whether incurred in Italy or abroad.

Foreign tax credit. If double taxation arises, unilateral measures allow relief from it. Taxes paid by residents abroad on foreign income (be it from isolated transactions or from the activities of a permanent establishment) are allowed as credits against net tax in an amount equal to that part of the Italian tax which is proportional to the ratio between foreign source income and aggregate worldwide income. However, if foreign taxes are higher than Italian taxes, Italian residents bear a non-deductible tax credit ('excess foreign tax credit') which cannot be carried back or forward.

If income produced in more than one foreign state is included, the tax credit is applied separately with respect to each state. Thus averaging of tax credit on an overall basis is not allowed, thereby making the tax planning of multinationals based in Italy rather inefficient.

Tax credits must be claimed in the return for the tax period in which the foreign taxes are definitively paid, that is when foreign assessment is final. If the tax due in Italy for the tax period in which the foreign income was included in the taxable base has already been settled, a new settlement must be prepared, taking into account any increase in foreign source income, and the credit will be applied to the tax due in the tax period pertaining to the annual return in which it was claimed. If the period of limitation for assessment has already expired, the credit is limited to that part of the foreign tax proportional to the part of foreign source income subject to taxation in Italy.

There is no right to credit in the event of failure to file a tax return or to report income produced abroad in the tax return.

The credit for taxes paid abroad by partnerships and similar entities belongs to the individual partners, associates, or participants in their quotas.

Subsidiaries. An Italian company may also decide to carry out its activities in another member-state through a newly incorporated entity, usually wholly owned or controlled (a 'subsidiary').

The subsidiary is treated as a resident company and its taxable income is all net income sourced in Italy and abroad earned during a financial year and resulting from the balance sheet with the adjustments required by the criteria set out by tax rules. All expenditures and charges which relate to the production of taxable income and properly allocated in the balance sheet are deductible.

Expenses are deductible if their existence is certain or their account is ascertainable in an objective way and if they have been entered in the profit and loss account.

Royalties paid to the parent company on patents, trademarks, know-how and similar rights, and service fees (i.e. management fees and technical advisory fees) are deductible by the subsidiary if the amounts are reasonable and computed at arm's length. Royalties paid by subsidiary to parent are subject to an effective domestic 21 per cent withholding tax (30 per cent on 70 per cent of the amount paid), subject to the provisions of the treaties.

Dividends paid by the subsidiary to the parent are not deductible in Italy and are subject to a domestic 30 per cent withholding tax. The treaties provide for lower rates. Directive no. 90/435 of 23 July 1990 eliminates such withholding tax on dividends (see section 5.4. 1.1 below).

Forty per cent of the profits distributed to resident parent company by 'related companies', as defined in article 2359 of the Civil Code, which are not resident in the territory of the state, are taxable but the entire amount thereof is calculated for the purposes of the rules relating to increases for so-called 'equalization tax'. Directive no. 90/435 mentioned above also eliminates double taxation by exempting those dividends.

Interest paid by subsidiary to parent company is deductible for the parent company. A domestic 15 per cent final withholding tax is levied on interest paid for normal financing of the subsidiary by the parent company, but the treaties usually lower the rate of withholding tax. Proposals for the harmonization of withholding taxes on interests has not come through at a European level, and Italy has not taken any initiative to harmonize the rates of the bilateral treaty.

Transfer price. The income components derived from transactions with companies not resident within the territory of the state and which control the enterprise directly or indirectly or which are controlled by the same company which controls the enterprise are valued on the basis of the normal value of goods transferred, of services performed and of goods and services received, determined in accordance with their 'normal value', if income is thereby increased.

Under Italian tax rules 'normal value' is the average price or consideration paid for goods and services of the same or similar type, in free market conditions and at the same level of commerce, at the time and place in which the goods and services were purchased or performed or, if there be none, at the time and place nearest thereto. In determining normal value, reference is made to price lists or tariffs of the party which has supplied the goods and services and, if there be none, to the indices and price lists of the various chambers of commerce and to professional tariffs, taking normal discounts into account. For goods and services subject to price control, reference is made to the regulations in force.

The link of interdependence between entities which empowers the Italian tax authorities to reallocate income is referred to as 'dominant influence'.

In a Circular Letter of 1980 (Circular 9/2267 of 22 September 1980) the Ministry of Finance indicated different methods of valuation to be used for each type of transaction (so-called 'safe harbours'). These methods are all based on the arm's-length principle. In accordance with the circular, rates of interests for loans paid by non-resident controlling companies must be 'normal'. Royalties or fees paid to the parent licenser are readily accepted if they do not exceed 2 per cent of sales proceeds; proof for royalties between 2 and 5 per cent is more burdensome, and royalties higher than 5 per cent are accepted only in exceptional cases that can be justified by the high technological level of the economic sector in question or by other circumstances.

5.3. 1.2 Taxation of non-resident companies

In general. In general residents of other member-states are taxed by the Italian government on income sourced in Italy. For individuals the following items of income are considered as earned within the territory of Italy:

(a) income from land and buildings;
(b) income from capital when paid by the state, by parties resident within the territory of the state, or by a permanent establishment within the said territory of non-resident parties;
(c) income from employment for services rendered within the territory of the state;
(d) income from independent personal services within the territory of the state;
(e) business income derived from activities undertaken within the territory of the state through a permanent establishment;
(f) miscellaneous income derived from isolated activities undertaken within the territory of the state or relating to assets located within said territory;
(g) income of partnerships which is attributable to non-resident partners, associates, or participants

Independently from the source rules listed above, the following are considered as income gained within the territory of the state when paid by the state, by parties resident within the territory of the state, or by permanent establishments within the territory of non-resident parties;

(a) pensions and similar allowances and termination indemnities;
(b) certain items of income which are assimilated to employment income;
(c) compensation for the use of intellectual property, patents, and trademarks as well as processes, formulas and information relating to experience acquired in industrial, commercial, or scientific fields;

(d) compensation earned by enterprises, companies, or non-resident entities for
     artistic or professional services performed on their behalf within the territory
     of the state.

For foreign corporations taxable income is that income which is deemed to be
sourced in Italy, net of deductible costs. The income which derives from activities
undertaken within the territory of Italy through a permanent establishment is
therefore taxable in Italy. Treaties also provide analogous source rules which
sometimes modify domestic rules. Source rules (domestic and treaty) will not be
changed by EC rules.

Permanent establishment. If a foreign European investor in Italy operates through a
'branch', it has a 'permanent establishment' in Italy. The term 'permanent establishment' is not defined by Italian law, but the treaties entered into by Italy with
other European countries include a definition of it, in accordance with the OECD
Model convention. No EC rule provides a definition of 'permanent establishment'.

Italian law conforms with the OECD model. In accordance with it, the term
'permanent establishment' means a fixed place of business in which the business of
the enterprise is wholly or partly carried out, including a place of management, a
branch, an office, a factory, a workshop, a place of extraction of natural resources,
a building site or construction or assembly project. The term 'permanent establishment' does not include the use of facilities or the maintenance of a stock of goods,
delivery of goods or merchandise belonging to the enterprise or for processing by
another enterprise, or the maintenance of a fixed place of business solely for the
purposes of collecting information, advertising, for the supply of information, for
scientific research, or for similar activities which have a preparatory or auxiliary
character for the enterprise.

A person acting in Italy on behalf of an enterprise resident abroad other than an
agent of an independent status is a permanent establishment if it has, and habitually
exercises, the authority to conclude contracts in the name of the enterprise, unless
those activities are limited to the purchase of goods or merchandise for the enterprise.

The branch exercises a so-called 'force of attraction' on all items income-sourced
in Italy and must prepare separate accounts of income arising from its operations.

The branch must comply with Italian accounting and tax rules (other requirements are set by civil law rules relating to *sede secondaria*), as well as with the rules
of the source country. Thus it might be necessary to maintain both foreign and
Italian financial statements.

Finally, the branch must file a tax return every year and its income must be
consolidated with the income of the parent company.

Transfers of funds from branch to parent company are not subject to withholding tax, but simply result from consolidated balance sheets. Therefore, branch
income is taxable in Italy and deferral is not allowed. In turn, tax credit is allowed
by the country of residence.

The branch can deduct the following costs: interest paid to the parent company
for financing which is directly connected with the branch's activities; royalties paid
to the parent company at the normal value of the intangible, which has been
provided by said parent company (application of transfer-pricing criteria); all

expenses, if they result from branch accounting and if they relate to the production of income, and are borne exclusively by the branch.

If the parent company is not located in the EC, on establishment of the branch, a 1 per cent registration tax is levied and the taxable base is the operating capital attributed to the branch. In the case of increases in operating capital, the 1 per cent registration tax is paid on the amount of increase.

Registration tax is not due if paid in another EC country or if the parent is located within the EC. This is the effect of the implementation in Italy of the directive of 17 July 1969.

Value added tax. The foreign company is subject to value added tax (VAT) for transactions effected in Italy and must invoice transactions (sales–services), record invoices issued and received, pay VAT quarterly, and file a VAT statement each year. VAT is neutral for branch and borne by the final consumer.

Subsidiaries. Subsidiaries of foreign companies are subject to the same tax treatment as resident companies (see section 5.3.1.1).

Subsidiary incorporation is subject to a 1 per cent registration tax on net capital. If subsequent contributions in cash are effected, the tax is 1 per cent of each contribution. If real estate, equipment or other movables represent a contribution, the rates are, respectively, 8 per cent, 4 per cent and 1 per cent. A concession tax is levied *una tantum* (once only) for registration in the Register of Business Enterprises and business tax related to the size of enterprise (ICIAP) is paid in a fixed amount once a year.

5.3.1.3 Tax treaties

Since Italy has entered tax treaties with most member-states the transnational transactions are, *vis-à-vis* each of these states, bilaterally regulated. These treaties are based on the source principle and give the power to tax income to the contracting state where the income is sourced, and provide for tax credit if double taxation arises. Furthermore, the treaties alleviate the tax burden on the flow of dividends, royalties and interest between companies located in two different member-states by lowering or eliminating the withholding taxes. Treaty provisions about dividends withholding taxes and Competent Authority procedure will be modified by directive no. 90/435 an 90/436 of 23 July 1990 (see section 5.4.1 below).

Italy has entered tax treaties with all member-states (except Portugal and Greece), thereby creating a network of bilateral conventions which co-ordinates the rules of the various domestic tax systems concerning international taxation. However, bilateral treaties do not eliminate all benefits to the flow of capital, so that it is still possible for multinationals to create international corporate structures serving the sole purpose of reducing the tax costs. Italy is not usually chosen by foreign multinationals as the location for intermediary and base companies because the tax burden for corporations is relatively high and the treaty network and domestic legislation do not make it advantageous for tax planning. Italian multinationals on the other hand, choose other member-states as the location for their intermediary companies.

5.3.1.4 Conclusions

The main problems which affect the Italian corporate tax rules on transnational transactions and which violate international neutrality are the following:

(a) the prohibition of the carrying-over or carrying-forward of foreign tax credit;
(b) the lack of rules defining the items of 'foreign income' for the purposes of applying tax credit rules;
(c) the lack of rules for correlative adjustments in intracompany transactions;
(d) the lack of co-ordination between domestic remedies and the 'mutual' agreements resulting from bilateral competent authority procedures;
(e) the lack of clear rules concerning accounting and tax requirements for permanent establishments abroad (or for permanent establishment in Italy of foreign companies);
(f) the partial exemption for dividends paid by a subsidiary abroad, which does not eliminate double taxation on those dividends;
(g) the lack of an indirect tax credit for items of income distributed to the resident company and which have borne abroad an indirect tax burden at the corporate level;
(h) the lack of co-ordination of the Italian imputation system with other systems adopted by member-states;
(i) the lack of specific tax rules for multinational groups;
(j) the levying of withholding taxes on investment income received by non-residents;
(k) the lack of rules on transnational mergers.

While items (c), (d), (f), (g), (h), (j) and (k) will be covered by new applicable EC rules (see section 5.4), the source of income rules, the tax credit regime, the tax treatment of permanent establishments and multinationals will be left to member-states. Thus Italy still has to accomplish the task of creating, by way of domestic rules, the conditions fostering international tax neutrality in relation to foreign source income.

5.3.2 Value added tax (VAT)

Italian VAT is harmonized with EC directives and, therefore, a thorough description of it will be provided in section 5.4 in the context of the impact analysis developed therein. As far as transnational transactions are concerned, the export of goods is VAT-exempt and VAT is paid by the member-state importing the goods from Italy. The rendering of services is subject to VAT if the person rendering the services is resident in Italy. However, certain exceptions to this rule are provided.

5.3.3 Excises and internal charges

In Italy excise duties (*'imposte di fabbricazione'*) are consumer taxes paid by the producer but transferred as costs on to the consumer. Various rates are applied to different products. The assessment and the enforcement system is obsolete and is based on detailed inspections and on a preliminary self-assessment by taxpayers. Within the tax system many other charges are levied that have a 'tax nature'.

As far as excise duties are concerned, it is difficult to provide a thorough description of these charges; in section 5.4, therefore, the main modifications of these charges will be described in the context of impact analysis.

It is difficult to assess in detail all Italian domestic rules in the area of excise taxes that have been affected by the EC process of integration. This process has developed in two sets of proposals; on the one hand, directive proposals relating to the harmonization of the tax base and structure of domestic excise duties; on the other, proposals dealing with tax rates, in an attempt to bring them closer together.

5.4 The impact of EC rules on the Italian tax system

5.4.1 Corporate taxes

Section 5.3.1.4 above has shown that several problems currently affecting the Italian tax rules on international transactions should be modified in the EC context. Direct taxation is a fundamental factor in creating the conditions for the free movement of goods, persons, services and capital in the single market. If the national tax system of one member-state treats the income arising from movement of labour and capital more (or less) favourably then investment decisions are distorted by tax factors and the situation of 'international tax neutrality' is not achieved. As mentioned above (section 5.2), the Community has not taken a clear stance in favour of full harmonization, but it has taken co-ordinated measures in the following areas: withholding taxes, dividends, tax treatment of parent companies and subsidiaries, taxation of transnational mergers, correlative adjustments.

5.4.1.1 The imputation system and withholding taxes

In 1975 the Commission prepared a proposal for a directive which envisaged the harmonization of withholding taxes on dividends flowing from a company resident in a member-state to a company resident in another member-state. The unification of the corporation tax rates was also proposed within the range of 45–55 per cent, in addition to a 45–55 per cent income tax credit on grossed-up dividends, and a uniform 25 per cent withholding tax. Under the proposal tax credit would have been applied to non-resident recipients receiving dividends directly or via an intermediate subsidiary of the parent company.

The proposal has not been approved because, by ignoring the problem of harmonization of rules for defining the taxable base, the harmonization of tax treatment of profit distributions is rendered useless.

Assuming the completion of the process of harmonization of rules on the taxable base, the introduction of such a directive in the Italian tax system would have extended tax credit to non-residents (currently non-resident recipients do not benefit from tax credit because they pay a withholding tax, unless they have a permanent establishment in Italy)

As far as the election of the imputation system and the range of corporation tax rates are concerned, the process of co-ordination has been carried out by member-states autonomously, but still great differences exist in the rates of tax credit and corporation tax. Thus, in order to trigger a modification of the Italian corporation tax in accordance with other member-states, rather than revive the old proposal, an autonomous process of tax co-ordination/competition is required.

In conclusion, since no EC rule is currently in effect, the need to co-ordinate the Italian imputation system with other national systems will be achieved by a change in domestic rules.

5.4.1.2 Parent companies and subsidiaries

In connection with the creation of a common system of tax credits and withholding taxes on dividends, the Commission has also envisaged the creation of a system of common taxation of parent companies and their subsidiaries.

Within the Common Market, when profits of a subsidiary located in one member-state are distributed to the parent company (located in another member-state) in the form of dividends, various situations of double or multiple taxation may arise (in Italy a partial double taxation occurs). Unless bilateral tax treaty rules apply, those profits are taxed in one country as the business income of the payer and, in the other country, as dividends when received by the payee.

The proposed Council directive in this area submitted by the Commission to the Council on 23 July 1975 introduced: (a) a common imputation system of corporation tax; (b) a common system of withholding tax on dividends.

As far as the harmonization of systems of company taxation is concerned, article 3 of the Proposal provided for a single rate of corporation tax not lower than 45 per cent and not higher than 55 per cent, with the possibility of derogations imposed for domestic reasons such as tax policy requirements.

Under article 4 of the proposal the recipient of a dividend who is resident of a member-state has the right to tax credit. The proposal, however, extends the benefit of tax credit to taxpayers resident in third countries if tax treaties between a member-state and those countries so provide.

Tax credit was linked to the corporation tax rate. Thus credit could vary between 45 and 55 per cent of the amount of corporation tax levied on the distributed dividend, and a compensatory tax would have to be charged to the corporation on distributed dividends which were exempt at the corporate level. The compensatory tax would not be charged if an advance payment of corporation tax (in an amount at least equal to the tax credit) were made.

The proposal also put forth rules relating to the withholding tax on dividends by setting its rate at 25 per cent on outbound flows of dividends, by barring withholding tax if dividends were distributed by a subsidiary to a parent company resident in a member-country, and by allowing member-states not to impose the withholding tax if the names of the recipients were communicated to the relevant tax administration.

The proposal resulted from the studies conducted at the beginning of the 1970s on the integration of corporation taxes; did not take account of the problem of harmonization of the tax base, and it has not yet been adopted. Nọr has there been a change in the Italian system.

Current domestic and treaty law existing in Italy does not eliminate double taxation on dividends paid by one unit to another unit of a multinational group. The exemption for dividends received from foreign-controlled corporations is a partial one and the withholding taxes, though reduced by the treaties and credited as foreign taxes, create an undue financial burden on corporations.

Had the 1975 proposal been introduced in its present form, it would not have had a relevant impact on the Italian tax system, which already adopts an imputation system (*'credito d'imposta sui dividendi'*, introduced by law n. 904, 1977) combined with a compensatory corporation tax (*'imposta di conguaglio'*, introduced by law n. 649, 1983), and which levies a withholding tax on dividends paid to non-residents.

The Council has recently issued a directive of 23 July 1990 (n. 90/435) on the common system of taxation applicable in the case of parent companies and subsidiaries of different member-states, which modifies the unfavourable tax treatment of groups of companies based or operating in Italy. The directive provides that dividends distributed by a subsidiary to a parent company are exempt in the state of the subsidiary (or deductible by the parent company) and are not subject to withholding tax neither in the state of payer nor in the state of payee (see points (f) and (j) of section 5.3.4 above).

The directive also allows the so-called 'indirect tax credit' in so far as it provides that it shall not affect the credit for the recipient of dividends of taxes previously paid on that income before distribution (see point (g) of section 5.3.4 above).

The directive set 1 January 1992 as the deadline for implementation by member-states. It is likely that the Italian legislation will amend the domestic rule which now allows partial exemption by simply modifying the requirements for full exemption. At present, so that the dividends may be partially exempt in the hand of the parent company, that company must have a holding of at least 25 per cent of the capital of the subsidiary. As far as withholding taxes are concerned, existing domestic and bilateral rules will be overridden by the new rules.

5.4.1.3 Transnational reorganizations

'Transnational reorganizations' involve companies of different countries and can consist of 'mergers', 'split-ups', 'transfers of assets' in exchange for stock (for definitions of these terms, see below). In general in a transnational reorganization a company (hereinafter 'acquired company') is absorbed into another company (hereinafter 'acquiring company'). Within the Common Market transnational reorganizations should not be affected by tax factors determined by different member-states, and as a result they should be tax-neutral. However, existing national legislation in this area differs greatly and is not adequate to prevent tax-induced distortion of the functioning of the Common Market.

The Commission and the Council have adopted a policy in favour of the creation of common European rules for reorganizations based on two principles: (i) the deferral of taxes on gains arising from the reorganization; (ii) the protection of the revenue interests of the country of the acquired company.

The EC policy-making bodies have also established a transnational merger to be the conversion of the acquired company in a 'permanent establishment' of the acquiring company, so that tax deferral for the company resulting from the reorganization necessarily implies tax deferral on the income arising from the assets of the acquired company. When these assets are disposed of, the state in which the acquired company is located imposes tax on realized gains.

In the process of creating common tax rules for transnational mergers, the Community was also faced with the following tax policy issues: (a) the attainment of coherent rules for treatment of reserves and losses of companies taking part in the reorganization; (b) the tax treatment of reciprocal participation in capital by companies taking part in the reorganization; (c) the elimination of double taxation on the profits of permanent establishments abroad of the companies taking part in the reorganization; (d) the attainment of neutrality for VAT purposes.

The proposed Council directive on transnational reorganization, submitted by the Commission to the Council on 15 January 1969, set up tax rules for treatment of reorganizations in general, and for transfers of assets and permanent establishments abroad in particular.

The proposal defined the term 'merger' as an operation whereby: (a) one company, following its dissolution without liquidation, transfers all of its assets to another company, in exchange for shares of the other company, or for shares and cash not exceeding 10 per cent of par value or book value of such shares; (b) two or more companies, following a dissolution without liquidation, transfer all of their assets to a company which they establish, in exchange for shares or cash, within the limits set above under (a).

In turn, a 'split-up' (or 'division') is defined as an operation whereby one company, following a dissolution without liquidation, transfers all of its assets to two or more companies, in exchange for transfer to its partners of shares or cash, within the limits set above at (a) of the previous paragraph.

Finally, 'transfer of assets' is defined as an operation whereby a company transfers all or parts of its assets without being dissolved to another company in exchange for shares.

For the purposes of this chapter mergers and split-ups are defined as 'reorganizations'. These definitions have been adopted by the directive no. 90/434 of 23 July 1990.

The basic principle of this directive (set out by article 4) was that member-states do not tax capital gains resulting from the reorganization: (a) if the assets involved in the transaction as well as those excluded are carried on the books of establishments of the acquiring company located in the same state of the acquired company; (b) if the acquiring company uses as the basis of its assets the value as stated on the tax return of the acquired corporation.

The Proposal also provides that this principle applied to tax-exempt reserves and losses of the acquired company carried on the books of the acquiring company. The Proposal specified (1) that losses, however, cannot be deducted by the acquiring company if they arise from its establishments located abroad; and (2) that if the acquiring company holds a share of the acquired company and vice versa, gains and the allocation of shares to its partners are not taxable.

As far as the principle of protection of interests of the state of the acquired company is concerned, article II of the Proposal allowed taxation of gains from reorganizations (when they are realized) to be imposed by the country of the acquired company if the assets disposed of are connected to its establishments abroad: the state where those assets are located waives its primary right to tax based at source in favour of the country where the company is resident. It should be remembered, however, that the proposal's rule of taxation by the country where the establishments are located is taken as the general rule.

The proposal was approved by Parliament ('Opinion', C 51, 29 April 1970) and was for many years before the Council for adoption. Various draft proposals were circulated and the Council finally issued a directive on transnational mergers in July 1990 (see below).

Currently the Italian tax system has rules on the treatment of domestic mergers but does not have rules on transnational mergers. Under domestic tax law a merger is tax-neutral. A merger between resident companies does not constitute either a realization or distribution of capital gains or losses on the assets of the merged companies, including inventory and goodwill. Capital gains and losses reported in the financial statement to assess the value of the merging companies are not considered for tax purposes. If the merger is effected by issuing to shareholders of the dissolving company securities representing the capital of the other company, gains and losses due to the exchange ratio or cancellation of the shares of the companies taking part in the merger are not recognized for tax purposes. The increased value of assets being transferred is not taxable up to the amount of the difference between the cost of shares and the net worth of the companies taking part in the merger. Special rules provide for tax deferral on certain reserves and funds transferred from one company to the other and specify when they are taxed. Other rules disallow the deduction of losses of the dissolved company by the other company.

In conclusion, in Italy the tax treatment of domestic mergers is tax-neutral and, in certain respects, advantageous (for example, tax deferral, stepping up of basis free of value of assets with no imposition of any tax on such increase of value.) Since there are no rules about transnational mergers (acquisition of a foreign company by an Italian company or vice versa), these mergers are considered to be tax-neutral in the same way as domestic mergers if the incorporating company is resident. On the other hand, the tax treatment of the acquisition of Italian companies by foreign companies is not covered by any tax rule (domestic or bilateral) and is left to the rules of the other state, thus creating a situation of potential disparity of treatment of similar transactions.

The Council directive no. 90/434 of 13 July 1990 on the common system of taxation applicable to mergers, divisions, transfer of assets and exchanges of shares concerning companies of different member-states will therefore complete domestic Italian rules dealing with international transactions, rather than modify them.

The directive is based on the same policies which underlie Italian legislation and, therefore, radical modifications will not be necessary. The first common policy is that tax rules must be neutral, so that tax restraints do not impede corporate reorganization for genuine business purposes. The second common policy is tax deferral of capital gains arising from the transaction until they are realized. The directive is based on two additional policies: the safeguarding of the tax interest of the state where the acquired assets are located, that is the state where the gains of the transaction are sourced, and the safeguarding of the concurring interest of the state of residence of the acquiring company. These two policies which relate to the transnational dimension of the merger do not conflict with existing policies and rules of the Italian tax system and confirm the trend set by the proposal of 1969.

As far as tax neutrality is concerned, the directive provides that a merger division or a transfer of assets does not give rise to any taxation of capital gains computed by the difference between the 'real value' of the assets and liabilities transferred and their 'value for tax purposes'. If the acquiring company has a holding in the capital of the acquired company, any gains accruing to the acquiring company on the cancellation of its holding are not taxable. The tax–neutrality of the reorganization does not prevent member-states from taxing gains arising out of subsequent acts of disposal. Therefore, subsequent realization of capital gains (sales of assets, distributions and other taxable events) are taxable by the country where they occur.

The tax deferral is the gain computed on the difference between the real value of transferred assets and liability which are 'effectively connected' with a permanent establishment of the acquiring company and located in the other member-state of the acquired company.

If exempt provision or reserves of the acquired company are from permanent establishments located in the state of the acquired company, they can be carried over by the permanent establishment of the acquiring company which is located in the state of the acquired company (principle of territoriality for transfer of losses and reserves of the permanent establishment).

On the other hand, if the assets transferred in a merger or division or a transfer of assets include the permanent establishment of the acquired company located in a member-state other than that of the acquired company, the power to tax the gains of the reorganization is attributed to the state of the acquired company and losses related to the permanent establishment abroad can be deducted by that company (principle of source taxation).

The directive also provides that member-states may not apply the common rules if the reorganization has as its principal objective or as one of its principal objectives tax evasion or tax avoidance. Italy does not have, at this stage, a general anti-avoidance clause which gives power to the tax administration to disregard the form of the transaction to look at its substance. Therefore, it is difficult to assess, when avoidance is suspected, in which cases Italy may waive the common rules in order to apply its own rules. The waiver operates for tax evasion schemes; since rules about tax avoidance and a package on tax treatment of reorganization are being prepared by the government, it is likely that an explicit clause to this effect will be inserted into the legislation.

5.4.1.4 Correlative adjustments

As far as dispute settlement in the area of intercompany transactions is concerned, Italy does not have domestic or bilateral rules on 'correlative adjustments'. So far, recourse has been made to the competent authorities procedure, which has not proved efficient.

The member-states have recently agreed on the text of a multilateral Convention on the elimination of double taxation in connection with the adjustment of profits of associated enterprises. The Convention will enter force two months after the date when the last instrument of ratification is deposited by the last signatory state to take the step.

The Convention establishes a correlative adjustment procedure for reallocation of profits arising from intracompany transaction of multinational groups located with EC boundaries.

Article 4 of the Convention provides that if an enterprise of a contracting state participates directly or indirectly in the management control or capital of an enterprise of another contracting state, or if the same persons participate directly or indirectly in the management, control or capital of an enterprise of one contracting state, and in either case conditions are made or imposed between the two enterprises in their commercial or financial relations which differ from those which would be made between independent enterprises, then any profits which would, but for those conditions, have accrued to one of the enterprises, but by reason of those conditions have not so accrued, may be included in the profits of that enterprise and taxed accordingly.

In this situation double taxation is eliminated if the excess profits are taxed only in one state or if the tax on those profits in one state is reduced by an amount equal to the tax chargeable on them in the other state.

The Convention modifies existing Italian domestic and treaty law, which currently only provides domestic judicial remedies and the ordinary competent authority procedure. Both remedies do not allow correlative adjustments, thereby failing to eliminate double taxation of income within multinational groups.

The Convention also modifies existing law with respect to the co-ordination between domestic remedies and treaty dispute settlement procedure. Currently competent authorities are not obliged to reach an agreement and the nature of the mutual agreements is still uncertain, as is their capacity to modify domestic law.

The Convention makes it clear that if the competent authorities fail to reach an agreement within two years they should set up an Advisory Commission which must reach a decision by a simple majority of its members not more than six months from the date on which the matter was referred to it. If mutual agreement is not reached the opinion of the Commission binds the contracting states.

The Convention also specifies that neither the request to the competent authorities for mutual agreement nor remitting to the Advisory Commission should prevent taxpayers from having recourse to domestic remedies, or the tax administration from initiating procedures for applying administrative penalties. This principle of autonomy of domestic and bilateral remedies does not apply if domestic procedures lead to a 'serious penalty'. In that case the competent authorities may delay the bilateral proceeding until conclusion of the domestic proceeding.

The competent authorities of any contracting state are not under obligation to carry out administrative measures at variance with domestic law or its normal administrative practice, to supply information which is not obtainable under domestic law or in its normal administrative practice, or to supply information which would disclose any trade, business, industrial or professional secret or trade process, or information the disclosure of which would be contrary to public policy or to the public interest.

The potential impact of the Convention on the Italian tax system is relevant in so far as it makes access to bilateral relief feasible. Bilateral relief is currently available only through the ordinary competent authority procedure, which has proved to be unsatisfactory because of administrative delays, the lack of obligation to reach a final decision, and the absence of correlative adjustment rules.

Any initial impact, however, will rely on the willingness of all other member-states to ratify the Convention; it is likely that it will take several years for the Convention to enter into force in Italy, as well as in other member-states. It is also difficult to forecast the effectiveness over a long period of time of the new procedure, since article 20 of the Convention provides that after four and a half years the member-states will meet to decide on the extension of the Convention.

5.4.1.5 Taxes on capital

The Council directive of 17 July 1969 provides for a harmonized 'capital duty' to be imposed on contributions to the capital of joint stock companies ('capital companies') and for the removal of taxes on securities transactions. 'Capital companies' within the meaning of the directive are – in addition to corporations, stock partnerships, and limited liability companies – all companies, associations, or legal entities operating for profit whose securities can be traded on a stock exchange or whose members may dispose of their shares without prior authorization and are liable only to the extent of their investment. Other companies, firms, associations, or legal entities operating for profit may be exempted from capital duty at the option of the individual member-states, even though they are considered capital companies under the directive.

Capital duty may be levied once only on any one operation by the member-state in whose territory the company's real seat of management is located or, for companies whose real seat of management is in a third country, by the member-state where the registered office is located. Where both offices are in a third country, capital transfers to a branch in the Common Market may be taxed by the member-state in whose territory the branch is located.

Despite the fact that EC directive no. 335 of 1969 has been in full force since 1969, the Italian domestic tax system has not been modified accordingly. In particular, a registration tax ('*imposta di registro*') has been levied on contributions of capital already taxed in another member-state as well as on loans raised by issuing bonds. The inaction of the legislation notwithstanding, judges have recently fully implemented the cited provisions of directive no. 335 of 1969 and have disregarded domestic legislation.

Finally, the new amended decree on the registration tax has conformed to the EC directive and has provided that the following operations are exempt from registration tax in Italy:

(a) the creation in Italy of the legal seat of a company having its place of management in another member-state;
(b) the transfer from another member-state of the place of management if the tax has been levied in the other member-state;
(c) the supply of working capital to a branch of a company having its legal seat or place of management in a member-state.

5.4.2 Value added tax (VAT)

In general the tax integration process in the area of VAT has proved successful and has resulted in the full implementation of EC directives in Italy as well as in other member-states.

VAT is a tax on consumption which is paid on every transaction (sales and rendering of services); it has a neutral effect on the distribution process because the tax liability of each taxable person carrying out economic activities is determined by subtracting the VAT paid on goods and services received from the VAT received on goods and services rendered to third parties.

At the time of adoption of the Treaty, Italy imposed a cumulative multi-stage tax (*imposta generale sulle entrate*, IGE), under which tax was levied at each stage of the distribution process so that the tax burden on the final consumer was determined by the stages of distribution; the more stages involved, the bigger the tax burden.

At each stage of production and marketing, IGE accumulated so that the amount of tax depended on the number of stages. Therefore, the tax levied on different consumers was unevenly distributed and was determined by the production and marketing structure of a given product.

When applied to international transactions this system made it extremely difficult to calculate internal taxes and drawbacks. Consequently, the IGE system in Italy (as well as the other accumulative consumer taxes in other member-states) was conflicting with article 97 of the Treaty. That article provides that member-states levying a turnover tax calculated on a cumulative multi-stage system may, in case of internal taxation imposed by them on imported products or of repayments allowed by them on exported products, establish average rates for products or groups of products provided that there is no infringement of the prohibition of discriminatory internal charges (article 95 of the Treaty) or of the obligation of exporting states not to repay internal taxation in excess of the internal taxation imposed by other countries on the exported products (article 96 of the Treaty).

Thus, the Community was faced with the problem of establishing average rates of cumulative turnover taxes. On the other hand, under article 97 paragraph 1, each member-state had the discretion – not the obligation – to establish average rates and repayments as well as to define the rules of consumer taxes.

In addition, individual taxpayers did not have the right, to be enforced in the national court, to challenge national legislation in that area.

This situation resulted in a serious obstacle to the implementation of free circulation of goods. In particular, in Italy the IGE system greatly altered the free flow of goods; since credit for taxes on purchases was not readily assessable, products imported in Italy did not receive the same treatment as domestic products.

Council directive no 68/221 of 30 April 1968 laid down criteria to establish average turnover tax rates, setting a deadline for implementation by member-states.

Article 2 of the directive prescribed that average tax burdens on a product be equal to the weighted average of tax burdens of the product at the different stages of production, and that the average tax burden for a group of products be equal to the weighted average of the average tax burdens of representative products of the group. Arts. 3 and 4 introduced criteria for determining the tax burden at final and intermediate stages; articles 9, 10 and 11 established the procedure for implementation.

Italy retained its IGE system and did not implement the directive, and the problems described above were not resolved. Subsequently, the Commission set aside the rate-averaging approach and adopted the policy of introducing harmonized VAT. Under Council directive no. 67/227 of 11 April 1967 ('First directive') such an obligation was imposed upon member-states and the deadline for implementation was set at 1 January 1972. Article 2 specified that the principle of the common VAT system involves the application to goods and services of a general tax on consumption exactly proportional to the price of the goods and services, whatever the number of transactions taking place in the production and distribution process before the stage at which the tax is charged.

Within directive no. 67/228 of 11 April 1967 ('Second directive') the main technical features of the VAT system were defined: (a) the tax is imposed upon 'deliveries of goods', 'performance of services' and 'imports of goods'; (b) the tax is applied to transactions effected 'within the country'; (c) the tax base is the consideration paid for goods and services and the custom value – inclusive of other duties – for imports; (d) each member-state sets the normal rate of tax; (e) deliveries of export goods and related services are exempt from tax; (f) the VAT paid for goods and services received and for imports is deductible from the VAT due by the taxpayer; (g) taxable persons are those who carry out commercial activities.

The directive also included guidelines for accounting and rules for transition to the new common system and set the implementation deadline for January 1970.

On 14 July 1969, Italy informed the Commission that it was not in a position to meet the deadline of 1 January 1970 and requested an extension of two years. In acceptance of the request (also made by Belgium), the Council issued, on 9 December 1969, directive no. 669/463 ('Third directive'), setting the deadline at 1 January 1972 and defining 'average rates' as the rates of charges on imports and repayment on exports which equalize the burden of VAT excluding the tax on sales by the final producer.

The procedure of implementation in Italy has been very cumbersome due to inefficiency in the tax administration and the complexity of IGE. Upon request, directive no. L283 was issued on 24 December 1971 ('Fourth directive'), extending the deadline to 1 July 1972. Upon further request, directive no. L162 of 4 July 1972 ('Fifth directive') was issued to extend the deadline to 1 January 1973.

With decree 633 of 26 October 1972 (entered into force on 1 January 1973), Italy implemented the Council directives on VAT. Decree no. 633 of 1972 has been amended several times in pursuance of subsequent directives (the amending laws were: no. 24 of 29 January 1979; no. 94 of 31 March 1979; no. 889 of 22 December 1980; no. 693 of 31 October 1980; nos. 891 and 897 of 30 December 1980; no. 17 of 27 February 1984.).

As a result of these laws the Italian VAT system conforms with EC rules, which, despite the lengthy implementation process, have had a direct and immediate impact on the Italian tax system. The impact has two dimensions: a 'domestic' dimension and an 'intracountry' dimension. The domestic dimension relates to the structure of new VAT on domestic transactions and the effects of the shift from IGE to VAT. The intracountry dimension relates to the effects of the Italian VAT rate structure on intracommunity trade and to the viability of the destination principle (exemption on exports and taxation on imports).

5.4.2.1 The Domestic impact

The 'transfers of goods' and the 'rendering of services' effected within the territory of the state by a person carrying out commercial or professional activities are subject to tax.

Decree 633 has also definitional rules which conform with EC directives. 'Transfers of goods' are acts which transfer the property of goods or which create or transfer quasi-proprietary rights (*diritti reali di godimento*) on goods.

In applying the directive, the following are considered to be transfers of goods: sales with a clause stating that ownership passes upon the payment of the final instalment; leases with a clause providing for the transfer of ownership; the transfer of goods pursuant to a contract under which commission is payable on purchase or sale; gratuitous transfers; the use by the taxpayer for private purposes or for purposes not related to the exercise of commercial activities; assignment to partners of goods.

In turn, the following are not considered as transfers of goods: transfers of cash, firms, assets, transactions related to corporate reorganizations, sales of newspapers and foodstuffs.

'Rendering of services' is the performance, upon payment of fees, depending on various types of contracts provided for by the Civil Code, and including all obligations, of doing, not doing, consenting to do or not to do.

Also considered as rendering of services are leases, licences of intangibles, loans, assignments of contracts. On the other hand, the issuance of debentures, the effecting of services related to corporate reorganizations, and brokerage services related to licences of intangibles are not considered to be rendering of services.

Decree 633 also has rules defining the place of taxable transactions and when those chargeable events occur in accordance with the principles set out by the directive, as well as rules establishing the functioning of the tax and bookkeeping requirements. Tax is charged to the person receiving the goods or services, who in turn has the right to deduct the VAT paid in respect of goods or supplies to him by another taxable person. Each taxable person effects the deduction by subtracting from the total amount of VAT due for the fiscal year the total amount of VAT in respect of which, during the same year, the right to deduct has arisen, and, to that end, must keep proper accounting.

During the seventies the administrative and compliance costs of VAT – compared with IGE – were high for the taxpayers as well as for the tax administration. After much criticism by small entrepreneurs, a 'forfeit system' was introduced for small businesses. Under this system the deductible VAT was determined by coefficients, and the taxpayer had only to record active transactions. The forfeit system allowed many taxpayers to evade payment of VAT; the system was therefore abolished and reintroduced in a modified form in 1985.

The problem of avoidance of VAT payment remains to be solved, but no studies are available on the difference between evasion of IGE and evasion of VAT. Yet the invoicing and bookkeeping requirements relating to VAT have had a positive impact on the assessment of taxable transactions for the purposes of income tax (this is the so-called *'controllo incrociato'* effected through the *'anagrafe tributaria'*).

VAT has rendered consumer taxation independent from the production and distribution system and has not modified the price level to a great extent.

5.4.2.2 The intracountry impact

Decree 633 provides that the supply of goods dispatched or transported to a destination outside Italy directly by the producer or by conveyors on behalf of a purchaser outside Italy are tax-exempt. Also exempt are supplies of goods and services (such as fuelling, provisioning, etc.) connected with international transportation.

The implementation in Italy of destination-based VAT has meant the reinforcement of border controls to assess tax on imports and verify the flow of exempt exportations.

5.4.3 Excise and other charges

With regard to excise duties, the implementation of proposed EC rules will bring about the following changes in the Italian law:

(a) the elimination of duties on various products and the creation of three groups of excises: on spirits (wine and liquors), tobacco, and mineral oil;
(b) the harmonization of rates, which will compel Italy to establish a new excise duty on wine, and to reduce the current rate of the excise on petrol;
(c) the modification of the enforcement/administrative structure, which will be based on 'fiscal warehouses' rather than on case-by-case assessments effected by the tax administration.

As far as 'other tax charges', are concerned, article 95 paragraph 1 of the Treaty provides that no member-state shall impose, directly or indirectly, on the products of other member-states any internal taxation of any kind in excess of that imposed directly or indirectly on similar domestic products. Article 95 paragraph 2, in turn, provides that no member-state shall impose on the products of other member-states any internal taxation of such a nature as to afford indirect protection on other products.

The EC Treaty, as far as internal charges on products are concerned, is based on a 'capital-import neutrality' principle on products imported from other member-states.

These principles of tax neutrality have a direct as well as an indirect effect. The Court of Justice has ruled repeatedly that article 95 must be applied broadly, thereby allowing the detection of any fiscal burden that might create discrimination against foreign products, or any unjustified advantage for goods which are exported (*Molkerei Zentrale Westalen/Lippe v. Hauptzollamt Paderborn*, Court of Justice, case no. 28/67, 4 April 1968; *Recueil*, vol. XIV, no. 3, p. 215).

Internal charges prohibited by article 95 do not include either import duties or charges having an equivalent effect (which are covered by articles 12 and 13 of the Treaty), or quotas (which are covered by article 30 of the Treaty).

The non-discrimination clause of article 95 is self-executing and creates rights for taxpayers that can be enforced by Italian courts. In combination with the general clause of paragraph 1, the non-discrimination clause makes non-tax burden unlawful as well as tax burdens which only affect the tax base.

The Court of Justice held that a tax imposed on imported spirits on the basis of a minimum alcoholic content of 70 per cent, where comparable domestic spirits were taxed on the basis of true alcoholic content, was a violation of the Treaty (*Commission* v. *Government of the Republic of Italy*, Court of Justice, case no. 16/69, 15 October 1969; *Recueil*, vol. XV, 1969–5, p. 377).

In another case the Italian Corte di Cassazione and the Court of Justice held that certain administrative charges (*diritti per servizi amministrativi*) were unlawful (Cassazione, sez. I, civ., 11 January 1989, no. 2949, in *Il Fisco*, 1990, p. 426; Court of Justice, case no. 70/77, 28 June 1988).

Since article 95 only prohibits internal charges which are higher than a certain limit – the charges imposed on domestic products – Italy is allowed certain leeway in equalizing the treatment of imported and exported products. Despite the total elimination of custom duties within the Community, the Italian legislation can use tax factors to compensate market disadvantages in limited sectors. Thus, the impact on the Italian legal system of the two clauses of article 95 is that it bars the Italian legislation from inserting creeping tax barriers into the free flow of goods; for this reason, article 95 is considered to be the basic rule of the Italian legal system regulating international trade.

PART II: FOREIGN RELATIONS

Chapter 6

Italian–European foreign policy

Luigi Vittorio Ferraris

6.1

Western Europe has represented for post-war and post-Fascist Italy an ideological choice, a source of legitimacy for the very existence of Italy as a political actor on the international stage. As former Prime Minister MA. M. Rumor proclaimed in 1969, 'The essential core of Italian foreign policy is and remains the European union'.

The framework of Italian foreign policy is thus summarized: a kind of alibi in the frequent periods of lacking initiative and at the same time an instrument to compel Italy to become a modern state. The European component thus plays its role and is supported and enhanced by the Western choice through the solid link with the United States and the fidelity to a market economy (although this is not always flexible enough). Europe is the *raison d'état*, which no one has the courage to infringe upon or to question.

Therefore, on the whole, up until the 1980s, any evaluation made of the function of the European component within Italian foreign policy has had to take into account the fact that the European choice was dictated primarily by the need to conduct an internal policy capable of transforming Italy, both socially and economically. Even though the transformation succeeded on the whole and Italy ranks among one of the most industrialized states and is listed as having one of the highest incomes per capita, it did not succeed in transforming its political structures with the same pace and with such satisfactory results. Hence a dichotomy, which affects public opinion and which explains the enthusiasm of the average Italian for Europe, a Europe from which they expect a great deal, perhaps too much. Many of the present difficulties inevitably stem from this imbalance between economy and political structures, an imbalance which exerts influence upon the international relations of Italy with Europe and with the rest of the world.

However, even in the difficult 1970s, when Italy seemed to many as being already on the verge of total political and economic collapse, torn apart by terrorism, social unrest and structural decay, the fundamental tenets of the European orientation did not waver – probably more so because the future appeared so uncertain. The reference to European obligations and to the ensuing strings represented more than once a subtle expediency to prevent any temptation to go astray, to give in to subversive forces and to the demagogy of the leftist parties.

The danger of ending nowhere was perceived in such a way that even the anti-European leftist parties, especially the Communist Party, started their evolution towards the West from a new appreciation of the role of the European component as a fundamental part of Italian foreign policy.

It became quite clear then that there was a real danger: one of a revival of past, deeply rooted habits and old doubts. In the beginning the European choice was not made unanimously: neutralist trends and Third World or Mediterranean illusions played a role consistent with two main components of Italian civil and political society: the socialist and the Catholic.

The debates on the function of the European choice make evident the always looming dilemma of the Italian profile as a nation which has come late into the world. There are immanent contradictions between the objective limits of Italian capabilities to act on the international stage with force and clarity on the one hand, and on the other there is the pretension or expectation of being taken as a great power. As consequence there is therefore a second contradiction in the deep-rooted belief of not being recognized as an important partner, due firstly to the animosity of others and due secondly to the lack of determination to pay the necessary costs connected with the pursuit of national interests.

These two levels of contradiction are the key to understanding the undercurrents of Italian policy towards the world as a whole, but particularly towards Europe: a mythical aim, a challenge, but also something foreign, where admiration combines with envy. It is not nationalism as an aggressive expression of identity against others, but rather a feeling of a people, both old and young. When such an intricacy of sentiments expresses itself in politics the dialogue is coloured by the reactions against any doubts or against any critical evaluation. Such reactions become a challenge to prove that Italy does not deserve such kinds of reservations on its capabilities. Strangely enough, these emotional reactions eventually succeed in proving the extraordinary promptness of ageing Italian structures to adapt themselves even at the cost of being forced to follow the leadership of others. It may be a lack of political will but it shows an acute understanding of the ways and means of conforming.

Glories of the past and hard realities of the present remain the two poles between which Italian psychology and Italian feelings move, giving to Italian foreign policy a profile which very often sounds to outsiders unconvincing or without any weight. This polarization which has been a curse for a long time is tending to become a challenge. For Italy European policy means the meeting of such a challenge.

6.2

If you take such a background into account, and leave to others the task of examining competently the various aspects of the Italian stance on the various chapters of Community policy, a general view of present Italian policy towards Europe, as a part of its foreign policy, should start with the consideration of two elements which have come into the limelight: a newly discovered, intense, and not always convincing faith in the Italian capability of mastering its own problems;

and an even deeper faith in the development of the Italian economy. Even when statistical figures seem to cast doubt or when social forces are not hesitating in dramatic utterances, great relevance is given to any news on the brilliant future of Italy ('in the year 2010 Italy will be the richest country in Europe'). Politicians extol the Italian future as an essential part of an allegedly extraordinary development of Europe as a whole (a newly discovered Eurocentrism) or maintain that Italy has surpassed either Great Britain or France or both in pro capita income. There is no need to give clear-cut evidence in support of such statements when such a deep feeling of confidence is felt fully by Italian public opinion, even when criticism of the government is loud. Public opinion at home is very critical of Italy, but at the same time a substantial part of the electorate, with its reluctance to support changes in the traditions and a strong feeling of attachment to the country, guarantee a surprising continuity of the political system, to the point that immobility is preferred to reform.

Though the fragility of the political system appears more and more as a fact, the feuds inside the government coalitions are sparked by motivations which are more and more unclear as they are connected with power politics and not related to real problems. The connection between organized crime and politics poisons the whole political texture. However, such facts do not exert a real influence upon public opinion, which shows a sort of fatalistic indifference to negative aspects of such pathological phenomena and accepts them as a part of real life.

In this general framework foreign policy as a whole, and particularly European policy, plays the role of solid reference point; it is, however, difficult to gauge which influence exerts itself most on daily political life. Italy is very much dependent on the export and import of goods, and, above all, is heavily dependent from abroad in the energy field. Therefore, the general situation in the world or a world crisis exerts a direct influence on the economic situation of the country. This dependence does not succeed in convincing the Italians of their own international role. International events command much attention even though they are without practical consequences upon the internal balance of power. On the one hand, Italian public opinion is unable to consider very highly the role of the potentiality of Italian foreign policy; on the other, the political class takes decisions of some magnitude (the presence of military forces in the Near East or in the Gulf), enjoying the passive support of the majority of the public. The reconciliation link between these two attitudes has to be found in the uneventfulness of debates on foreign policy or even more in the absence of foreign policy in the electoral campaigns, even for the elections of the members of the European Parliament. Debates on foreign policy in the Chamber are a rarity and governmental decisions on foreign policy generally meet with approval.

6.3

Hence the traditional elements of Italian foreign policy are still paramount, as long as we take into consideration Italy's position on the enlarged European stage. These are:

- The link with the United States has always been the necessary reference for ensuring internal stability and is still considered essential. Despite all possible critical remarks of erratic connected to American decisions, as a last resort Italy will be always on the side of the United States. The Gulf crisis has been the most recent evidence of such an attitude.
- The old inclination towards an opening to the Soviet Union as a means of balancing the pro-American attitude and of weakening the communists has now found a new legitimacy. This is due to the democratization of the Soviet system and the collapse of the Soviet empire. Gorbachev is much loved and confidence in his capabilities is very high (sometimes in an acritical way), even in diplomatic circles, where the objective is to build the so-called 'common European house', a myth which gets support from many political sectors.
- The traditional Italian game between fidelity to the United States and its *Ostpolitik*, which gave room for some manoeuvring, has been impaired by the co-operation between Washington and Moscow. On the one hand, the disappearance of confrontation between the two countries has brought about a total change of stance from the Communist Party (to the point of compelling its leaders to change its name and the aims it was to pursue); on the other, it has given way to a feeling of uneasiness at the risk of a diminishing role in the Mediterranean and the Near East. The ambiguity of Italian–Arab politics was laid bare at the end of the cold war by the inability to follow a possible autonomous policy within the framework of the decisions of the Community, starting with the Declaration of Venice of 1980.

To resume the initiative, Italy, under the impetus of Foreign Minister De Michelis, launched a project for a Conference on Security and Co-operation in the Mediterranean, to be modelled on the successful example of the CSCE and its Helsinki Final Act. This proposal has received, so far, only lip-service and has revealed the vacuity of attempts to act without the consent of the United States and of Israel. Even though acting according to the orientations of the community and claiming to be on good terms with all concerned parties, Italy has, on the whole followed a path which is more and more suspicious for Israel.

6.4

The European option remains a central element of Italian politics. The belief in an imminent strengthening of the European structure (political union and monetary-economic union) is the main driving force; as is the means to impose upon the Italian political system the choices, which the system would not have the courage to take if it were left alone. For that reason any surrender of national sovereignty is considered acceptable. The implementation of Community decisions takes a long time due to the reluctance of the bureaucracy, made inefficient by a lack of foresight on the part of the political class, and even more so because of the lack of flexibility of the administrative machinery. New laws were passed in 1989–90 to expedite the approval of Community decisions and their implementation.

The rather naïve belief that Italy could move ahead at full speed during its tenure of the Chairmanship of the Community in the second half of 1990 was partially shattered by the Gulf crisis.

However, thanks to European orientation, Italy was able to accept the process of German unification (a symbol of the disintegration of the communist system) without undue problems, though admittedly after a period of uncertainty. The unification process was also considered a useful means with which to mobilize the forces towards European unity, having abandoned the utopia of a parallel development of the two processes.

The second step has been the insistence on the search for a new peace and security order in Europe without infringing upon NATO as the essential instrument of security. In this mood Italian opinions were rather oscillating. Importance was given to an enlargement and an institutionalization of the Helsinki CSCE process. At first it was thought that a conference should be held in 1990, then later that the task of initiating a process towards the institutionalization of the CSCE context should be given to the CSCE Paris Conference in November 1990 (to ensure general security in Europe), and finally it was thought that at most the instrument of the Paris Charter should be used.

Such insistence meant the fundamental pursuit of three aims:

– The persuasion that the general economic balance in Europe was not to be changed. There existed, therefore, contradictory fears between too great an influence of the new enlarged Germany and, at the other end of the spectrum, worries in case of a weakening of the DM or of inflation in the united Germany. Hence the present difficulties, in the improving situation in Eastern Germany, are viewed closely. Germany seems not to be as strong as some were inclined to fear.
– The willingness to seek a European security system should not collide with the functions of the Atlantic Alliance. Thus, although not unanimously within the ruling political groups, the search for a so-called European architecture should try to reconcile these two contradictory objectives. The aim of building a European security system with military dimensions, perhaps enhancing the function of the Western European Union (WEU), meets with two different reactions: yes to the security dimension of political union as an indispensable element, but not at the expense of making the Atlantic Alliance and NATO an empty shell.
– Thirdly, an all-embracing European architecture could also include the Soviet and East European dimension and prevent immediate choices concerning the too early admission to the Community of countries that are not yet mature enough to take over all the obligations ensuing from such membership.

6.5

Once again, from a European angle some new elements are appearing inside Italian foreign policy:

(a) As a result of evolution in the East, there is a new appreciation of the situation in Central Europe. This arises from the fear of being pushed to the fringe of the European context and being reduced to a Mediterranean dimension. This new Italian sensitivity for Central Europe expressed itself through the initiative called 'Pentagonale', the members of which are Italy, Yugoslavia, Hungary, Czechoslovakia and Austria. After a good start, this attempt to connect Italy with the grey zone between NATO and the Soviet Union seems to be weakening.

(b) Italy has demonstrated a desire to play an active role in the Near East through the partial mitigation of the pro-Arab attitude of the 1980s, but with little consistency in a clear political line.

Italy is acquiring the psychology of a power with an economic and political weight on the European and world scenery. However, three limitations are clear:

(a) The increasing strength of Germany's position seems to highlight the diminishing role of Italy, which so far has been strictly connected with the German dimension. A new realignment with France is not succeeding because France is more interested in keeping in close touch with Germany.

(b) The difficult internal development of Italy (due to the North–South divide), where state intervention to control the situation is becoming more and more evident, prevents the political class from attaching greater importance to foreign policy.

(c) The presence of objective limitations of general consent to any activity in foreign policy, which could exceed the vision of short-sighted interests. Such limitations are underlined by the pacifist attitude of the Church and of influential Catholic sectors.

On the whole, Italian foreign policy has its central pillar in the European policy, that is to say in the legitimacy that the Community gives to the dimension of Italy in the international scene. Without the strong connection with the Community the Italian position within it will not only be weaker but will lose its function to serve national interests.

The Italian political class is moved primarily by its fight for internal power and daily foreign policy is subservient to the internal fight for power and influence. Important decisions were taken in the 1950s and with a great sense of responsibility. The major choice has been to be a European country sharing responsibilities with the rest of Europe and avoiding the temptation of neutralism or of the Mediterranean spell. Each step in the economic and political field finds its justification in the loyalty to the European choices, which are on the whole common choices and which Italy is always disposed to accept. In brief, through Europe and the decisions taken in the framework of the Community institutions Italy is able and willing to be herself.

Chapter 7

Italy and the EC at the UN

Silvia Bartali

7.1 Introduction

The purpose of this chapter is to assess the effect on Italian foreign policy of participation in European Political Co-operation (EPC), the diplomatic procedure that involves intergovernmental contacts between the twelve member-states of the European Community with regard to foreign policy co-operation in areas outside the scope of the Treaty of Rome. The aim is to determine to what extent being part of this co-operation process may hinder or foster national interests, and how this erosion or widening of national competences could be considered in terms of a cost–benefit analysis.

In particular, this chapter will analyse the Italian international profile in the United Nations General Assembly (UNGA). This specific choice is due to the fact that the UNGA can be considered as the unique international forum with diplomatic weight derived from its ever-widening membership (159 members), where East meets West and North meets South.

The analysis of costs and benefits involves, as a first step, the identification of national interests involved in this particular area. That is why a separate section will be devoted to the description of the general lines of Italian foreign policy.

Furthermore, the UNGA is the major arena where the EC states can meet the 'rest of the world', and where they may demonstrate their political solidarity and show EPC to be an aspect of Community policy which is growing in importance. A special section is devoted to the description of internal procedures and rules governing the relations between the European national capitals (in particular Rome) and New York.

Since the early days of EPC, 'speaking with one voice' at the United Nations and in particular during the annual session of the UNGA has been a major topic on the agenda of the EC states. One of the most important indicators for demonstrating the common or divergent positions of the twelve on foreign policy questions is through the roll-call vote on UN resolutions.

A further section describes in detail, the Italian voting behaviour over a period of seventeen years. (It was not until 1973 that EPC became a real base for co-ordination of national policies.)

In the last section, the cost–benefit analysis will weigh the national targets against the international constraints. Is the loss of national autonomy offset by the benefit of access to the international decision-making process?

7.2 Italian foreign policy: main characteristics and future developments

Before analysing the Italian position in the UNGA and interpreting its voting behaviour, it is necessary to outline the main objectives and characteristics of Italian foreign policy.

From the immediate post-war period onwards, the basic direction of Italian foreign policy has demonstrated a marked consistency in three principal areas of involvement. It can be said that it is articulated in concentric circles (Garruccio, 1983, p. 9): the Western Circle (Atlantic Alliance), the European Circle (European Community), and the Third World Circle (especially Mediterranean countries). Italian foreign policy took on the so-called 'low-profile' image, characterized by an overwhelming American hegemony. This has put a question-mark over the degree of autonomy or even the very existence of an Italian foreign policy. The causes which explain this position and its persistence over time will be analysed in the course of this chapter.

This low profile is rooted in Italian insecurity which stems from the nation's structural, economic and political weaknesses, old and new. As a rule, these have reduced its capacity for taking the initiative internationally, as is very clear from the analysis of the voting behaviour in the General Assembly of the UN (see section 7.4.2). Italy became a member of the UN on 14 December 1955. A primary cause of the particular policy followed by Italy was the weakness of the immediate post-war state. There is no doubt that Italy has supported the process of West European integration from the beginning. Its rationale for doing so was more concrete than idealistic: namely, the view that the fragile and divided post-war Italy would derive from membership of the North Atlantic Treaty Organization (NATO) and of EC both political gains – joining the club of the Western allies – and economic advantages – anchoring its predominantly agricultural economy to more advanced ones.

As recalled by G. Andreotti, then Foreign Minister at the 41st session of the UNGA, 23 September 1986: ' ... L'Italie est partie intégrante des deux grands et libres systèmes politiques qui existent dans le monde occidental, l'Alliance Atlantique et la Communauté Européenne. Cela renforce notre capacité de participer à la vie et à l'activité du plus vaste système multilatéral: celui des Nations Unies...' International organizations offered attractive opportunities for Italy at that time. Institutions whose formal structures do not reflect the coercive power behind the individual members, and which do not grant formal influence (voting rights, vetoes, and committee memberships) precisely according to capabilities and world roles, are definitely biased in favour of smaller and weaker states. Because Italy lacked a military and industrial foundation comparable to that of the other powers of the period, these ambitions could only be achieved by proposing itself as an indispensable element to counterbalance the force of the adversary; hence the concept of 'balance of powers'. Within the multilateral organization, Italy tried to create a situation balanced enough to allow the space necessary for its presence. Confronted with the possibility of playing a more active role in European politics, a second reason to take into consideration is the fact that a country like Italy is strongly conditioned by its geopolitical position. Unlike Germany, Italy is not a key front-line state in Central Europe; it is a Central/Southern European country which is likely to have a more specific interest in the Balkans and in the Mediterranean dimension of European security problems. Also, Italy is not, like France and Great Britain, a traditional 'major' European power with a historical national vocation. Clearly this has been a weakness and is reflected in Italy's recurrent fears of 'exclusion'. But this weakness can become an advantage because of its more flexible attitude towards international events. Other important causes are to be found within the characteristics of the functioning of the political regime: on the one hand, the existence of a predominant party, Democrazia Cristiana (DC), which has governed the country since the first elections of the post-war period; and, on the other hand, the presence of an opposing party, Partito Comunista Italiano (PCI), now Partito Democratico della Sinistra (PDS), which both acts and is seen by the majority of the electorate as being against the system. This explains the iron alliance with the United States: a defensive weapon against domestic opposition; the absolute coincidence of American and European interests which was assumed as a pivotal point of foreign policy itself; and Italy's lack of autonomy in international politics.

'Foreign policy depends on the particular parallelogram of forces which prevail inside every state and this parallelogram is susceptible to change' (Garruccio, 1983, p. 20). Today the picture seems to be changing. The trend towards a more active Italian foreign policy stems from at least three factors: the first is the achievement of a domestic consensus on Italy's international position, already evident in the mid-1970s, when the Italian Communist Party formally accepted Italy's NATO and EC membership; the end of the old ideological cleavage between government and opposition obviously eliminated one element of domestic fragility in Italy's foreign policy. The second factor is Italy's economic growth in the early 1980s, which has made it one of the major European economies. Finally, there has been a profound change in the international setting exhibiting above all growing differences between European politics on the one side, and that of the United States and several European nations on the other.

Having analysed the main lines and tendencies of Italian foreign policy, it is now going to be seen how they are reflected in the voting behaviour in the UNGA.

7.3 Italy, EPC and the UNGA

Bearing in mind that Italy is a member both of the UNGA and of EPC, it would seem necessary, before beginning a detailed analysis of the Italian international profile in the General Assembly, to give a preliminary description of how the two structures (EPC and the UNGA) are co-ordinated and what their reciprocal influences are.

7.3.1 The EPC network in the UNGA

In strictly institutional terms the European Community has two distinct sets of machinery for framing its policies and responses to the outside world. The first and the oldest one, the 'Community method', covers the formal provisions of the Treaty of Rome (arts. 111, 113, 131, 136, 238). The second, developed since 1970 and institutionalized in the Single European Act (SEA) (*EC Bull.*, Supplement 2, 1986), is the Political co-operation procedure which involves intergovernmental contacts between member-states for foreign policy co-operation in areas outside the scope of the Treaty of Rome. The aim of EPC is to maximize the Twelve's influence in international affairs through a single coherent European approach. The EC members have developed a machinery for the collective participation in the daily work of diplomacy through the exchange of information, exposition of viewpoints, and negotiations to bring positions closer together. Furthermore, in cases of open disunity, there is now an expectation by the Twelve that divergent positions will be revised, as clearly stated in art. 30(2d) of the SEA: 'The High Contracting Parties shall endeavour to avoid any action or position which impairs their effectiveness as cohesive force in international relations or within international organizations.' This is particularly true in the framework of the United Nations.

The EC countries are all represented both in the General Assembly and in its seven Main Committees. The consultations of EPC in the UN have two aims. Firstly, they enable the Twelve to diffuse the European positions and to strengthen the influence of the EC states in the UN. Moreover, the consultations help to avoid contradictions between the national positions of member-states. Thus they can act as a united front. In the session period of the UNGA (from September to December), EPC meetings of Ambassadors take place weekly or even more often. Experts can join these meetings when a specific agenda point is dealt with. The number of formal and informal meetings in the framework of the UN has considerably and constantly increased over the last seventeen years: from 173 in 1975 to 490 in 1989 (Lindemann, 1978, p. 127; EPC Secretariat, Brussels). Important instruments for EPC in the UNGA are the joint declarations on agenda items and on voting. The former define the detailed position of the EC states on issues discussed in the UN. They are the starting point for further diplomatic actions. An example is the common EC speech of the Minister of Foreign Affairs of the EC state which holds the Presidency of the Council of Ministers and of EPC. This speech is made 'on behalf of the Community and the Member States'. In 1975 the Presidency spoke for the first time. Since then, practice and official documents have confirmed and systematized this role (see the 'Statement by H. E. Mr Gianni de Michelis, Minister of Foreign Affairs of Italy, on behalf of the European Community and its Member States' at the 45th Session of the General Assembly, New York, 25 September 1990). Joint declarations which explain the vote of the EC states reflect the EPC interpretation of the resolution. They contain possible reservations to certain paragraphs and possible different interpretations of certain states. Only with the help of such declarations can some EC states decide to abstain in a given case in order to avoid a negative vote. The number of joint declarations has considerably increased over the last seventeen years: from two in 1973 to 333 in 1988 (Lindemann, 1978, p. 127). As long as the concept of concerted diplomacy is the basis of EPC and as long as the final target of a European Foreign Policy is not achieved, joint declarations seem to have only a minimal effect in the UN because they represent the lowest common political denominator. On the other hand, the very existence of a common language in the UNGA is an important stimulus for EPC itself. Normally the EC states show agreement on the fundamentals of the questions. Differences of opinion emerge when specific aspects and the means to be used are discussed, as we will see in the next section.

7.3.2 The functioning, rules and links between Rome and New York

In spite of an impressive network of communications, a considerable amount of declarations on international events and important progress in co-ordination, we cannot yet speak of the Twelve as a cohesive actor on the international scene. Where there are clashes between the 'acquis politique' and areas of a genuine national interest, the latter invariably rank higher (Pijpers, Regelsberger and Wessels, 1988, p. 264). On the same subject is worth mentioning the editorial of E. Gazzo (Agence Europe, 6 December 1989, p. 1).

It is necessary to know whether, in the area of foreign policy-making, as conducted by a sovereign State, systems can be imagined which enable the application of a certain degree of 'gradualism', or a partial and limited exercise of various powers and prerogatives. According to us, such a possibility does not exist. ... In other words, in terms of foreign policy it is, literally, all or nothing. ... the Member States of the EC established through the SEA a 'European Cooperation in the field of foreign policy' defined in art. 30. Within the framework of that cooperation, they strive to 'formulate and implement in common a European foreign policy'. Their efforts sometimes achieve results, but the latter can only be in the form of 'common actions' or declarations. In other words, they exploit the existence of a 'joint action capability'. Of course this can be an 'advanced' form of cooperation, which implies the more or less explicit acceptance of common objectives. But nothing else: national sovereignty in the field of foreign policy remains total.

However, information, transmitted in good time, combined with a rapid clarification of position on the spot, is of great tactical value. It is possible to identify a convergence of views from originally differing positions of member-states in important areas of international politics. Participation in the UNGA serves as a sort of testing ground. Here 'speaking with one voice' is demonstrated or denied in the clearest way, either by the voting behaviour, through contributions to debate, or by voting declarations. Political issues, which are the specific concern of the UN, can arise in the context of the Community. In this respect, mention should be made of the discussions between EC foreign ministers and heads of state and government meetings within the framework of EPC and the European Council. They can convey their points of view directly to the political bodies of the UN via their permanent representatives in New York. They can, when working together, speak with a single voice through the ambassador representing the state which currently holds the Presidency of the Council.

At the administrative level, the function of shaping the Italian position in the UNGA and negotiating it with the other members of the EC is in the hands of a special branch of the Foreign Office: the Political Affairs Directorate (*Direzione Generale degli Affari Politici*), where there is an office charged with ensuring that the flow of communication takes place between Rome and New York. In the final analysis, therefore, EPC remains the Foreign Ministry's responsibility. Theoretically the permanent representative in New York cannot shape the Italian position; he can only negotiate a position already shaped in Rome. The exchange of communications between the Permanent Mission and the Ministry of Foreign Affairs should be carried out in such a way that the national position can then be adjusted according to the circumstances. However, very often the Permanent Mission ends up, if not helping to shape the Italian position, then at least influencing it. On the other hand, the constant pressure to unite faced by the EC states in New York can create problems for EPC. The Twelve often fail to harmonize their positions in New York, in the Political Committee or at the foreign minister level. The UN delegations are in general more convinced of the necessity of joint action than are their governments back home in the capitals of Europe. It happens quite often that a common position of the Twelve UN delegations in New York, which has resulted after long and difficult negotiations, is made impossible by instructions from national capitals. The result is then an uncommon voting behaviour.

The degree of unanimity reached by the Twelve involves hard work on the part of the Political Committee which is assisted by a group of UN specialists from among the Foreign ministers of the Twelve. When delegations receive further or new instruction from their governments, they express the opinions of their partners in return. They also make propositions for their own national position. In the case of non-controversial questions, these propositions are very often taken fully into account and copied into the new instructions. However, controversial issues are negotiated in the meetings of the ministers of foreign affairs and the Political Committee. The result is transformed into identical instructions.

Political events in the UNGA move quickly and co-ordination towards a joint vote can only be successful when the guidelines for a common policy have been laid down in advance with the Political Committee and the Twelve delegations in New York are left with enough freedom of action to agree on their position within these guidelines. On questions of significance for national policy, all Community states follow instructions from their own governments and unless there is greater consultation between the Political Committee, its specialist groups and the delegation in New York, a common basis for policy will be even more difficult to find. Belgium, Luxembourg, Italy and the Netherlands, rarely vote against the majority position. Their national governments allow their delegations freedom to align their vote at the UN with the majority position. We have to bear in mind that, in contrast to other areas of international politics where EPC is practised, the UNGA shows certain structural limitations. Here, Political Co-operation is confronted with a wide spectrum of international problems that are on the agenda of the UN, and it is difficult to produce a common position on such a large variety of topics. Furthermore, the Twelve represent a numerical minority in the UNGA, which consists of a total of 159 member states. The power and the influence lie with the group of the Third World (seventy-seven), which possesses the majority to dominate the UNGA. It is now time to analyse the voting pattern.

7.4 Italian foreign policy and voting behaviour in the UNGA

7.4.1 The voting procedure

Decisions in the UNGA are normally 'made by a majority of members present and voting' (article 18.3, UN Charter). Decisions on 'important questions shall be made by a 2/3 majority of the members present and voting' (article 18.2, UN Charter). A list of 'important decisions' is given in article 18.2 of the charter. Abstentions and non-participation in the voting do not count as votes. Abstentions can mean mild doubt, disinclination to declare openly support or opposition, strong opposition to some parts of the resolution, or lack of timely instructions from home. The precise meaning of an abstention becomes clear when an explanation of the vote is given afterwards.

Divergent voting of individual states is the result of national factors, differences in national priorities concerning foreign affairs, differences in national interests, character of the government in power. If the twelve member-states of the EC/EPC often fail to harmonize their positions in New York, the result is then an

Table 7.1 *Divergent voting behaviour: Italy, 1973–89*

	Minority of:					
	1	2	3	4	5	Total
1989	0	0	0	3	1	4
1988	0	0	0	2	2	4
1987	0	0	0	0	1	1
1986	0	0	0	1	2	3
1985	0	0	0	1	2	3
1984	0	0	0	1	0	1
1983	0	0	1	7	0	8
1982	0	0	2	4	0	6
1981	0	0	0	4	0	4
1980	0	1	6	8	0	15
1979	1	3	3	14	0	21
1978	0	0	2	6	0	8
1977	0	2	3	4	0	9
1976	0	1	2	5	0	8
1975	1	0	5	2	0	8
1974	0	3	3	1	0	7
1973	0	1	0	2	0	3
	2	11	27	65	8	113

Source: Bartali and Thijn, 1990.

uncommon voting behaviour. Divergent EPC votes can take three forms. The first is the 'two-way split', which consists of a vote split into two ways: no–abstention, or yes–abstention. The second the 'yes–no split' which is also a two-way split, but it is a more extreme form of splitting. In this case, the EC states are completely opposed; it is a 'diametrically opposed vote'. Finally, the 'three-way split' shows a voting split into three ways, some states voting in favour, some against and others abstaining. The EC states try very hard to limit the number of 'three-way splits', which involves long consultations in order to persuade one or more dissenting states to abstain. The divergent voting behaviour can be illustrated with the help of a 'minority table'. Table 7.1 shows whether a state voted or abstained alone against all the other EC states (minority of 1) or whether two states voted or abstained against the ten others (minority of 2), and so on (Bartali and Thijn, 1990).

The number of 'diametrically opposed votes', the most clear sign that the EC states disagree completely, has been diminishing over the last seventeen years. With regard to Italy, we can record only two opposed votes: in 1974, it voted with France against a relatively insignificant resolution about the salaries and allowances of the UN staff, while all the other EC states were in favour (GA resolution 3358A (XXIX) 18.12.1974). In 1978, together with Belgium, Luxembourg and France, it voted against a non-controversial resolution about the revised budget appropriations for the biennium 1978–9; all the other EC member-states were in favour (GA resolution 33/180A 21.12.1978).

Looking at the voting pattern of individual EC member-states, they can be divided into two categories (Stadler, 1989, p. 14): those states that are very active in achieving common positions and are prepared to make concessions in order to reach that goal can be considered to belong to the 'mainstream'. The core of the EPC mainstream is formed by Benelux and Italy. These countries are the most integrative of all EC states. Small states such as Belgium, the Netherlands or Luxembourg can increase their influence when acting in a bigger group. Also, Portugal has integrated very quickly into the EPC majority group. Germany is part of the EPC mainstream, too, its total deviating votes always being between two and twelve. Other states that are not very active and manifest themselves very often as dissenting states are the 'non-conformists'. The United Kingdom and France can be considered non-conformists: they often have special interests when security and disarmament questions are concerned, they are permanent members of the Security Council, and both are nuclear powers. Another common characteristic is their special relation to the former colonies. Denmark expresses its non-conformist attitude especially with regard to disarmament, and social and human rights issues. Ireland is an outsider when it comes to security and military questions because it is a neutral country and it does not belong to the NATO. Spain has special interests in the Middle East and Latin America because of its geographical position and its historical links. All the Spanish 2-minority votes in 1989 were expressed together with Greece on Middle East issues. Greece is the top non-conformist, its number of deviating votes being highest in the fields of security, disarmament, the Middle East, South Africa, decolonization, and human rights.

7.4.2. The voting behaviour of Italy in detail

It is interesting to notice that Italy, despite its geographical dimensions has more or less the same integrationist attitude as the Benelux countries. This is due to the fact that in a broad sense the 'size' of a state applies not only to the geographical dimensions or to the population, but also to its power sources: military, economic and political. We have already seen that the Italian military situation is one of great dependence on allies. Economically, Italy belongs to the seven most industrialized countries but it has limited markets and almost no natural resources – the reason why it depends on outside sources of supply. Also, politically the 'polarized pluralist' character of the Italian political system is based on the existence of one or more 'anti-system' parties which tend to erode 'the legitimacy' of the regime it opposes. Such conditions have impeded Italian foreign policy from assuming initiatives of greater scope. In such conditions the place assigned to Italy is undoubtedly modest, its powers and freedom of manoeuvre very restricted. It is therefore natural that a country like Italy has tended to rely more than others on non-coercive means of interstate influence, supranationality and multilateral means rather than on military, economic and individual initiatives.

The integrative attitude of Italy in EPC, when one considers the voting behaviour in the UNGA, is quite impressive: since 1980 it has not expressed any 1- or 2-minority votes, and since 1983 any 1-, 2- or 3-minority votes (see Table 7.1). Its total divergent votes, in the analysed period, have always been under the 10, except for 1979 (21) and 1980 (15) (see Table 7.1). The divergent Italian votes are a result of its specific geographic, historical and economic relations. If we analyse more closely the few times Italy has voted in a different way from the majority of the other EC member-states (archives of the UN Information Centre for the Benelux, Brussels), we can see that in 1975 it gave a 1-minority vote in favour of a resolution concerning general and complete disarmament, while the other EC states abstained: '... the General Assembly requests the Secretary-General to take appropriate steps for the strengthening of the Disarmament Affair Division, including the addition of staff necessary for the effective carrying out of its increased responsibilities...' (GA resolution 3484 (XXX) 12.12.1975). This can be explained by the fact that Italy has always been in favour of maintaining international peace and security through arms control and disarmament. Rome played a quite active role both in the planning of the Stockholm Conference on confidence-building measures and disarmament and in the framework of the Conference on Security and Co-operation in Europe (CSCE) negotiations which resulted in the Helsinki agreement of 1975 – a cornerstone for dialogue between the United States, the Soviet Union and Europe on disarmament and human rights. Another important decision has been its participation in the nuclear non-proliferation negotiations, to prevent further expansion of nuclear weapons, which in 1968 resulted in the Non-Proliferation Treaty (NPT). This decision was taken despite the nationalistic mainstream which considered the act of renouncing possession of atomic weapons an irrevocable surrender of sovereignty and their possession a real way of exercising that sovereignty in the international arena. Furthermore, Italy favoured the conclusion of the Intermediate-Range Nuclear

Forces (INF) Treaty on medium-range, land-based missiles, which it considered a historical turning point towards nuclear disarmament. Recently the Italian Foreign Minister, G. de Michelis, proposed enlarging the model of co-operation of the CSCE to include the Middle East countries:

Over and above these present grave crises, the time has also come to begin reflecting on the introduction in the Middle East of a collective system capable of guaranteeing stability, security, economic and social development and recognition of the rights of all peoples ... without wishing to transfer the CSCE model ... we consider that it would be worth endeavouring to introduce in that area principles and measures capable of reducing military imbalances, which are in general the prelude to other military adventures. (from the 'Statement by H. E. Mr. Gianni de Michelis, Minister of Foreign Affairs of Italy, on behalf of the EC and its Member States' at the 45th Session of the General Assembly, New York, 25 September 1990)

Italy has demonstrated its interest in stimulating the growth of an integrated European defence through a fusion of the present Western European Union (WEU) competences in the framework of the EC (*La Repubblica*, 24 September 1990). Italy is not an independent power, it has no illusions about its capacity to defend itself independently; that is why the principal means by which it compensates for its lack of military power tends to be an alliance with the major powers in case of international crises and constant support for worldwide disarmament as a general principle. A clear example of this attitude was shown during the Iraq–Kuwait crisis. From the outset of this international affair, the twelve member-states of the EC represented by Italy, the European country holding the Presidency of EPC at the time, tried to maintain a firmly united position towards Saddam Hussein, reflected in the voting pattern at the UN. The EC states affirmed their full support for the implementation in all aspects of the UN Security Council Resolutions and a parallel and co-ordinated action with the United States and the international community. On this basis they tried all possibilities to reach a peaceful solution.

The Community reaction was the most far-reaching and perhaps the swiftest in its history. The Twelve were first to decide sanctions, they put their political weight behind their own decisions and the decisions of the others to deploy forces, they granted transit facilities and they contributed towards the adoption of decisions by the UN, which remains the fundamental reference point for their action. This crisis has demonstrated the EC's ability to mobilize its structure to face an exceptional challenge, but at the same time has provided an incentive to improve even further the Twelve's capacity to act unitedly on the world scene, which constitutes a further guarantee of effectiveness for the UN (from the 'Statement by H. E. Mr. Gianni de Michelis, Minister of Foreign Affaires of Italy, on behalf of the EC and its Member States' at the 45th Session of the General Assembly, 25 September 1990)

It is true that 'action' was less impressive. For with regard to military initiatives, while supporting America in acting on the UN Resolutions to do whatever was necessary to counter the Iraqi aggression, the Twelve in practice, apart from Britain, kept their distance from the Americans. Their responses reflected both the feeling that the Europeans should assume a separate and distinct European position, and also, paradoxically, an urge (notably in the case of France) to assert each nation's right to act in what it perceives to be its own interest. Only Britain and France sent troops of their own, while several other members joined the naval blockade under the auspices of the WEU (Italy sent ten tornadoes and six warships). And although Britain and France both took military action, they failed to do so in concert. Britain put its forces in the Gulf under direct American command; France kept its troops under independent command. But, as we know, the Community has no legal basis to play a military role. Its half-detached foreign policy wing, EPC, cannot discuss defence. It is interesting to quote from an eminent review: 'The EC longs to stop looking like a political pygmy. The Kuwait saga has given it the chance to display a foreign policy that amounts to something more than the sum of 12 divergent views' (*The Economist*, 22 December 1990). In spite of the underlying ambiguity of French foreign policy since the Gulf situation first erupted, characterized by a Western diplomat in Paris as 'the Elysée two-step, one move towards solidarity, then another swiftly back' (*The Times*, 3 January 1991), the Twelve agreed not to negotiate with Iraq. They clearly stated that they considered any act committed against one or several of them as affecting them all. The EC member-states under the Italian Presidency have demonstrated solidarity by acting according to the principle of 'all for one, and one for all'. The EC–Gulf unity has been reaffirmed by the twelve EC foreign ministers meeting in Brussels on Tuesday, 18 December, when they cancelled a session with Tariq Aziz, the Iraqi Foreign Minister. The reason for this was that they knew that Bush had invited Tariq Aziz to Washington and that Secretary of State Baker was ready to go to Baghdad. Seeing the Bush plan as opening the door for unilateral initiatives, they cancelled the planned session in order to send a clear signal to Baghdad that there were no divisions between Europe and the United States on the issue of Iraq's unconditional withdrawal from Kuwait. But this episode exposed strains in Europe's united front for the first time. French, Spanish, Greek and Italian ministers argued strongly that the planned meeting with Gianni de Michelis, the Italian Foreign Minister representing the Presidency, should go ahead. Britain, the Netherlands and Luxembourg were opposed. In the end, the thesis that European and American members of the anti-Iraqi alliance had to remain united prevailed. During the European Council of Rome on 14–15 December, the heads of state and government of the Twelve, led by the Italian Presidency, agreed on a common policy. One declaration reaffirmed support for all UN Security Council resolutions, saying that Iraq must leave Kuwait unconditionally by 15 January. At the previous summit (European Council conclusions of the Presidency, Rome, 27–28 October 1990), all members had agreed not to negotiate with Iraq for the release of hostages. The Gulf has thrown into sharp relief the huge difficulties confronting the Community in attempting to move towards economic and political union. What would be the position of any nation that felt impelled in such a crisis to follow its own interest or moral perceptions against the decisions of the majority? What would be the consequences of ignoring national feelings? The Gulf has provided further evidence of the need for new approaches to European political and defence co-operation. Europe will move towards a common defence policy as long as it does not interfere with national policies, weaken NATO, or affect the neutrality of Ireland – these were the summit conclusions of 14–15 December.

To return to the voting pattern in the UNGA, in 1979 Italy gave a 1-minority vote abstaining on a non-controversial resolution relating to the programme budget for the biennium 1980–1 (GA resolution 34/233, 18.12.1980). This reaction against raising budget expenditure is quite often expressed and can be explained by Italy's national debt problems.

To assess the real impact on Italian foreign policy of membership of EPC, it is interesting to analyse Italian voting behaviour in the UNGA over a period of seventeen years against that of the other States of the EC. It is quite evident that Italy follows other EC member-states with relation to the issues discussed. For example, during the 1970s it formed with the Netherlands, Denmark and Ireland the so-called 'progressive minority voting bloc' (Foot, 1979, p. 353). These four states were always together on resolutions concerning Namibia, South Africa, or decolonization, voting in favour or abstaining on resolutions where the other states were abstaining or against. Five minority votes out of the eight came from Italy in 1976 (GA resolutions: 31/6F and 31/6G 9.11.1976; 31/148 20.12.1976, where these four states and the majority of the UNGA voted in favour and the rest of the EC member-states abstained; GA Resolutions: 31/6H 9.11.1976 and 31/ 146 20.12.1976, where the four abstained and the other EC member-states voted against). It is interesting to quote some passages from Res. 31/6H: 'The General Assembly ... Proclaims that any collaboration with the racist regime of South Africa constitutes a hostile act against the oppressed people of S.A. and a contemptuous defiance of the United Nations and the International community ... Calls upon Member States still engaged in economic collaboration and trade with the racist regime of South Africa to implement the relevant General Assembly resolutions and to cease forthwith any such collaboration with that regime...' Two minority votes out of the nine came from Italy in 1977 (GA resolutions: 32/9G 04.11.1977, where the four voted in favour and the rest abstained; 32/105G 18.12.1977, where the four abstained and the rest voted against), three out of the eight in 1978 (GA resolutions: 33/23 29/11/1978, where the four abstained and the rest voted against; 33/38A 13/12/1978 and 33/137 19.12.1978, where the four voted in favour and the rest abstained). In resolution 33/38A on Southern Rhodesia, 'The General Assembly ... calls upon the Government of the United Kingdom, in the discharge of its primary responsibility as the administering Power, to take all effective measures to enable the people of Zimbabwe to accede to independence in accordance with their deep aspirations and not under any circumstances to accord the illegal regime any of the powers or attributions of sovereignty...'There were five minority votes out of twenty-one from Italy in 1979 (GA resolutions: 34/42 21.11.1979; 34/46 23.11.1979; 34/92C 12.12.1979; 34/93R 12.12.1979, where the four voted in favour and the rest abstained; 34/ 150 17.12.1979, where the four abstained and the rest voted against), three out of fifteen in 1980 (GA resolutions: 35/29 11.11.1980, where the four voted in favour and the rest abstained; 35/118 11.12.1980, 35/206D 16.12.1980, where the four abstained and the rest voted against). In particular, Res. 35/118 concerns the plan of action for the full implementation of the Declaration on the Granting of Independence to colonial countries and peoples. It is worthwhile noticing that in two cases (GA resolutions: 33/183E 24.12.1979; 35/206D 16.12.1980), where the Netherlands, Denmark and Ireland voted in favour and the other EC member-states against. Italy alone abstained to avoid a diametrically opposed vote.

On the other hand, Italy 'formally' belongs to the bigger states, and as such it must defend specific interests. That is why it often abstained along with France, the United Kingdom and Germany on resolutions where the General Assembly urged the Security Council to consider the matter of achieving the cessation of further foreign investments and financial loans to South Africa, while the other states voted in favour (GA resolutions: 33/1830 24.12.1979, 34/93Q 12.12.1979, 35/206Q 16.12.1980, 36/1720 17.12.1981, 37/69H 09.12.1982, 38/39I 05.12.1983). The same happened concerning the arms embargo (GA resolutions: 36/172F 17.12.1981, 38/39G 5.12.1983) where France, Germany, the United Kingdom and Italy voted against and the rest abstained: 'The General Assembly ... calls upon Member States to monitor effectively and to reinforce the mandatory arms embargo against South Africa and to prohibit all military and nuclear co-operation with South Africa by Governments, corporations, institutions and individuals.' There was an identical situation regarding the establishment of a nuclear-weapon-free zone in South Africa: Denmark, France, the United King-dom and Italy abstained, the rest voted in favour (GA resolutions: 34/78 03.12.1979, 35/148 12.12.1980, 36/88 09.12.1981, 37/76 10.12.1982, 38/65 15.12.1983, 39/55 12.12.1984, 40/83 12.12.1985).

Italy voted with France and Ireland on Palestinian questions (GA resolutions: 3210 (XXIX) 14.10.1974, where these three states voted in favour and the rest abstained; 3376 (XXX), 10.11.1975, 3414 (XXX) 05.12.1975, where the three abstained and the rest voted against, 3419C 08.12.1975, where these states voted in favour and the rest abstained; 31/20 24.11.1976, 32/40A 02.12.1977, 34/65A 29.11.1979, 35/207 16.12.1980, where the three abstained and the rest voted against), abstaining when the other states voted against and in favour when the others abstained. In resolution 34/65A 1979, these three states abstained and the rest voted against the 'invitation of the Palestinian Liberation Organisation (PLO), the representative of the Palestinian people, to participate ... in all efforts, delib-erations and conferences on the Middle East which are held under the auspices of the UN on an equal footing with the other parties'.The same applied in Resolu-tion 35/207 1980 where 'the General Assembly strongly condemns Israel's aggres-sion against Lebanon, and the Palestinian people' and 'calls for strict respect for the territorial integrity, sovereignty and political independence of Lebanon within its internationally recognized boundaries'. That is very well explained by the fact that Italy has an obvious and vested interest in better relations with the Middle East. Historically, prosperity and peace in such a region have always had a positive spill-over on Italian development. The policy of the Italian government towards what is now the Arab World has, since its inception, focused on the aim of taking advantage of its unique geographical position in order to develop a sort of special relationship with the whole Mediterranean basin (the *mare nostrum* idea), but without ignoring the fact of acting in this area in accordance with a pattern set by other European powers. In the first half of July 1979, Italy, for the first time since the Second World War, sent its soldiers to the Middle East. Since then direct

Italian military involvement has been growing: it has taken part in the Sinai international peace-keeping force, and in the multinational peace-keeping force in Lebanon. Furthermore, the Italian government has agreed in principle to provide the logistical support for the operations of the US Rapid Deployment Force, if necessary.

Linked to the Mediterranean dimension is the Third World feature of Italian foreign policy. While maintaining its position in Western Europe, it can offer itself as a bridge between Europe and the Arab World, between North and South. The solid relation it has with Europe, its limited colonial heritage and its affirmed faith in multinational institutions offer Italy the possibility of lending a greater dimension to its choice of co-operation themes, which go beyond the national sphere. Looking at the Italian voting record at the UN, we see constant support for co-operation and development of the poorest regions in the world. In 1974, for example, it abstained with the Netherlands, France and Ireland on the final resolution concerning the Charter of Economic Rights and Duties of States (GA resolution 3281 (XXIX) 12.12.1974), the other EC states being against:

The General Assembly adopts and solemnly proclaims the following Charter: Every State has the sovereign and inalienable right to choose its economic system as well as its political, social and cultural systems ... Has and shall freely exercise full permanent sovereignty, including possession, use and disposal, over all its wealth, natural resources and economic activities ... All States have the duty to promote the achievement of general and complete disarmament under effective international control ... It is the right and duty of all states, individually and collectively, to eliminate colonialism, apartheid, racial discrimination, neo-colonialism...

The same attitude can be found out in the following years (GA resolutions: 33/137 19.12.1978, on the need to develop policies to ensure the increased flow of resources to developing countries; 34/150 17.12.1979 and 35/166 15.12.1980, on consolidation and progressive development of the principles and norms of International Economic Order; 35/60 05.12.1980, on the UN Conference on Trade and Development; 38/25 22.11.1983, on transmission of national experience in achieving far-reaching social and economic changes for the purpose of social progress; 40/164B 16.12.1985, on the establishment of a new world information and communication order; 43/156 08.12.1988, on the improvement of social life through the complete elimination of such fundamental elements hindering economic and social progress and development as colonialism, neo-colonialism, racism, and all forms of racial discrimination and inequality and exploitation of peoples). In 1989 Foreign Minister de Michelis suggested that, beginning in 1993, the EC should allocate 1 per cent of its aggregate GDP to development aid, distributing 25 per cent of these funds to Eastern Europe, 25 per cent to the Mediterranean countries, with the remaining 50 per cent going to other developing countries (*La Stampa*, 12 December 1989). The rationale is that only balanced development in the poorest states can guarantee Italian and European long-term security.

In the 1980s, the integrative character of Italian foreign policy in the UNGA and in EPC in general became stronger and stronger. This can be explained by the fact that at the beginning the open acceptance of EPC was difficult because of the fear of 'committing a sort of political heresy' (Bonvicini, 1983, p. 75) with regard to Italy's traditional stance in favour of a process of supranational integration. It was argued that the intergovernmental method adopted for EPC risked eroding the Community's authority and negatively affecting the integration process. But the course of events gradually overcame such fears and, with its institutionalization in the SEA, the idea that sooner or later EPC and the EC would become a single body and that we could speak of a single European foreign policy came forward. On resolutions condemning the apartheid regime and practice of the South African government, Italy was often joined by Spain, Ireland and Denmark (GA resolutions: 44/27H 22.11.89; 43/50J 05.12.1988, where the four States voted in favour with the majority of the UNGA states, the United Kingdom against and all the other EC states abstained). Sometimes these four states were joined by Greece (GA resolutions 38/39D 05.12.1983; 37/69C 09.12.1982), also on resolutions related to disarmament (GA resolutions 43/78D 06.12.1988; 41/59D 03.12.1986; 41/60B 03.12.1986). Regarding resolutions concerning assistance to the Palestinian people, Italy often voted with Ireland, Greece and Spain (GA resolutions 43/178 20.12.1988; 42/160E 08.12.1987; 41/63G 03.12.1986).

Looking more closely at Italian voting behaviour in the UNGA, some remarks must be made. Because of the reasons we have already illustrated, the very nature of Italian foreign policy encourages it to vote in line with other states. By participating in EPC, Italy gains access to and influence in international decision-making and thus also increases its weight inside its national system. If development of EPC was on the whole welcomed by the Italian government and political forces, this is due to an awareness that the constraints imposed by EPC on Italian foreign policy are considerably less than the room for manoeuvre and the liberty deriving from it. From a cost–benefit viewpoint, the present analysis suggests that the participation of Italy in the framework of EPC, and in particular in the UNGA, is generally consistent with the national policy objectives relating to external relations.

7.4.3. The exception proves the rule: the Falkland Islands case

On 2 April 1982, Argentinian forces invaded the Falkland Islands. The reaction of the United Kingdom was to break off diplomatic relations and to ask the Community partners to ban Argentinian imports. The imposition of an import ban was announced by foreign ministers, the precise text was agreed upon on 14 April and entered into effect two days later. Rarely has the Community moved so rapidly. The occasion when it did act with speed was on the occasion of the invasion of Kuwait by Iraq – Iraq invaded Kuwait on 2 August 1990, and the Twelve issued a declaration on 4 August in the framework of Political Co-operation, condemning outright the invasion of Kuwait, and on 8 August they enacted the Council Regulation no. 2340/90 and the Council Decision 414 of the Representatives of the Governments of the Member States of the ECSC preventing trade by the Community as regards Iraq and Kuwait (OJ no. L 213, pp. 1ff.). The regulation suspended imports into the Community of all products originating in Argentina and was applicable for one month (regulation no. 877/82, 16 April 1982). In taking their decision, the EC states were strongly influenced by moves made at the UN. The Security Council Resolution 502, drafted by the United Kingdom ambassador to the UN, called for the immediate withdrawal of Argentinian forces and for both parties to seek a diplomatic solution.

As to the voting behaviour of the Twelve in the UNGA on the Falkland crisis, two resolutions should be mentioned with regard to the Italian standpoint. In the first (GA resolution 3160 (XXVIII) 14.12.1973). Italy and Ireland voted in favour and the rest of EC member States abstained.

The General Assembly invites the Government of Argentina, and the United Kingdom of Great Britain and Northern Ireland to proceed without delay with the negotiations … with regard to the implementation of the Declaration on the Granting of Independence to Colonial Countries and Peoples with a view to finding a peaceful solution to the problem of the Falkland Islands (Malvinas) … Urges the Government of Argentina and the United Kingdom, therefore, to proceed without delay with the negotiations, in accordance with the provisions of the relevant resolutions of the General Assembly, in order to put an end to the colonial situation…'

In the second (GA resolution 40/21 27.11.1985), Italy, Spain, France and Greece voted in favour, the United Kingdom against and the rest of the EC member-states abstained.

The General Assembly requests the Governments of Argentina and the United Kingdom of Great Britain and Northern Ireland to initiate negotiations with a view to finding the means to resolve peacefully and definitively the problems pending between both countries, including all aspects on the future of the Falkland Islands (Malvinas), in accordance with the Charter of the United Nations…

If we analyse the Italian position we notice that the decision to support sanctions had very largely been the responsibility of the Foreign Minister, Sr. Colombo. It rapidly came under fire. It was not primarily an economic issue, even though sanctions were seen as likely to impose heavy burdens on some Italian industries such as the leather industry. Of greater importance were the numbers of Argentinians of Italian extraction. The argument was of particular relevance to the Italian Deputies because of the parliamentary bill in preparation that would allow all Italians living abroad to vote in national elections. This would enfranchize well over a million Argentinians of Italian extraction. Few Italian parties could look on continued support for sanctions with any great enthusiasm. The result was that Italy withdrew from the common position under art. 224 of the EC Treaty and it did not apply regulation 1176/82 18 May 1982, which renewed the sanctions, denying an overriding Community jurisdiction with respect to such measures.

This is an example of how, on questions of significance for national policy, all Community states follow instructions from the government at home, and how, notwithstanding the extensive transfer of sovereign powers to the Community, the member-states remain fully-fledged subjects of international law. They retain their 'original' capacity to act in the international sphere. Also Italy, one of the most integrative EC member-states, is able to sustain a common diplomatic stance as long as the needs for sacrifices are not too high, and as long as the enterprise does not demand a high degree of commitment. Although the procedures which have developed within its framework were incorporated in the SEA, EPC remains a voluntary set of arrangements to concert and co-ordinate the foreign policies of member-states without infringing on their separate sovereignties and vital interests. If Political Co-operation is today accepted by member-states, this is because the benefits of the exercise largely outweigh the costs.

7.5 The advantages of a collective diplomacy: a cost–benefit analysis

The fact that Political Co-operation, both inside and outside the UNGA framework, is gradually playing a larger role in national foreign policies can be explained and justified in terms of the number of objective advantages which it affords to all member-states and the greater effectiveness in their international actions. It provides governments with a detailed knowledge of the partners' viewpoints on international developments, thus widening individual perspectives and facilitating decision-making. It is indisputable that all those participating in the system greatly appreciate the circulation and discussion of information collected and verified by their respective diplomatic services. As well as access to this 'data-bank', the synergic reflex that has developed in the diplomatic machinery of all the member-states has made it easier for each to predict the likely behaviour of the others, at the same time giving them added opportunity to influence their positions. It is especially the geographically small and the politically weak countries that profit from Political Co-operation, which offers considerably more information on international developments than a government would be able to collect alone, thus strengthening each country's single voice in the choir of the Twelve.

The question remains whether national governments, in this case Italy, have lost sovereignty as a result of acting within the framework of EPC, and whether this loss can be balanced by the advantages it offers. The cost is a possible reduction of autonomy in foreign affairs. It derives from the need to adjust positions of principle on issues over which the state has no specific interests in order to meet the interests of the other partners. There is a price to pay for EPC: it is a certain divergence from historical tradition, a certain bending of national principles, a certain departure from the 'purity' of national foreign policies. Nevertheless, we must observe a resolute attitude on the part of member-states if sensitive or crucial interests are touched on. Often reactions of the EC countries to international crisis inside or outside the UNGA (e.g. Afghanistan, Lebanon, the Falklands, South Africa) have given proof of the Twelve's heterogeneity and their limited room of manoeuvre when they are forced to go beyond their policy of declaratory diplomacy. There are classic examples of stepping out of the common position: Denmark, Ireland and Italy over the Falklands; Greece's non-acceptance of sanctions against the Soviet Union after martial law in Poland; France's and the United Kingdom's refusal to impose sanctions on South Africa.

From an international relations perspective, we can interpret EPC according to the regime theory. The major criterion is 'rational' problem-solving in a given situation. The nation-state is still the basic unit and the major actor, but not necessarily for all time and on all occasions. Other levels of government such as the Community are and will be used as long as they contribute to problem-solving effectively. Political Co-operation develops in a way which leads to its most efficient use. Over time mutual acquaintance and the habit of co-operation have undoubtedly grown. Nevertheless, participants in the system, however committed they are, approach their task with a fundamental obligation to their national states, their parliaments, their dignity and their objective interests. They are representatives of their 'foreign' offices, and foreign affairs still begin at national, rather than EC frontiers.

7.5.1 Italy: an integrationist perspective

To assess in the most analytical way the impact of EPC on Italian foreign policy, we have decided to analyse the Italian voting behaviour in the largest international arena in the world: the UNGA. It is now necessary to strike a balance and to weigh the pros and the cons, taking into account national objectives.

We have seen that, in the difficult search for its 'international identity', Italian foreign policy must reckon with some categories of 'constraints' or 'limitations' of action that derive from causes either of an external or internal order. Among the constraints of international origin, there are those that spring almost automatically from the perimeter of Italy's 'strategic and political interests', that is, from its geopolitical context. Essentially, they concern the spatial confines determined by the capabilities of the country's political, economic and military projections.

Another set of 'constraints' to which Italy is exposed in the extension of its foreign policy potential concerns those that stem from belonging to a double alliance system, NATO and the EC, as well as supporting treaties of any type, in the UN and other negotiating bodies. The ambiguities and structural weaknesses peculiar to the Italian system have generally not allowed the country to play an active role, either by making positive proposals or by offering guarantees – on the contrary they have reinforced a tendency to seek guarantees elsewhere, tying Italian foreign policy to the United States, to a European framework, to the great democracies, or to the industrial world, as the moment or the circumstances dictate. All this places voluntary limits on the political initiative of the national government *vis-à-vis* the outside world. Obviously it involves freely accepted rules that have, among other things, a twofold characteristic: that of constraint on the *épanouissement* of a completely independent foreign policy, and at the same time of offering the opportunity to directly and from within on the structure of alliances or signed pacts in order to adapt them through negotiation and in a pacific way to new requirements. There has been a constant dimension in Italian foreign policy – the desire to continue to belong to a 'club' whose members recognize each other at international summit meetings and through the large international institutions. This has often been criticized and dismissed as a mere wish to be present: for Italy, it is better to be inside rather than outside the system. This constant, however, is justified by the awareness that Italy constantly risks being pushed to the outer margins of the international system, and by the desire to take political precautions by all available means against the threat of being edged out. If, for example, we consider the few occasions when Italian initiatives for a reform of the UN have been tried over the last twenty years, we notice that they were inspired above all by the intention to overcome in some way Italy's inferior position as a non-permanent member of the Security Council. Very recently, Foreign Minister de Michelis proposed that the EC should have a permanent seat in the UN Security Council: '... considering the progress so far achieved in European integration, thought should also be given in my view to institutional adjustments, within the UN, capable of granting a more visible role to an entity like the EC which Italy wants to see endowed with supranational structures for conducting foreign policy' ('Statement by H. E. Mr. Gianni de Michelis, Minister of Foreign Affairs of Italy, on behalf of the EC and its Member States' at the 45th Session of the General Assembly, New York, 25 September 1990). Of course, this will increase EC influence in the UNGA and, indirectly, also the Italian voice.

In particular, the foregoing survey shows that, in the field of foreign policy, the benefits resulting from the Italian membership of EPC overshadow a limited number of disadvantages. Italian efforts to consolidate the impact of EPC in the world, particularly *vis-à-vis* the Middle East and the United States, have been unstinting, partly through a recognition that without that mechanism Italy is likely to have even more difficulty in achieving recognition as a middle-range state of equal rank to Britain and France. By participating in EPC, Italy gains access and influence on international decision-making, thus also increasing its weight inside its national system. The cost–benefit relation in EPC can be illustrated by way of Figure 7.1. On the one hand, there is a gain through the increased capacity to influence policy outputs, and, on the other, there is a loss in decision-making autonomy. EPC is increasingly considered an essential foreign policy instrument, the constraints of which are far outweighed by the freedom of manoeuvre it provides. It is difficult to assess exactly this relationship, but it is easy to understand that, for a country like Italy, the participation in international circles ensures that the national balance sheet contains more credits than debits. A state with a deeply rooted national identification, boasting a strong and prestigious army, an efficient

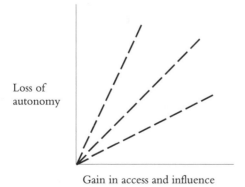

Figure 7.1 *The cost–benefit relation of Italy's membership of EPC*

bureaucratic apparatus and a stable executive capable of developing its programs with relative coherence and continuity, has obviously a much greater potential to act autonomously and with authority on the international scene than one lacking these qualities. And the former will inevitably feel a heavier burden from acting within the framework of EPC than the latter.

Another important element is the Italian supranational attitude which implies greater flexibility in the face of international events and a less strong feeling of being restricted or conditioned over the use of national power and sovereignty prerogatives. The multilateralist conviction and supranational standing is strongly rooted in Italian society. In Italy, 71 per cent of the population supports the United States of Europe (Inglehart, Reif and Rabier, 1987). When the Italians voted in the European Elections in 1989, they were also asked about the strengthening of the European institutions in a referendum that became famous all over Europe. The question asked was along the following lines: do you wish to see the Communities transformed into a true union, endowed with a government responsible to Parliament and entrusting this Parliament with a mandate to write a draft European Constitution to submit directly for ratification to competent bodies in Community member-states? The percentage of positive answers was amazingly high: 81 per cent of the total against 11.9 per cent of negative answers. This referendum clearly showed the strong support of the Italian public for a European Union. Thus it is natural that Italy supported and supports a strong and efficient EPC.

Other instrumental reasons for favouring EPC are the common European positions which emerged as a result of EPC. These soon proved useful as a sort of 'cover' for national foreign policy decisions. Thus, in their general policy statements, successive Italian governments have increasingly used the 'preamble' supplied by EPC declarations when stating their positions on international issues. Italy's bilateral foreign policy has also been brought into line with EPC declarations. It was discovered that EPC could be used not only as an *a priori* point of reference for government activities, but also to bolster foreign policy initiatives which Italy had taken on its own. Knowing which elements of the package deal can arouse Italian interest, which partners are convenient to ally with, which institutional strategies to promote, and understanding which domestic forces can be relied upon to provide supports in these endeavours are the chief problems to solve in day-to-day diplomatic life.

Italy, with all the limitations and contradictions it has faced, and for the reasons we have illustrated, has always supported the traditional idea of supranationalism, and schemes for a reordering of the world of nation-states whereby national sovereignty would be abolished have always been quite popular. Italy has been the cradle of European federalism with such personages as E. Rossi, E. Colorni, A. Spinelli, and even in 1918 Einaudi criticized the idea of a new League of Nations which left intact the sovereignty of the member-states. Italy has always shared the awareness of smaller countries, that one's own problems can only be solved by joint action, on a multilateral basis, at the same time knowing that the cost of the transfer of competence and the shift of power are largely counterbalanced by the advantage of speaking with one voice in the international arena.

Bibliography

Ago, P. (1987), 'La Politica Estera Italiana nel Mediterraneo', *Comunitá Internazionale*, vol. XLII: 156–66.

Aliboni, R. (1985), 'Italy and the new international context: an emerging foreign policy profile', *The International Spectator*, vol. 20, no. 1, Jan.–March: 3–17.

Bartali, S. and Thijn, I. (1990), 'EPC in the General Assembly of the UN: one voice or twelve voices?', unpublished paper, Bruges.

Bonvicini, G. (1983), 'Italy: an integrationist perspective', in C. Hill (ed), *National Foreign Policies and European Political Cooperation*, Royal Institute of International Affairs, London pp. 71–81.

Cremasco, M. and Luciani, G. (1985), 'The Mediterranean dimension of Italy's foreign and security policy', *The International Spectator*, vol. 20, no. 1, Jan.–March: 27–33.

Dassú, M. (1990), 'The future of Europe: a view from Rome', *International Affairs*, vol. 66, no. 2: 299–311.

Donini, G. (1988), 'Italy and the Arab World' *The International Spectator*, vol. 23, no. 3, July–Sept.: 174–80.

Edwards, G. (1984), 'Europe and the Falkland Islands crisis 1982' *Journal of Common Market Studies*, vol. 22, no. 4, June: 295–313.

Foot, R. (1979), 'The European Community's voting behaviour at the United Nations General Assembly', *Journal of Common Market Studies*, vol. 17, no. 4, June: 350–60.

Francioni, F. (1983), 'Sharing of Community and Members States' powers in the field of foreign policy', in F. Francioni and G. Grottanelli dé Santi (eds), *National and Supranational Powers in the Shaping of Community Policies*, Istituto di diritto pubblico e internazionale, Facoltá di Giurisprudenza, Universitá degli studi di Siena, Milan, pp. 53–72.

Froment-Meurice, H. and Ludlow, P. (1989), 'Towards a European foreign policy', CEPS Sixth Annual Conference, 29 Nov.–1 Dec. 1989, Brussels.

Garruccio, L. (1983), 'What lies behind the main options?', *Politica Internazionale*, vol. 3, no. 1: 5–13.

Hurwitz, L. (1975), 'The EEC in the United Nations: the voting behaviour of the eight countries, 1948–1973', *Journal of Common Market Studies*, vol. 13, no. 3, March: 224–43.

IAI Report (1984), 'The evolution of the major factors influencing international politics and Italy's options for the 1980s' *The International Spectator*, vol. 19, no. 3–4, July–Dec.: 171–89.

Inglehart, R., Reif, K. and Rabier, J. R. (1987) 'The evaluation of public attitudes towards European integration: 1970–1986', *Revue d'Integration Européenne*, Montreal, vol. 10, no. 2–3.

Lindemann, B. (1978), 'EG-Staaten und Vereinte Nationen: Die politische Zusammenarbeit der neun in den UN-Hauptorganen', Munich: Oldenbourg Verlag.

Milza, P. (1985/6), 'L'Italie a-t-elle une politique étrangère?', *Politique Internationale*, vol. 30: 319–34.

Panebianco, A. (1983), 'The domestic origins of a low-profile stand', *Politica Internazionale*, vol. 3, no. 1: 14–31.

Parsons, A. (1983), 'The Falkland crisis in the United Nations, 31 March–14 June 1982', *International Affairs*, vol. 59, no. 2, Spring: 169–78.

Pijpers, A., Regelsberger, E. and Wessels, W. (1988), *European Political Cooperation in the 1980s: A Common Foreign Policy for Western Europe?*, Dordrecht: Martinus Nijhoff.

Santoro, C. M. (1985/6), 'Italian foreign policy: a comprehensive overview', *Politica Internazionale*, vol. IV, no. 2: 89–100.

Silvestri, S. (1984), 'Italy', in D. Allen and A. Pijpers (eds), *European Foreign policy-making and the Arab–Israeli Conflict*, The Hague: pp. 31–6.

Stadler, K. D. (1989), Die Europäische Politische Zusammenarbeit in der Generalversammlung der vereinten nationen zu beginn der Achtziger Jahre, Florence, European University Institute, Working Paper No. 89/371: 98.

Vedovato, G. (1979), Politica estera italiana e scelta europea: Firenze, Le Monnier.

Chapter 8

Foreign commercial policy

Francesca Martines

8.1 Introduction

The purpose of this chapter is to discuss the advantages and disadvantages that single member-states, and Italy in particular, might derive from EC membership in the field of foreign trade – in this context, commercial relations with 'third' countries, those outside the Community.

The study will be divided into the following sections:

– the Treaty of Rome provisions concerning commercial policy and the questions arising with regard to interpretation and to the extension of the transfer of competence from member–states to the Community; the Community practice.
– foreign trade policy in Italy, in particular the institutional organization and the competence of the institutions involved.
– the negative and positive effects of Community commercial policy.
– the linkage of foreign, trade and domestic policies through sanctions.
– a final evaluation of the impact of Community commercial policy on member-states.

8.2 The commercial policy in the Treaty of Rome.

The establishment of a commercial policy is expressly provided for in the Treaty of Rome establishing the European Economic Community in article 3.b and in more detail in articles 110–116.

Article 3 is a basic provision in the context of the whole Treaty: it lists the actions which the Community is empowered to take in order to fulfil the rather general objectives set out in article 2 ('[the] harmonious development of economic activities, a continuous and balanced expansion, an increase in stability, an accelerated raising of the standard of living and closer relations between the States belonging to it'). One of these actions is 'the establishment of a common custom tariff and of a common commercial policy towards third countries' (3.b). This provision should be read together with article 3.a establishing 'the elimination, as between Member States, of customs duties and of quantitative restrictions on the import and export of goods, and of all other measures having equivalent effect'.

Although the expression 'customs union' is used for the first time in the Treaty only in Chapter I, in articles 3.a and 3.b the internal and external components of customs union are defined. These two aspects are closely connected. It should in fact be taken into account that the Treaty provides for the assimilation, in terms of free circulation of goods, of products originating in member-states to those imported from third countries that have complied with all requirements applied at Community borders regardless of the member-state where the importation has taken place.

In the hypothetical case of a heterogeneous regime applying at frontiers, third countries could export their goods into Community territory via the member-state applying the least restrictive regulations. In order to avoid such a risk and the deflection of trade that would probably result, the same conditions have to be applied in terms of tariffs (hence the common customs tariff) and trade regulations (common commercial policy).

The common commercial policy is not, however, merely an element – though essential – for the correct functioning of the free circulation of goods within the Community; it is also related to the Common Market and the Economic Union as well. The former is based on the four basic freedoms (free circulation of goods, services, persons and capital) and on a common policy for trade, agriculture and transport. Commercial policy is thus not only limited to the functioning of the customs union, but it is the expression of the economic potential of the Common Market. This may explain why the rules governing trade are provided for in that part of the Treaty concerned with the integration of economic policies which, once fulfilled, should result in the creation of the Economic Union.

None of the articles of Chapter 4 of the Treaty devoted to commercial policy provides for a definition of commercial policy.

Article 113, the key and most discussed provision of this chapter, reads: '... the common commercial policies shall be based on uniform principles, particularly in regard to tariff rates, the conclusion of tariff and trade agreements, the achievement of uniformity in measures of liberalization, export policy and measures to protect trade such as those to be taken in case of dumping or subsidies.' It emerges from this provision that the common commercial policy is made up of contractual and autonomous measures. This has been expressly stated by the Court of Justice in the *Massey-Ferguson* case (case 8/73 12 July 1973, ECR 1973: 897 at p. 908): 'the proper functioning of the custom union justifies a wide interpretation of Articles 9, 26, 27, 111, 113 and to the powers that these provisions confer on the institutions to allow them thoroughly to control external trade *by means taken both independently and by agreements*' (emphasis added). The autonomous measures taken by the Community in the field of trade are not limited to those listed in the above-cited article. The Community has developed a complex system of rules covering customs duties and customs legislation, imports from market economy countries and from state-trading countries, exports, export credits and export aids, safeguard and surveillance measures, dumping duties, and illicit commercial practice (Megret, 1976; Bourgeois, 1985; Steenbergen, 1980; Kapteyn, 1989).

As far as the other articles of Chapter IV (Commercial Policy) are concerned, the opening provision, article 110, has been interpreted as a declaration for a free-trade-oriented commercial policy. A reading of articles 18 and 29 and of the preamble (the sixth paragraph seems to confirm such an interpretation. It has been held (Giardina, 1965, p. 907) that these articles do not contain legal obligations and the member-states are free to change this orientation, provided they respect the obligations deriving from the engagements undertaken towards third states, which can, however, constitute quite a strong restriction of this freedom, (particularly under GATT). According to the opposite thesis (Pescatore, 1969, p. 922), the member-states and the institutions are bound by this choice. The question is particularly interesting in the light of the Court of Justice case-law on the interpretation of the notion of commercial policy. The expression 'development of international trade' has been interpreted as a general aim to be pursued by the common commercial policy, an aim that may be fulfilled by different means, the liberalization of trade being only one possible instrument. In Opinion 1/78 the Court stated in fact that 'although it may be thought that at the time when the Treaty was drafted liberalization of trade was the dominant idea, the Treaty nevertheless does not form a barrier to the possibility of the Community's developing a commercial policy aiming at a regulation of the world market for certain products rather than a mere liberalization of trade' (Opinion 1/78 ECR 1979: 2871ff.).

Articles 111 and 112 applied during the transitional period. Article 111 provides for the transfer from member-states to the Community of competence concerning tariff matters, and for a co-ordination among member-states of their commercial policy towards third countries in order to prepare the conditions for the establishment of a common commercial policy at the end of the transitional period. Article 112 provides for the harmonization of member-states' export-aid measures towards third countries. Neither of the two provisions was applied during the transitional period (Megret, 1976, p. 370).

Article 115 is based on the assumption that even at the end of the transitional period it would be unlikely that a common commercial policy would have been fully achieved and hence national commercial measures would continue to be applied. Under this article member-states may adopt protective measures against indirect imports from another member-state of products originating in a third country against which they apply restrictive measures, provided that these have been authorized by the Commission.

Article 116 lies outside the proper field of commercial policy, providing for the co-ordination of member-states' actions within the framework of international organizations of an economic character where the Community is not represented.

What, then, is commercial policy? Why is that question so important at Community level? For an answer we must refer to the nature of Community powers to act in this field.

With regard to external trade, the Community competence has been recognized as exclusive by the Court of Justice. This means that from the end of the transitional period member-states are no longer empowered to take autonomously any commercial measure affecting trade with third countries. The reason for the unacceptability of a concurrent competence with member-states is justified by the same reasons leading to the establishment of a commercial policy in the Treaty, namely the uniformity of the regime to be applied in relation to import and export measures with third countries in order to make the free circulation of goods within the Community possible. It should in fact be remembered that article 9 equates products originating in the member-states with those in free circulation in the Community (that is, products duly imported from third countries having met the requirements laid down in Article 10). Such assimilation is possible only if the same conditions of importation (set down in article 113) and customs are applied. This concept has been unequivocally expressed by the European Communities' Court of Justice in one of its early judgments on commercial policy:

> the provisions of articles 113 and 114 ... show clearly that the exercise of concurrent powers by the member-states and the Community in this matter is impossible ... to accept that the contrary were true would amount to recognizing that, in relations with third countries member states may adopt positions which differ from those which the Community intends to adopt, and would thereby distort the institutional framework, call into question the mutual trust within the Community and prevent the latter from fulfilling its task in the defence of the common interest. (Opinion 1/75 ECR 1975:1355; case 41/76 ECR 1972:1921).

Since member-states have lost any power to act in this field they will try to limit the notion of common commercial policy: it is in fact clear that the more extensively the notion of commercial policy is interpreted, the more limited the margin of action for member-states will be.

The interest of member-states to limit Community action may explain the ongoing dispute between the Council (the institution where member-states voice their interests) and the Commission over the choice of a criterion to classify commercial measures.

According to the Commission, commercial measures are those which regulate international trade exchange, regardless of the aim they pursue. According to the Council, only measures aimed at the modification of the flow of trade can be classified as commercial. However, neither of the two theories is completely satisfactory; to present the question in terms of instruments and objectives may in fact be misleading. First of all, because of the subjective element lying behind the reasoning; what can be considered as scope can also be interpreted as an instrument to pursue different and, in the extreme hypothesis, contradictory objectives. The fact that in the course of the years the two institutions have partially modified their respective theories so as to adjust them to the Court of Justice case-law demonstrates the difficulty in finding a definitive solution to the question.

Although avoiding a clear choice between the two theories, the Court of Justice has enlarged the field of Community action through a wide interpretation of the notion of commercial policy based on the principle of the identity of commercial policy for a state acting in the international context and for the Community and on the evolution of the notion: if in international trade relations more complex instruments are applied, the Community cannot be deprived of such instruments. In case 45/86 (26.03.1987 ECR (1987): 1439) (Auvret-Finck 1988), for instance, the Court has affirmed: 'Article 110 lists among the objectives of commercial policy the aim of contributing "to the harmonious development of world trade", which presupposes that commercial policy will be adjusted to take account of any changes of outlook in international relations.'

Moreover, when the Council acts on the basis of article 113 it must do so by a qualified majority. This means in principle that a single member-state cannot oppose the adoption of the act if it considers that this is contrary to its own interests. For years this rule has practically been ignored as a consequence of an inter-institutional crisis.

As far as agreement-negotiating procedure is concerned, the Council issues the negotiating directives – actually prepared by the COREPER, the committee of permanent representatives – which the Commission is compelled to follow. A special committee (the 'article 113 committee') acts as liaison between the Council and the Commission and is present during the negotiations. Members of this committee are the general directors of commercial policy of the member-states or – at a lower level – their subordinates. Most important, the procedure for the adoption of community acts is by majority vote. This interrelation may also explain the difficulties in achieving a common commercial policy, which in the end will only be possible when the economic policies of the member-states become truly integrated.

8.3 Foreign trade policy in Italy

Italian foreign trade lies entirely under state control and responsibility. The main competence is exercised by the Ministry for Foreign Trade (established with *decreto legislativo luogotenenziale* 12.01.1946, no. 12 and by *decreto ministeriale* 2.09.1946), which is responsible for the execution and co-ordination of import and export programmes, for the negotiation of commercial treaties and conventions, for currency movements related to imports and exports, for the examination and approval of financial operations related with exchange of goods with third countries. It acts in concert with other ministries (Treasury, Foreign Affairs, for example). It is organized into five General Directorates (commercial agreements, currencies, exchange development, imports and exports, and general affairs). A very important role is played by the inter-ministerial committee for foreign economic policy (CIPES). It is responsible for the definition of and the co-ordination of the general guidelines on foreign trade policy, insurance and export credits, supplies policy, and any other economic activities with third countries. Members of CIPES are the Ministers of Budget, of Foreign Policy, Treasury, Industry, Agriculture, Foreign Trade, Trade, and for the Co-ordination with Community policies. The former competence of CIPES in the field of development co-operation policy has been transferred to the inter-ministerial committee for development co-operation (CICS) created by the act no. 49 of 26 February 1987. The clear distinction made by this act between international trade and co-operation with developing countries, a matter reserved exclusively for the national competence, would appear to be in contrast with the above-mentioned case-law of the Court of Justice.

Other institutions operate in the field of foreign trade. The Italian exchange bureau (*Ufficio italiano cambi*), which acts under the supervision of the Ministry of Foreign Trade, is responsible for currency movements and financial operations related to commercial exchange. The Institute for Foreign Trade (ICE), which also acts under the supervision of the Ministry of Foreign Trade, has the task of furthering and developing international exchange. It also provides assistance and information for commercial operators. Its activities include the study of foreign markets and of the customs, commercial and fiscal norms applied abroad, technical assistance and promotion (Franchini, 1987).

When the Community was created, Italian commercial policy was based on the rule of the prohibition of imports and exports unless they were explicitly authorized. The aim of this rule however, was more the control of foreign trade than the prohibition in absolute terms of imports and exports. The instruments applied were customs duties (competence of the Ministry of Finance) and quotas. The Ministry of Foreign Trade's activity was mainly directed at the determination of annual quotas and the issuing of imports and exports licences.

8.4 The consequences of Community commercial policy for member-states

One of the ways of examining the costs of a common commercial policy is to consider the loss of sovereignty for member-states.

It could be argued that such an approach could be followed to evaluate the impact of any community policy. This is only partially correct. First of all, in the field of trade the Community has exclusive competence to act (as discussed above) and the decisions are taken by the Council acting on a majority vote, and, finally, whilst for the Community the definition of the notion of commercial policy is a central issue, states have never been required to frame such a policy with regard to their other spheres of action. Although this may, of course, be explained by the fullness of competence enjoyed by a state and by the more limited competence of the Community, it should be remembered that foreign trade can hardly be isolated from the other components of state economic policy and that it is perceived by a state as an important instrument of its foreign policy: in other words, it touches the very core of state sovereignty.

It could be observed, moreover, that Italy has limited its power of action in adhering to other commercial and economic international organizations. However, the restrictions arising from membership of the Community as compared to other economic organizations (GATT, OCSE) are of a different nature and have different consequences. The activities of commercial organizations operating at an international level are mainly directed towards the application of technical mechanisms for the regulation of international trade relations within a free trade approach (Colle and Gambini, 1972).

Community membership means not only the loss of sovereign powers in the field of commercial relations – as discussed above – but also the first step towards a tighter form of integration.

As an example of the loss of sovereignty for member-states, autonomous measures such as quotas and customs duties and agreements with third countries will now be discussed.

8.4.1 *Autonomous measures*

8.4.1.1 Customs duties

The common customs tariff, expressly provided for in Articles 3.a and 18–29, came into force on the 1 July 1968 after a transitional period allowing the progressive equilibration of customs duties of member-states. Since that date member-states have lost any competence to modify unilaterally customs duties and any charges having the same effect as customs duties (case 37–38/73 ECR 1973: 1609).

When the Community was established each member-state – with the exception of Benelux which constituted a single customs territory – applied its own customs tariffs to goods imported from third countries. For Italy, whose tariff rates were higher than Germany's and Benelux's (France, like Italy, applied a rather high level of tariff protection), the establishment of a common customs tariff meant a reduction of customs duties previously applied as well as modification of customs legislation (Panebianco, 1974; Torricelli, 1974).

A reduction of customs duties was the result of tariff negotiations undertaken within the General Agreement on Tariff and Trade. In this respect it should be pointed out that the process of reciprocal reduction tariff was set out in the Treaty itself. In fact, article 18 reads:

The Member States declare their readiness to contribute to the development of international trade and the lowering of barriers to trade by entering into agreements designed, on a basis of reciprocity and mutual advantage, to reduce custom duties below the general level of which they could avail themselves as a result of the establishment of a customs union between them.

Any tariff system requires customs legislation, in particular a tariff nomenclature (a description of goods to which duties apply), a uniform system for the valuation of goods (customs duties are commonly calculated as a fixed percentage of the value of imported goods), and rules on origin (particularly relevant for the application of preferential agreements). Although the Treaty does not explicitly regulate these aspects, the Community has exclusive competence to issue rules in the field of customs legislation.

In a recent case the Court of Justice stated that the Council competence as regards tariff modification (articles 113 and 28) implies the power to modify tariff nomenclature (case 165/87 ECR 1988) (Olivier and Yataganas, 1987). The International Convention on the Harmonized Commodity Description and Codying System (which has replaced the Brussels nomenclature) could then have been correctly adopted on the basis of articles 28 and 113 without having recourse to implied powers (article 235). The Community has exclusive competence in the interpretation of the nomenclature as regards member-states. The uniform application of customs duties could in fact be endangered by the existence of different administrative practices of member-states.

In the *Massey-Ferguson* case the Court held that 'the functioning of customs union requires the uniform determination of the valuation for customs purposes of goods imported from third countries so that the level of protection effected by the

Common Customs Tariff is the same throughout the Community' (op. cit.). Common rules for the calculation of the value of goods have been enacted by Regulation 1224/80 (OJ L134 1980:1), replacing Regulation 803/68 and introducing a new system (based on the transaction value of imported goods) to comply with the 'Agreements on implementation of Article VII of GATT' concluded with the aim to avoid barriers that could derive from the application of different methods of customs valuation (OJ L71 1980:1).

In judging the consequences for member-states of the loss of competence as regards customs duties one should not reason only in terms of trade protection since this instrument may be applied to pursue different objectives: the reduction of customs duties has, for instance, been used by the Community as an instrument of development co-operation policy and of regional integration.

In the first case one should mention agreements concluded by the Community with developing countries in Africa and in the Mediterranean (Lomé Convention and co-operation agreements with the Maghreb and Mashrak countries), which provide for the granting (without reciprocity) of tariff reduction or for the abolition of products imported into the Community and originating in these countries, and the Community System of Generalized Preferences which also provides for the duty-free entry of products originating in developing countries (on a non-contractual basis) (Lebullanger, 1988).

As regards the System of the Generalized Preferences, it is worth mentioning that the Court of Justice of the Community has interpreted the System as being covered by the common commercial policy, regardless of the development co-operation aims pursued (case 45/86, cited above).

The agreements concluded by the Community with European Free Trade Association countries between 1972 and 1973 (Austria, Sweden, Switzerland, Iceland, Norway and Portugal before the latter's EC membership) and creating a free-trade area – that is, the elimination of custom duties for industrial products and processed agricultural products – aimed at closer economic integration with the Community's natural partners in Europe.

8.4.1.2 Quantitative restrictions

These represent the second major instrument by which to control foreign trade flow. In principle, member-states have lost their competence as far as the application of quantitative restrictions are concerned. In this respect, however, a common commercial policy has not yet been achieved, and national quotas still exist. These are in effect the heritage of national quotas that existed in the pre-Community period.

The Community import regime is based on the principle of liberalization of imports with the exception of a number of products listed in the regulation and for which member-states are allowed to impose quotas, while modification of quotas takes place after a consultation procedure if no objections are raised by the Community or by other member-states (as regards imports from state-trading countries, under the Community regime a list of products which are liberalized is established, and national import quotas are determined by a Council decision).

Until very recently, the two most important groups of quotas applied by Italy concerned imports from Japan and from Eastern European countries. In 1989 a process of liberalization took place within the Community as regards imports from Japan (with the exclusion of cars) and Eastern European countries.

Quotas on the import of Japanese cars constitute a very sensitive issue for Italy because of the economic importance of the national car industry. Italy applies a significant quantitative restriction on Japanese car imports (2200 units per year) which are part of national quotas allowed under Regulation 288/82 (written question 2119/80 OJ C303 1981:4).

The importation into the Community of Japanese products and of cars in particular is a point that illustrates the difficulties of setting up a common regime. There seems to be a preference amongst member-states to employ individual national policies as regards Japanese competition, in particular in certain industrial sectors such as cars, by means of quotas and the conclusion of voluntary export restraint agreements, the new protectionist instrument for modern trade. This is due to the different interests at stake and to the feared effects, in terms of social and economic adjustment costs, that a common policy would be likely to produce. A common policy towards Japan would probably be accepted by those countries with national import restrictions on Japanese cars – member-states that are important car producers, in particular Italy and France – only if a certain level of protection could be assured at Community level, a policy which is less likely to be welcomed by those countries that, being mainly car importers would (Netherlands, Luxembourg, Denmark and Ireland) opt for a liberalization of imports (Koopmann , 1990). It should not be forgotten that a common policy could probably reinforce the bargaining power of the Community when dealing with the question of the export of European products into the Japanese market.

8.4.2 Agreements with third countries

Since the end of the transitional period, member-states have, in addition, lost their competence to conclude commercial agreements with third countries. It is perhaps in this respect that the loss of competence is particularly strongly felt since member-states are deprived not only of an important instrument of foreign trade but of foreign policy as well.

In this section some observations will be made on the difficulty of substituting national agreements with Community instruments – the problem of co-operation agreements and their relations with trade agreements – and the widening of markets and the problems that may result.

The existence of member-states' national agreements at the time of the creation of the Community could obviously not be ignored – during the transitional period a range of measures were adopted to avoid the situation whereby a common commercial policy might be jeopardized by the existence of bilateral trade agreements concluded between member-states and third countries. These were: the inclusion of the so-called EC clause ('should those obligations under the Treaty establishing the European Economic Community which relate to the gradual establishment of a common commercial policy make this necessary, negotiations shall be opened as soon as feasible in order to amend this present Agreement as appropriate') in member-states' bilateral trade agreements, the establishment of a consultation procedure on the negotiations of trade agreements conducted by member-states with third countries (JOCE 1971, p. 274), and the harmonization of the duration of these agreements (Kovar, 1970).

The adoption in 1969 of decision 69/464 (OJ, English special edition 169, II:603) on the progressive harmonization of member-states' bilateral trade agreements – which in substance, allowing for the possibility under certain conditions of member-states to conclude bilateral trade agreements, extends the transitional period as far as conventional trade policy is concerned – indicates that the establishment of a common commercial contractual policy was a very difficult task to be achieved. The reasons were the reluctance of member-states to lose control of a fundamental instrument of foreign trade and also (a political reason) the refusal of Eastern European countries to recognize the Community (up until the recent Joint Declaration of COMECON and the Community on the establishment of official relations (25.06.1988. OJ L157 1988, pp. 34–5), which opened the road to the conclusion of co-operation agreements with most of these countries).

It should also be pointed out that not all national trade agreements could have been assumed by the Community, even after the transitional period. Indeed, member-states would probably wish to maintain the bilateral and national character at least of some of these agreements which in certain cases date back to the last century. Since the end of the transitional period the Council every year has enacted a decision authorizing member-states to extend for one year the provisions governing matters covered by common commercial agreement contained in the friendship, trade and navigation treaties and similar agreements concluded between member-states and third countries (Decision 89/150 OJ L58 1989:63). The authorization is conditioned to the absence of Community norms regulating the same matters with those countries. As far as Italy is concerned, all agreements whose renewal has been authorized have been concluded before 1957, with the exception of an exchange of note with New Zealand and a friendship, commerce and navigation agreement with Panama, concluded respectively in 1967 and 1965.

8.4.2.1 Co-operation agreements

When discussing member-states' loss of competence with regard to commercial agreements, one must consider that the pure commercial agreement has lost much of its relevance and that member-states as well as the Community tend to make use of more complex forms of agreements such as co-operation agreements. To what extent are member-states free to negotiate agreements of this type if one considers that they usually regulate trade relations as well? In this regard only a consultation procedure has been established under Decision 74/993 (OJ L208 1974:23) concerning the co-ordination agreements concluded by member-states with third countries. This procedure aims at the co-ordination of these agreements and should prevent the insertion of commercial clauses into these agreements. The Commission itself recognized that the procedure is not a sufficiently effective means to conduct a true Community co-operation policy (Written Question 939/ 79 OJ C156 1980:11).

If in theory the Community could conclude co-operation agreements under article 113 – the Court of Justice (Opinion 1/78, op. cit.) having extended the Community competence to conclude under article 113 agreements regulating matters other than trade when these have a subsidiary or ancillary nature – it has in fact concluded co-operation agreements under article 238 (with ACP countries – Lomé Convention – and with the Mediterranean countries) or under the double legal basis of articles 113 and 235 (framework co-operation agreements). In the first case, member-states have exercised their control in signing the agreements together with the Community; in the second case, the Community has limited itself, recognizing the member-states' competence to act in those matters not covered by the common commercial policy (although the problem of defining it remains).

The framework co-operation agreements concluded in Asia and Latin America and, more recently, with some Eastern European countries (Poland, Hungary, Bulgaria, Czechoslovakia) (Fernandez Sola, 1990) contain a clause first used in the agreement signed with Canada: 'without prejudice to the relevant provisions of the Treaty establishing the Community, the present Agreement and any action taken thereunder shall in no way affect the powers of the member States of the Community to undertake bilateral activities with (name of the Country) and to conclude, where appropriate, new economic cooperation agreements with (name of the country).'

As regards these type of Community co-operation agreements, member-states have a double advantage: they may profit from the bargaining power of the Community and at the same time they remain free to negotiate bilateral agreements within the framework created by the Community. The only limits to their action are the common commercial policy and the compatibility with the Community agreements. In this respect the framework co-operation agreements with Eastern European countries provide that: 'Provisions of this Agreement shall replace the provisions of the Agreements concluded between member States of the Community and (name of the country) to the extent to which the latter provisions are either incompatible with or identical to, the former.'

Two last observations may be made with regard to commercial agreements. One of the most important advantages created by the Community for member-states is the widening of markets and the creation of opportunities for their undertaking. This has been first of all the consequence of the 'legacy' of privileged relations that member-states, like France and the United Kingdom, have brought to the Community.

Thus the origin of the agreements concluded by the Community with African countries (Lomé Convention and co-operation agreements with the Maghreb and Mashrak countries) is to be found in the colonial type of relations maintained by France at the time of the Community's creation. The interest of France in maintaining close economic links with its overseas territories led to the insertion in the Treaty of articles 131–136 providing for the association of 'non-European countries and territories' having with certain member-states 'special relations' and to the declaration of intention to associate independent countries of the franc area (Morocco and Tunisia) contained in Annex IV of the Treaty.

After the independence of some of these countries the association (providing for the unilateral granting by the Community of certain advantages for these territories) was replaced by association agreements (concluded at the Yaoundé Conventions). The Community's relations with African countries were further transformed as a consequence of the United Kingdom's accession to the Community which led to the conclusion of the first Lomé Convention which included the Anglophone countries of the African continent.

In addition, the contractual relations with India and the Indian subcontinent and the setting up of regular contacts with ASEAN (Association of South East Asian Nations) countries – leading to the conclusion of a framework agreement in 1980 – can be considered as the follow-up of the United Kingdom's accession to the Community.

It should, however, be taken into account that since the flow of trade, a consequence of the opening-up of markets, operates in two directions (from and towards Europe), certain sensitive national sectors may well have suffered from the increased level of competition that the opening-up of the markets has caused. In the case of Italy this can be illustrated by making reference to the co-operation agreements concluded by the Community with the African Mediterranean countries of Maghreb and Mashrak (respectively Morocco, Algeria and Tunisia, and Egypt, Lebanon, Syria and Jordan). As far as trade in agricultural products is concerned, the agreements give preferential treatment to imports coming from these Mediterranean countries, ranging from a reduction to the abolition of customs duties (according to the products). It should be noticed that although in general terms the imports from Mediterranean associated countries only account for 1 per cent of all agricultural imports from third countries, some of these products do compete directly with those grown in certain member-states and in Italy in particular (wine, fruits such as citrus fruits, apricots, vegetables, in particular tomatoes, olive oil). Moreover, import levies, the mechanisms created within the framework of the common agricultural policy, and which apply at the external borders to imports of products competitive with Northern European agricultural produce such as butter, milk and meat, offer a higher level of protection than do customs duties which apply to fruit and vegetable imports (Fennell, 1987). The pressure and the interests of European (Italian) producers may explain the existence of a number of provisions in the above-mentioned agreements, such as quotas, import calendars, which tend to limit the concessions offered.

Moreover, the over-production of milk and cereals finds a market in the same Mediterranean countries which need to import such products to feed their growing population and because they devote their agriculture to the growing of products that can find a market in the EC (Basile and Cecchi, 1988, p. 35).

So far only the bilateral contractual policy of the Community has been taken into account. In what follows a few observations will be made concerning the relationship between GATT, the EC and Italy.

The General Agreement on Tariff and Trade is the most important instrument regulating trade at international level. The liberalization of markets, the basic principle of GATT, is to be fulfilled through the application of the most-favoured nation clause, the abolition of non-tariff restrictions and of other non-tariff barriers, and through tariff reductions to be negotiated at international level (the so-called 'rounds'). The General Agreement also provides for some exceptions to the principle of free trade in the case of regional integration agreements (article XXIV) and of developing countries (Part IV of the General Agreement). Agreements implementing some of the GATT Articles have been concluded (such as the Anti-Dumping and Subsidies Codes) and complete the system.

Although not formally a member of the General Agreement, the European Community 'has assumed the powers previously exercised by member States in the area governed by the General Agreement', thus, 'the provisions of that agreement have the effect of binding the Community' (Steenbergen, 1981). The Community has actively participated in tariff negotiations and is part of the agreements concluded under the aegis of GATT.

The bargaining power of the Community in international organizations is much greater than could have ever been reached by single member-states.

Member-states' national positions are co-ordinated at Community level until a common position is reached. During the negotiations, which are led by the Commission acting as spokesman for member-states, consultations take place at the level of permanent representatives. Member-states remain parties to the Agreement (which is open only to states and not to international organizations), the Community as a result having 12 votes at its disposal. This can of course be considered an advantage if one considers the hypothesis of a single vote for the whole Community. This is true only in part, since it is obvious that the negative vote of an economic area such as the Community would carry greater weight than the vote of one state.

According to the case-law of the Court of Justice, GATT provisions do not have direct effect, that is they cannot be invoked by an individual before a national judge (case 21–24/1972 12 December 1972 ECR 1972:1219; case 9/73 24 October 1973 ECR 1973:1135; case 267–269/1981 16 March 1983 ECR 1983:801) (Borracchini, 1988).

There is no common position within the Community as regards the effects of GATT provisions. According to the Court however,

it is important that the provisions of GATT should, like the provisions of all other agreements binding the Community, receive uniform application throughout the Community. Any difference in the interpretation and application of provisions binding the Community as regards non-member countries would not only jeopardize the unity of commercial policy ... but also create distortions in trade within the Community, as a result of differences in the manner in which the agreements in force between the Community and non-member countries were applied in the various member States.

In Italy, GATT articles have been considered as self-executing (Cassazione 6 July 1968 n. 2293, Riv. Dir. Int. 1969:325; 8 June 1972 n. 1773, ibid., 1973:600; 21 May 1973 n. 1445 Foro it. 1973, I:2443; 20 October 1975 n. 4304; Corte Costituzionale n. 96 1982 and n. 219 1985). This case-law has the advantage of assuring the best possible application to the General Agreement, but on the other hand may cause disturbance at Community level. In this sense, for instance, was an Italian Court's decision (Tribunale of Milan, 2 April 1982, *ANIC e SNIA VISCOSA* v. *American Cynamid Co.*), which placed a ban on imports of acrylic fibres and polyester yarns from the United States justified on the ground of the violation of several GATT provisions (Steenbergen, 1981: pp. 337–44; written question 485/80 OJ C283 1980:4):

> The Commission considers that the situation created by the judgment given on 2 April 1980 … could if implemented, lead to considerable unjustified differences in treatment between undertakings within the Community and to barriers to trade in the common market. In addition, coming at a time when the Commission had initiated an action under Article XXIII of the General Agreement on Tariffs and Trade in response to the US measures, the judgment may make the defence of the Community interests within GATT more difficult (written question 485/80 OJ C283:4).

8.5 Foreign policy and trade policy: the example of sanctions

It has already been stressed that commercial policy is closely linked with foreign policy. Sanctions, with their double component – economic instrument/political objective – may provide an illustration of the links between foreign policy, trade and domestic interests.

It should be remembered that the Community does not have competence in the field of foreign policy. The consultation and co-ordination of member-states' diplomacy takes place within the framework of the European Political Co-operation, a multi-level structure which, having worked on a pragmatic basis for some fifteen years, has been the object of an agreement between member-states which forms part of the Single European Act concluded in 1987. Although liaison with the European Communities is very close (through the involvement of the European Commission, the COREPER, and the diplomatic representations of the Community in third countries), the EPC remains a separate structure which responds to the logic of inter-governmental co-operation.)

Sanctions are restrictive trade measures concerning imports and exports taken by a state against another state as a consequence of the latter's illegal behaviour as a means to induce it to desist from such behaviour.

The adoption of sanctions by member-states involving a measure of commercial policy are permitted under Community law by article 224. The adoption of sanctions by the Community is based on article 113. These two provisions do not exclude each other: article 224 provides for the consultation procedure which allows member-states to reach the political agreement and give the community act the political force which is needed for a correct and effective application. The preamble of regulation 877/82 (OJ L102 1982:1) suspending imports of any product originating from Argentina (following the Falklands crisis) refers to: a decision within the framework of the EPC, consultation under article 224 should the adoption of a Community act be decided, article 113 as the legal basis for the regulation (Pertek, 1983; Kuyper, 1982).

The sharing of responsibility with its European partners at both international and domestic level against the opposition of economic interests may probably be considered an advantage by a member-state. Effectiveness of sanctions could also be better assured by Community sanctions as far as speed (legislative machinery in certain member-states could postpone the adoption of the measures) and economic weight are concerned. State identity would of course be 'diluted', which could be a reason for a member-state to adopt measures unilaterally, giving them a more national character.

The Italian position in the case of sanctions against Argentina will be discussed as an example of the influence of domestic economic interests on community actions.

Following the Falklands conflict, the Community adopted a regulation providing for the suspension of imports from Argentina (cited above). While the adoption of the sanctions received the unanimous consent and approval of all member-states, the extension of the sanction was opposed by Italy and Ireland which dissociated themselves from the Community regime under article 224. Italy then resumed economic relationships with Argentina. The reasons for such a decision are rooted in the close economic interests that Italy has in this country. A second most important foreign investor after the United States, Italy has a large number of Italian citizens established in the country and a high percentage of its population is of Italian origin. Moreover, after the embargo, the first counter measures against Italy (exclusion from public procurement, suspension of payments due for the building of a hydroelectric plant etc.) by the Argentinian government were announced.

In this case Community commercial policy has not constituted an obstacle for Italy (or any other member-state) to dissent and pursue its own interests.

It has, of course, to be pointed out that the case of sanctions is special in so far as it is a matter concerning foreign policy and thus in this case the Community does not have exclusive competence to act.

8.6 Concluding observations

It clearly emerges from the above observations that a definitive evaluation in positive or negative terms of Community membership as far as trade is concerned is difficult to make.

First of all, when evaluating the impact of community commercial policy on member-states, one should take into account, together with the advantages and disadvantages, the loss of opportunities and the increase in costs stemming from national institutional deficiencies. In Italy's case, these deficiencies have been the absence of an institutional reform assuring in the first instance co-ordination between ministries and institutions involved in trade, thus avoiding overlap of competences, and the inadequate technical preparation of officials from these establishments participating in EC working groups and committees.

A second element to be considered is the dualism existing between those sectors which, projected towards an international dimension, have favoured Community integration and the establishment of a common commercial policy and those economically weaker sectors which, on the contrary, have curbed this process, fearing the competition that would ensue from the opening-up of the markets. In this respect it would be more appropriate to discuss the advantages or disadvantages for certain economic sectors than for a country (Italy) in general. Indeed, certain sectors derive advantages from the opening-up of the market, in particular the exporters of high-technology goods and those undertakings that have invested in those countries with which the Community has concluded co-operation or commercial agreements (ACO, Mediterranean, Latin America). On the other hand, as seen above, in the case of agricultural producers of Mediterranean products, other sectors have suffered from the competition of those same countries' exports into the Community.

Finally, it is evident that since the achievement of a *common* commercial policy is a long way off, national measures continue to be applied. This means that member-states maintain in practice a certain amount of freedom to pursue, through such measures, their national objectives according to their own notions and interests of foreign trade policy.

When speaking of national measures, reference may be made in particular to quotas. The existence of quotas at national level is the precondition for the application of the safeguard clause provided for in article 115. When invoked, this article allows the member-state concerned to exclude products under protection (that is, covered by national quotas) from the principle of the free movement of goods (articles 9 and 10 of the Treaty); in other words, these products cannot be imported from other member-states even if they have been put into free circulation. (According to the Court of Justice in case 41/76 ECR (1976):1921, a member-state must obtain the express authorization of the Commission for the adoption of restrictive import measures, a less rigorous condition of application seems, however, to have emerged from case 174/84, *Bulk Oil* v. *Sun Int.* ECR 1986:559.)

In theory, article 115 should cease to be applied as soon as a common commercial policy has been fully achieved.

Although a very important move towards the achievement of a common commercial policy seems to have been made by a recent judgment of the Court of Justice (case 51/87 *Commission* v. *Council* 27.09.1988 ECR (1988) p. 5954) – where the Court admitted that the regime of national quotas (in this case sub-quotas deriving from the Community quota under the generalized system of preferences) may cause distortions and deflections of trade and that, 'as the common commercial policy now stands', may be compatible with Articles 9 and 113 only when certain conditions are met – the establishment of a common commercial policy is jeopardized by the existence of diverging interests of member-states and by their willingness to maintain as much control as possible over their foreign trade. This seems to be a very central question if two much-discussed judgments of the Court of Justice (*Tezi Texitel* case 59/84 and 242/84 ECR 1986:887, 993) – where the Court recognized the possibility of invoking article 115 even in the case of quotas derived from a Community regime (national sub-quotas deriving from Community quotas under the Multifibre Agreement), justifying the application of this provision through the lack of uniformity of the imported goods regime – have been justified as a way-out for the Court of Justice from the diverging choices of member-states between free trade and protectionism (Timmermans, 1986, p. 104) and as a way to ease 'the member States' acceptance of the transfer of power from themselves to the Community' (Cremona, 1990, p. 295). Since the application of national import restrictions adopted under article 115 presupposes the existence of customs control at internal borders, the question of the establishment of a common policy becomes even more topical against the perspective of 1992.

Abbreviations

AFDI	Annuaire français de droit international
CMLRev.	Common Market Law Review
ECR	European Court Reports
DCSI	Rivista di diritto comunitario e degli scambi internazionali
OJ	Official Journal of the EC
JWTL	Journal of World Trade Law
Rev. d'Int.Eur.	Revue d'intégration Européenne
RMC	Revue du Marché Commun
RTDE	Revue trimestrelle de droit Européen
Ybook of Eur. Law	Yearbook of European Law

Bibliography

Auvret-Finck, J. (1988), Note, RTDE, vol. 1:162–82.

Basile, E. and Cecchi, C. (1988), *Modelli commerciali e scambi agricoli*, Milan: F. Angeli.

Bianchi, P. and Giordani, M. G. (eds) (1989), *L'amministrazione dell'industria e del commercio estero*, Bologna: Il Mulino.

Borracchini, P. (1988), 'Ancora su alcune incoerenze interpretative del GATT', DCSI, vols. 1–2:113–34.

Bourgeois, J. H. J. and Laurent, P. (1985), 'Le "nouvel instrument de politique commerciale": un pas en avant vers l'élimination des obstacles aux échanges internationaux', RTDE, vol. 1:41–63.

Colle, B. and Gambini, T. (1972), *La sovranità economica limitata*, Bologna: Il Mulino.

Coombes, D. (ed.) (1979), *European Integration, Regional Devolution and National Parliaments*, London: London Policy Studies Institute.

Cremona, M. (1990), 'The completion of the internal market and the incomplete commercial policy of the European Community', *Eur. Law Rev.*, vol. 1:283–97.

Demaret, P. (1988), 'La politique commerciale: perspectives d'évolution et faiblesses présentes', in J. Schwarze and H. G. Schermers (eds), *Structure and Dimension of European Community Policy*, Baden-Baden, pp. 60–110.

Dewost, J. L. (1982), 'La Communauté, les dix, et les sanctions économiques: de la crise iranienne à la crise des malouines', AFDI vol. XXVIII:215–32.

Fennell, R. (1987), *The Common Agricultural Policy of the EEC*, Oxford: BSP Professional Books.

Fernandez Sola, N. (1990), 'Relations avec les pays de l'AELE et de l'Est: aspects juridiques', RMC, vol. 335:208–15.

Flory, M. (1981), 'Commercial policy and development policy', in *Thirty Years of Community Law*, Brussels: *European Perspectives*, pp. 375–97.

Franchini, C. (1987), *La disciplina giuridica del commercio con l'estero*, Padua: Cedam.

Giardina, A. (1965), 'Commentario all'Articolo 110', in R. Quadri, R. Monaco and A. Trabucchi (eds), *Commentario del Trattato istitutivo delle Comunita' Europee*, Milan Giuffré: pp. 904–11.

Gilsdorf, P. (1989), 'Portée et délimitation des compétences communautaires en matière de politique commerciale', RMC, vol. 326:195–207.

Guillarmond, O. J. (1987), 'Expressions juridiques au sein du système européen de libre-échange, du rapprochement de l'AELE et de la Communauté', in *Liber amicorum Pescatore*, Baden-Baden: Nomos, 299–318.

Kapteyn, P. J. G. (1989), 'Verloren', in P. Van Themaat (ed), *Introduction to the Law of the European Community*, Deventer: Kluwer, pp. 788–838.

Koopmann, G. (1990), 'Protection for the European car industry?', *Intereconomics*, vol. 2: 53–5.

Kovar, R. (1970), 'La mise en place d'une politique commerciale commune et les compétences des Etats membres de la Communauté Economique Européenne en matière de relations internationales et de conclusion des traités', AFDI, vol. XVI: 783–828.

Kuyper, P. J. (1982), 'Community sanctions against Argentina: lawfulness under Community and international law', in D. O'Keefe and H. Schermers (eds), *Essays on European Law and International Law*, Deventer:Kluwer, pp. 141–66.

Lebullanger, J. (1988), 'La politique communautaire de coopération au développement', RTDE, vol. 1: 123–57.

Louis, J. V. (1988), 'La CEE et ses Etats membres dans les relations extérieures', *Rev. d'int. Europ.*: 203–35.

Mattera, A. (1986), 'L'achèvement du marché intérieur et ses implications sur les relations extérieures', in P. Demaret (ed.), *Relations extérieures de la CEE et marché interieur: aspects Juridiques et fonctionnels*, Colloque, Bruxelles: Story-Scientia, pp. 202–24.

Megret, J. (ed.) (1976), *Le Droit de la CEE, Vol. VI, Politique Economique*, Brussels: ULB.

Oliver, P. and Yataganas, X. (1987), 'The harmonised system of customs classification', *Ybook of Eur. Law*, vol. 7: 113–29.

Panebianco, M. (1974), *Codice del mercato comune*, Milan: Giuffré.

Pelkmans, J. (1984), *Market Integration in the European Communities*, The Hague: Martinus Nijhoff, pp. 220–51.

Pertek, J. (1983), 'Les sanctions politiques à objet économique prises par la CEE à l'encontre d'états tiers', RMC, vol. 266: 205–16.

Pescatore, P. (1969), 'La politique commerciale', in *Les Nouvelles Droits des Communautés Européennes*, Bruxelles: Larcier n. 2298, pp. 317–942.

Steenbergen, J. (1980), 'The common commercial policy', CMLRev. vol. 2: 229–49.

Steenbergen, J. (1981), 'The status of GATT in community law', JWTL, vol. 4: 337–44.

Timmermans, C. W. A. (1976), 'La libre circulation des marchandises et la politique commerciale commune', Colloque annuel, College d'Europe Bruges 1986, sur les Relations extérieures de la Communauté Européenne et Marché Intérieur: aspects juridiques et fonctionnels: 91–108.

Torricelli, A. (1974), 'Programmazione del commercio con l'estero in Italia nella legislazione e nell'assetto organizzativo degli ultimi vent'anni (1948–1970)', in F. Merusi (ed.), *La legislazione economica italiana dalla fine della guerra al primo programma economico*, Milan: F. Angeli, pp. 737–848.

Usher, J. A. (1986), 'The single market and goods imported from third countries', *Ybook of Eur. Law*, vol. 6: 159–82.

Volker, E. L. M.(ed.), (1983), *Protectionism and the European Community*, Deventer:Kluwer.

Yannopoulos, G. N. (1985), 'The European Community's external commercial policy: internal contradictions and institutional weakness', JWTL, vol. 5: 45–65.

PART III: POLITICAL AND LEGAL SYSTEMS

Chapter 9

The impact of EC integration on the Italian form of government

Giovanni Grottanelli de Santi

9.1 European integration: costs and benefits applied to constitutional change

Any analysis of 'costs and benefits' requires some introductory remarks and, if not a definition, at least a suggestion of what we mean by these two terms. Naturally a definition may well vary according to the different fields of knowledge. For our purposes we can leave aside the question of the negative implications of the term 'costs' and of the positive and desirable ones of 'benefits' and simply accept that we are facing a trend towards the political, institutional and economic integration of the European continent, and that ultimately the achievement of such a trend is 'desired' and somehow in that sense considered 'beneficial'. The question of costs and benefits, then, may well find a satisfactory answer simply by looking at what changes EC development and institutional existence have brought to the Italian state, i.e. by looking at some of the alterations that over the last thirty years have taken place and trying to see how much 'power' has been lost in the evolution from a 'sovereign' national state to prospective member-state of a future European federation.

The following notes are confined to an evaluation made from a constitutional point of view; other aspects (economic, social or political) are inevitably connected and may well influence such an evaluation but they can not be dealt with here for obvious reasons.

A short description of the Italian form of government would seem necessary in order to appreciate the functions and specific powers that have been most affected by the European progress towards integration.

By 'form of government' we assume the way power is shared and exercised at the top level of the Italian state according to the Republican Constitution of 1948. But when we say this, and accordingly go on to distinctions about the 'form of government (e.g. 'parliamentary' as differentiated from forms where the executive power is the direct result of the popular will, as in the United States, we naturally take it for granted that Italy has, like other countries of Western Europe, a 'democratic' form of government or that power is exercised according to the 'will of the people', that is that the legislative assemblies and the executive may only exercise their powers so long as they are the result of free elections held at regular intervals or at any time they appear necessary.

Mention will also necessarily be made of the kind of decentralization adopted in Italy which, although it does not make Italy a federal state, is nevertheless so advanced as to be considered typical of the Italian state.

9.2 The Italian form of government: the parliamentary system 'corrective powers' and regional decentralization

The Italian form of government is commonly defined as 'parliamentary' in the sense that among the various branches of government the leading and dominant role is vested in the two assemblies (*Camera dei Deputati* and *Senato*) which together form the Italian Parliament. The two assemblies are not significantly different and they are both elected by universal suffrage. Their main power is of course the legislative one; their two other most relevant functions are: (1) to retain or dismiss through a vote of confidence the Prime Minister chosen by the President (and his Cabinet as well as individual Ministers); and (2) to elect (by meeting together in what is considered 'a third organ', i.e. '*Parlamento in seduta comune*') the President of the Republic every seven years.

The power relationship between Parliament and the executive power (*Presidente del Consiglio* and *Consiglio dei Ministri*) through the vote of confidence (or of no confidence) is common – in its main features – to most parliamentary systems in Western Europe, from the oldest (Great Britain) to the very recent one of the 1978 Spanish Constitution. The Italian parliamentary system, however, has two additional organs which, while not as important as the two legislative assemblies in the balance of power, do nevertheless exercise a very relevant role and in a sense 'reduce' the image of the 'pure' and 'absolute' parliamentary sovereignty: the President of the Republic and the Constitutional Court.

Parliamentary power is in fact far from being absolute: the whole system must function according to the provisions of the Constitution and no statute or act adopted by the two assemblies may contradict or violate the constitutional provisions. In their different roles and ways the President and the Court may be regarded as the 'guardians' of the Constitution, ready to intervene and 'correct' the excesses in which both Parliament and the Executive might indulge. The early dissolution of Parliament, when no acceptable coalition in the executive seems to be supported by a parliamentary majority; decisions of conflicts of power (e.g. between President and Parliament or between the Judiciary and Parliament); or the declaration of the unconstitutionality of a statute (involving its being 'struck from the book', are all examples of corrective actions that may be taken to ensure the respect of the Constitution.

Indeed, in spite of the presence of these two 'corrective' powers (President and Constitutional Court), we may say that Italy is no exception to the general rule in all modern states where in practice (although not formally) a dominant position has to be recognized and is conceded to the Executive (*Presidente del Consiglio* and *Consiglio dei Ministri*) as long as stable parliamentary support is available. Parliament by itself may check the activity of a Cabinet and sometimes cause its resignation, but naturally cannot decide in a detailed way the policies to be 'followed' by the

Executive. In fact, according to the general constitutional situation of most Western European countries, the legislative activity of Parliament is, for most of the time, focused on Cabinet bills; we cannot say, however, that the chief function of the two assemblies is limited to examining and amending the proposals of the Executive. A lot of work is devoted to parliamentary proposals (the overall production of acts of Parliament is comparatively quite high) or to other activities of a different nature (administrative, inquiries, vigilance committees, etc.).

One of the main features of the Italian political and constitutional setting is naturally represented by the electoral system; proportional representation, although not required by the text of the Constitution, has nevertheless so far been firmly established by parliamentary statute. That system, as everybody knows, favours a certain proliferation of political parties with the predictable consequences, some of which are commonly regarded as negative (e.g. instability of the Executive, a strong negotiating power of small parties needed to achieve parliamentary majorities, etc.).

Although since the second half of the 1980s the situation has much improved, Italy has long been seen as a country where ministerial crises were frequent and coalition governments short-lived. It has to be noted, however, that the negative sides of the 'unstable governments' in Italy are certainly counterbalanced – at least to a large extent – by the permanence of politicians (in terms of decades), i.e. their tendency, regardless of their successes or failures, never to retire and by the growing role of public administration *vis-à-vis* 'political level' proper), the latter phenomenon being common to the entire Western World. Finally we should note here that for all its defects proportional representation has probably smoothed the sharp and over-strong confrontational character of the two-party electoral system – no small result in a country like Italy with the biggest communist party in the Western World and where the same communist party until fairly recent times refused to accept the idea of liberal parliamentary democracy.

Mention has already been made of the Italian system of government as characterized by a very high degree of decentralization. In the wave of democratization after the Second World War, the national territory was divided into regions. These were endowed with legislative and administrative powers (the judiciary has remained entirely and exclusively national). Five out of the twenty Regions have a 'special' autonomy, which means that they have more powers and depend less on the centre than the other fifteen 'ordinary' Regions.

The interrelationship between state and regions is based on the enumeration of regional powers established by the Constitution and revised on several occasions by parliamentary law.

Italian regional legislative assemblies operate within the framework of fundamental principles expressed in the national corpus of legislation (article 117, para.1 Const.). Pre-emptive tendencies can be found in any federal state and no doubt are very evident in a regional one like the Italian Republic; there is no need to discuss for our purposes here the amount of constitutional litigation that has developed in the country especially with regard to the admissible degree of national interference in the fields regarded – according to the Constitution – as 'regional'.

Over the last thirty to forty years a fairly strong tendency towards constitutional reform has developed in the country: different proposals have been made by various political parties; an *ad hoc* parliamentary committee has presented an open but fairly detailed text of constitutional amendments; finally, some initiatives have been taken (1990) to reform the electoral system by referendum, thus circumventing the natural hesitation of the two assemblies to reform themselves, but it is of course difficult to assess how successful they will be. On the other hand, at least passing mention should be made of the fact that even without constitutional reform Italian society has changed considerably since the Second World War, thus diminishing certain sharp differences that existed up till that period between it and other European countries. Labour law, welfare legislation and family law may be pointed out as some of the most significant sectors that have been dealt with either by Parliament or by the Constitutional Court (and very often by both) from the 1970s onwards. One might say without fear of appearing complacent that Italy has never in her history achieved as in the last forty years such progress in equality and economic prosperity while remaining a democratic country. In fact, although there have been some alarming attempts at totalitarianism, we may say that for nearly half a century no government has governed without the support of parliamentary confidence and all parliaments have always been the result of free elections.

The greatest achievement of all, a successful test of democracy, we might say, might perhaps be the triumph over the terrorism that pervaded the 1970s, defying the natural and obvious temptations and without recourse to emergency powers or exceptional legislation.

9.3 Italian constitutional change and EC development

We now should turn to the main question of this chapter and try to describe in what sense the existence and the development of the EC have influenced the Italian form of government; in what sense the 'benefits' of progress towards a free common market and possibly a European federal union have been counterbalanced by costs and losses of power of the various branches of government, by a change in their mutual relationship or by a loss of their representativeness of the popular will.

It is fairly well known how the 'direct effect' and the 'supremacy' of Community law have been accepted and introduced in the Italian legal system without a constitutional amendment. To achieve this result the constitutional principle stated in article 11 of the Constitution has been invoked; the principle in question welcomes the constraints on national sovereignty rendered necessary on the basis of reciprocity, by the creation of organizations that promote peace and justice among the nations.

The restrictions on national powers were initially the object of some extremely important Constitutional Court decisions and in more recent times, as we will see, of parliamentary legislation. However, we may say that from the late 1950s on, day after day, a fairly constant (and sometimes abundant and rushing) stream of Community legislation has been flowing into our system, changing the regulation of entire sectors, introducing new principles, etc., with the state structural apparatus remaining apparently unaffected.

'Apparently unaffected' immediately implies that changes have taken place in matters of substance, indeed, that the constitutional reality has changed, and here we have to ask ourselves in relation to which state have such changes taken place. Certainly, we are not talking in terms of the pre-fascist parliamentary democracy nor the pre-Second World War fascist regime. The Italian Republic of 1948, the one that really matters to us here, was hardly 9 years old when the Rome Treaty was signed. It is not an exaggeration to say that the modern Italian state and the other Western European countries developed to a great extent over the same period. Yet they seem to have developed independently and without an interaction that might well have been possible considering that Italy was in a state of transition and change.

The main factor of this 'separate' development may be seen to have arisen from the birth and development of a welfare state from the early 1950s on, often coldly distant when not opposed to private initiative. At the origin of these developments lay a system of ideas which was certainly ill at ease with that of the free market on which the Rome Treaty rested and rests. When the Treaty was signed, the Constitutional Court had been functioning only for a year and therefore was obviously very far from exercising any relevant influence on the constitutional life of the country. Furthermore, the Italian Regions, endowed, as we have pointed out, with legislative power and nowadays vital agents in making EC directives effective in the country, had simply not been created – in spite of the fact that the Constitution devotes many articles to them – and one of our leading scholars doubted even in 1969 that they would ever be created at all (C. Mortati, *Istituzioni di diritto pubblico*, 8th edn. Padua, CEDAM 1969, pp. 824–5). The Regions properly started to function only in the 1970s and rapidly became – important in the present context – one of the main channels of expenditure in the fields in which European Community action has been particularly active.

Finally, we may note that in 1957 'government by decree' (subject to parliamentary ratification) had by no means become one of the distinctive features of Italian constitutional life as was going to happen in the following decades.

It is no exaggeration, therefore, to say that the contemporary Italian state and the rest of the EC to a great extent developed at the same time, and very often what was needed was a change in the mentality of public administrators rather than abolition, reform or restriction of 'state powers' in order to allow the expansion of Community powers.

9.3.1 Change without new national legislation: EC law and Italian judicial review

Obviously, as in any other member-country of the EC, the power structure in Italy has been strongly affected by regulations. EC regulations mean – as everybody knows – law produced outside the Italian constitutional system and directly effective in Italy; this great innovation has changed both the picture of the Italian system of production of norms and indeed the very hierarchy of norms.

As we have noted, and theoretically thanks to a rather stretched and artificial interpretation of art. 11 of the Constitution, regulations take precedence over national law and no special law or constitutional amendment has been deemed necessary for the purpose. The Italian Constitutional Court, having changed its initial opinion, took the view that in the case of conflict Community regulations prevail over prior or subsequent Italian legislation. Only in the case of a violation of fundamental rights may Community law be reviewed by the Constitutional Court.

The restriction on national powers stemming from the supremacy of Community law is a general theme on which many and important decisions of the Constitutional Court have been adopted. For our purposes we need not investigate the theoretical foundation of the supremacy of Community law; we may well accept it as a fact and note among the various consequences (all devastating from the point of view of Italian national sovereignty) that of Courts conforming to and having to accept interpretations of Community acts adopted by the European Court of Justice and *also* accepting the retroactive or non-retroactive validity of those decisions. The constraint on the freedom and independence of the national judiciary is naturally a consequence of the constraint on the national legislation, but this does not make it less striking and meaningful.

The Italian Constitutional Court, in a series of rather revolutionary decisions, has affirmed the direct applicability of the principles expounded in its interpretative function of the European Court of Justice (ex article 177 of the Rome Treaty). It has also affirmed that Community norms have direct applicability 'in the way they are interpreted' in the decisions of the Court of Justice (ex article. 169 of the Rome Treaty).

9.3.2 Community directives and Italian legislative intervention: an opportunity for the expanding role of the Executive

It might be debatable whether the Italian form of government has changed and continues to change more through regulations or through directives. This latter source of Community law, unlike regulations, has – as everybody knows – no direct effect, at least in principle, and requires the co-operation of national legislation. Directives are binding as to the result to be achieved and leave a margin of choice to national government concerning the time and way in which they will be applied.

The peculiar development of directives has blurred considerably their distinction from regulations and one of the current themes of Community law is 'the problem' about whether in given circumstances a direct effect has to be attributed to them.

For our purposes we may simply note that as long as they require the mediation and intervention of national government in order to achieve their ends, directives determine a change in the institutional roles of Parliament and of the Executive. This, as we will see, is particularly evident in the recourse to delegation made necessary by the flow of directives geared to the harmonization of legislation; such a flow is from the viewpoint of 'costs and benefits' undeniably of primary importance.

In a sense we could say that the impact of directives upon the Italian form of government has only strengthened and intensified an already existing tendency, namely that of the executive's role expanding at the expense of Parliament.

It is in the 'government by decree' that this peculiarly Italian tendency is particularly obvious. According to article 77 of the Italian Constitution, the government has the power to adopt measures having the force of a legislative act, but only for a limited period of time (sixty days) and subject to parliamentary ratification. Although very widely criticized, this power of the Executive can be seen as a remedy to the lack of clear majorities in Parliament.

On the contrary, the delegation of legislative power to the Executive has never been a common or frequent feature of our system. Although provided for in the Constitution (article 76) and used on some important occasions , we can say that the number of delegations has been minimal over the last twenty years when compared to the number of governmental legislative decrees.

It seems fairly evident that Community directives have become a further opportunity for the expansion of the role of the Executive; many of the matters and problems regulated by directives are highly technical and this of course calls for an administrative national filter rather than a parliamentary one. In 1987 an extremely wide and far-reaching use of delegation to the Cabinet was granted by Parliament (L. 16 April 1987 no. 183) for the adaptation and implementation of EC directives. The same law also established the principle that whenever a subject matter could be dealt with without parliamentary legislation the speedier recourse to administrative rules should be adopted (article 11). The same law has even conferred force of law on some Community directives (article 14) which, apart from raising considerable perplexities of a constitutional nature, may well be seen as a parliamentary abdication in favour, in the long run, of the executive and administrative power.

9.3.3 Rationalization and further steps of the Executive expansion of power in the law of 1989

The implementation process of EC norms is very likely going to change after the adoption of the law no. 86 of 1989. This law deals, as declared in its title, with the Italian participation in the Community normative process and with the procedures of implementation of obligations deriving from Community membership.

The law is an attempt to rationalize the ways in which Italian legislation conforms (or fails to conform) to Community norms (article 2). Every year a general overall evaluation must be made in a special parliamentary bill (mainly through the initiative of the Minister for Community Affairs) and at a special parliamentary session, and remedial action should be, if and when needed, promptly adopted. Italy does not have a very good score in the implementation of Community law and this act of Parliament is meant to change dramatically the present situation.

We certainly cannot comment and expound the contents of the law here, but for our purposes we should note the following:

(a) The use of legislative delegation from Parliament to the Cabinet is intensified considerably in order rapidly to put into practice all Community legislation which needs some sort of normative implementation. Matters which are expressly devolved to Parliament by the Constitution are excluded.

(b) The implementation of directives through administrative action will be also increased and will play a far greater role than in the past (article 4). As the advice of the competent parliamentary committees is required, the participation of Parliament in Cabinet action is sought and provided for. However, in the case of parliamentary inaction (forty days), the Cabinet will proceed. A major weapon of deregulation seems therefore to provide great opportunities for improving the present very slow and often unsatisfactory process of implementation.

In a general way we might say that present political tendencies may appreciably change the 'form of government': (1) the Minister for the Co-ordination of European Affairs may be shedding his Cinderella status to acquire a relevant position within the Cabinet with considerable powers and wide margins of discretion for their exercise; (2) the uses of legislative delegation, until now extremely limited if compared with other European countries (e.g. Great Britain), are bound to increase and while the degree of participation of parliamentary committees will have to be ascertained, this will bring unavoidably more (or rather 'even more') power and discretion into the hands of the executive; (3) finally, as we will note with a little more detail in the next section, the 1989 legislation will affect the relations between state and regions, but no significant change seems to be evident in the trend of a consistent constraint of regional powers.

9.3.4 Form of government and regional autonomy: regional power and foreign/ Community relations

In the brief description of the Italian form of government mention has already been made of the strong centralizing tendencies that oppose a full and satisfactory implementation of the kind of decentralization envisaged by the 1948 Constitution. Bearing in mind Italian history, it would perhaps be appropriate to speak of tendencies 'not to decentralize' rather than to 'centralize', for indeed Italy has been very centralized ever since its national unity and it became more so with fascism. After their creation in the 1970s the Regions could say they were entitled to more powers, but in no way could they complain about being deprived of those 'constitutionally regional' powers (i.e. as envisaged in the text of the 1948 Constitution) they had never exercised.

The story of federal states, and which is relevant to regional Italy, is always an unavoidably controversial one when one has to examine the power to deal with foreign affairs and the possible encroachments or conflicts between central authorities and local government powers. Even in a country like Italy where certainly American judicial precedents are not of common usage (to use an understatement), the Supreme Court decision on *Missouri* v. *Holland* (252 US 416) has become fairly well known among law students and scholars.

The basic assumption of that decision is almost identically the same as that to be derived from the current and consolidated judicial interpretation of the Italian Constitutional Court and from the consensus of the greatest part of law scholars: state decisions in the field of international relations may not be challenged by considerations of federalism and, which concerns Italy, of regionalism.

There does not seem to be much scope in developing what this 'fundamental' assumption means for the preservation of regional autonomy: it is one thing for the Regions to see their field of competence curtailed by the provisions of an international treaty, and another to see the same happen as a result of the daily flow of Community law. Community law – as it has been specifically stated by the Italian Constitutional Court – may well even change the separation of powers between the nation and the Regions as described in the text of the Constitution so long as fundamental rights are not violated (see the decisions no. 187 of 1977 and no. 399 of 1987; see also decision no. 232 of 1989 and ord. no. 132 of 1990). Perhaps we might simply add here that Community policies and norms very often coincide exactly with the most important and qualifying powers that the Constitution has assigned to the Regions (e.g. agriculture). Similarly, Community powers reduce regional powers with regard to the protection of the environment, thus reducing the fairly satisfactory space the Regions had carved out for themselves through legislative and judicial interpretation.

Naturally we are not concerned here with the loss of a certain amount of power to the Community, but rather with the loss of the Regions to the central State in the name of Community norms. Indeed, the implementation of Community law was first considered purely a matter of national concern and jurisdiction even when regional powers were involved (see DPR no. 616 of 1977). This approach, whether justified or not, provided an extra opportunity for the Italian Parliament and central administration to interfere with the exercise of regional powers and to impose a uniform overall implementation over the entire Italian territory. Such general and national implementation of Community law binding all the Regions (rather than separate regional implementations) received the blessing of the Constitutional Court. In most cases the regional role is reduced to the adoption of norms of implementation of state norms implementing Community rules with a margin of discretionary power that does not need any comment. The case of 'special' Regions, i.e. those with a more marked degree of autonomy, is somewhat different; a wider and more consistent power directly to implement Community norms is indeed recognized in such Regions (Val d'Aosta, Trentino–Alto Adige, Friuli–Venezia Giulia, Sardegna, Sicilia).

Tendencies now seem to be a bit different and we can say that the Regions are certainly heading towards a much more satisfactory degree of power-sharing in the implementation process. The state law of 1989 (no. 86) we have already mentioned now allows a general power of the Regions to implement directives, though this within the limits of the general principles that will be pointed out either by the 'general law for the implementation of Community norms' that every year will have to be adopted by Parliament, or by other specific state law implementing directives.

Indeed, the law of 1989 is full of caution and certainly does not mean an entire reversal of trends (e.g. compared with law no. 183 of 1987), but it is fair to say that there is a different and more open outlook as regards to regional decentralization.

In a sense the limited role of the Italian Regions in the implementation of Community norms corresponds to the limited role that the Regions have in the shaping of Community policies and legislation.

So far, regional aspirations to some sort of independent policy activity beyond the national boundaries have not gained much acknowledgement or satisfaction. Regional power in the field of foreign relations has been considered constitutionally admissible provided it remains confined to the promotion of some economic activity or to the exchange of information under the close control of central authorities. This activity has been nicely defined as of 'mere relevance on the international level' ('attività di mero rilievo internazionale delle Regioni' Const. Court no. 179/1987). In fact the power in question reminds one much more of a tradesman advertising his goods rather than some sort of departmentalized foreign policy.

As to what directly concerns the regional participation to the shaping of Community law and policy, we may note that a certain improvement may be on the horizon at least if we compare the situation of the 1990s to the one officially acknowledged in the 1980s. The law of 1989 provides for a 'conference' (article 10) between state and regional representatives to be called at least once every six months and to be dedicated to Community matters 'concerning' the Regions and their Provinces. It seems that similar occasions – official as they may be – will not go much beyond the exchange of information, the attempt to co-ordinate policies, the formulation of proposals with the view to the possible adoption of norms at Community level. No direct link or significant channel of communication between the Community and the Regions is even remotely mentioned or envisaged; if we consider the general situation we have described we suggest that it probably could not have been otherwise.

Finally we should also mention the possibility, envisaged by article 6 of the law no. 86 of 1989, of the Presidents of the Regions taking part at a national level in those Cabinet meetings during which certain important decisions adopted by the EC council or EC Commission will be discussed and action taken against them or directives adopted for their implementation. In these cases the Presidents of the Regions interested in such decisions may be heard in the course of Cabinet meetings and may express their (not binding) opinion.

The political atmosphere seems therefore, all aspects considered, more favourable to the Regions than in the past. In the light of present-day reality no more than this should perhaps be said; it would certainly seem advisable to give the trend time and see whether consistent progress is going to be made towards decentralization in the framework of European integration.

9.4 Tentative conclusion

The aim of this chapter was to summarize the changes that the development of European integration have or may have induced in the Italian form of government. The original idea of the Italian form of government, as we have seen, has not been seriously affected; the formal divide between legislative, executive and judicial powers seems to have remained the same regardless of the existence of European Community authorities. Legal and political phenomena such as European production of norms with direct effect on the country and Italian judicial (or administrative) decisions implementing European decisions in the widest variety seem to be simply additional to the ordinary and complex routine of the state; the hierarchy of norms may have changed – a process of pre-emption is indeed taking place – but no evident and corresponding mutilation has appeared in the jurisdiction of national organs. If all of a sudden European norms and processes and organs were to disappear, Italian law books would remain exactly the same; they would not have to be restructured except for the necessary omissions.

In a sense this is like saying that – with the obvious exception of the 'direct effect' of Community regulations – the Italian state is still the great interpreter or mediator through which Community law penetrates and expands, is understood and becomes applicable within the national legal order.

Nevertheless, impressive and consistent change is taking place in a rather unassuming way, without altering in any way the form of government; the state supreme mediator and interpreter remains 'sovereign' only in appearance. This is particularly evident if we consider together with that most striking instrument (direct effect of Community norms) those others through which the legal system is or can be affected by Community norms (harmonization, co-ordination, co-existence). More and more, while the formal authority remains 'national' the effective control of the decisions lies elsewhere, a phenomenon which is not entirely dissimilar from that of the legislative acts through which national budgets or estimates are adopted every year – it is well known how by far the greatest part of the budgets is rigid and fixed and may in no way be varied or touched by the 'sovereign' assembly entitled to vote them.

'Foreign policy' may provide a good example of a sector once regarded as reserved to the nations and where it is becoming very difficult for each member-country to follow their own inclination and not to adopt the line dictated in each specific case (e.g. the Falklands crisis in 1982 or the Gulf crisis in 1990–1) by 'European solidarity'.

Another sign of progress towards Europe of great importance and yet in the unassuming way we have underlined before may be seen in the tendency to evaluate the behaviour of member-countries not only on the basis of what they do or do not do (e.g. conforming to or violating European norms), but according to the way in which they do it; from this point of view developments of federal standards like *loyauté federale* or *Bundestreupflicht* considered applicable at a European level seem extremely meaningful.

Early attempts at European unity after the Second World War seemed to be directed at sharp historical turning points and rather traumatic (if not revolutionary) transfer of powers; they also seemed to set the pattern of thought for the future decades: supranationality was going to be measured in terms of decisions taken not unanimously but by a majority vote. It may well be that for some time to come progress will be achieved in a less spectacular way and yet one in which every single step forward may formally or in theory be revoked but is *de facto* a point of no return.

A short bibliographical note

The Italian form of government as briefly described in section 2 of this chapter is commonly accepted among Italian law scholars; for further reading on the subject, see among the best current textbooks, with their relevant bibliographies:

G. Amato and A. Barbera (1986) *Manuale di diritto pubblico,* il Mulino, Bologna,

T. Martines (1990) *Diritto costituzionale,* Giuffré Milan, 6th edn; L. Paladin (1990) *Lezioni di diritto costituzionale,* CEDAM Padua: For commentaries and interpretations of the new law no. 86/1989 (mentioned in section 3.3) by A Tizzano, S. Bartole, R. Bin, G. Conetti and L. Daniele (1988) (though published while the bill was going through Parliament), see *Foro it* vol. IV: 492ff. The *Legge comunitaria* for 1990 is indicated as L.29 dicembre 1990 no. 428.

Regional decentralization was at first considered as a subject as part of Italian constitutional law; with the growing importance of the Regions in the 1960s and 1970s regional law came to be considered as a separate subject matter in university curriculums although always unavoidably linked to constitutional law. For a general picture about the Regions, see L. Paladin (1985), *Diritto regionale,* CEDAM Padua: 4th edn. As regards the relationship between Community law and the Regions, see P. Caretti (1979), *Ordinamento comunitario e autonomia regionale,* Giuffré, Milan: F. Bassanini and P. Caretti (1981), 'Autonomie regionali e poteri comunitari', in AA. VV., *Comunita' europee e ruolo delle regioni,* Giuffré, Milan: A. d'Atena (1981), *Le regioni italiane e la Comunita' economica europea,* Giuffré, Milan: B. Conforti (1990), 'Giustizia comunitaria e regioni', *Giustizia e Regioni,* Facolta' di Giurisprudenza di Bologna, *Atti del convegno di Bologna 1–2 dicembre 1989,* Padua, pp. 215ff; F. Teresi (1990) *Comunità europee e regioni: il primato del diritto comunitario e le competenze legislative regionali,* in Istituto Gramsci Siciliano, Sez. Giuridica, Lo Statuto siciliano dopo 40 anni, Padua, pp. 93ff.

For a recent brief and yet exhaustive exposé of the subject of regional participation in the field of foreign relations dealt with in section 3.4, see V. Lippolis (1989), 'Regioni, treaty-making power e giurisprudenza della Corte costituzionale', *Giur.cost.* pp. 1206ff. and P. de Sena (1989), 'In tema di attività "internazionalé" delle regioni?' *Foro it.* vol. I: 2121.

In Italy the revolution in the hierarchy of norms as a result of participation in the European Communities has taken place essentially through a series of judicial decisions of the *Corte Costituzionale.* The most important of these decisions, reference to which is made in section 3.1, are the following: no. 170/1984 (direct applicability of Community regulations, supremacy over national law); no. 113/1985 (direct applicability of legal principles as expounded by the European Court of Justice ex article 177 of the Treaty of Rome); no. 389/1989 (direct applicability of Community norms as interpreted by the European Court of Justice ex article 169 of the Treaty of Rome).

The Constitutional Court decisions are all published in the special series of the *Gazzetta Ufficiale della Repubblica Italiana, Serie Speciale, Libreria dello Stato,* Rome, and also, after some delay but with annotations and commentaries, in the law journal *Giurisprudenza costituzionale* published by Giuffré, Milan.

Chapter 10

Italy and the EC: the legal protection of fundamental rights

Francesco Francioni

10.1 Introduction

In a volume dedicated to the assessment of costs and benefits of member-states' participation in the EC, the treatment of human rights policy presents a particularly difficult task. It is not possible, first of all, to evaluate in quantitative and statistical terms the gains and losses resulting from European integration with regard to a field where the performance of the Community cannot be measured by reference to tangible economic data but rather in terms of advancement of individual freedom and human dignity. Secondly, the conceptual and ideological relativism surrounding the doctrine of human rights – it is hardly necessary to recall here the debate over the priority of 'Western' civil liberties or of social economic rights, or even of the more recent collective rights (Cassese, 1984 pp. 293–311) – involves the epistemological problem of which vantage point to adopt in order to assess improvement or impairment of human rights in the European integration process. Further, the original treaties establishing the European Economic Community did not contain a charter of fundamental rights, although of the four fundamental freedoms of the 'common market' three actually concern individual rights (freedom of movement, freedom of establishment, freedom to provide services).

Despite these difficulties, the importance of the subject of fundamental rights is apparent at least from two points of view. *De Lege lata*, it is important to see how the process of transfer of sovereign powers from member-states to the EC has affected the ability of individuals – in this case, of individuals within the Italian jurisdiction – to enjoy and defend their fundamental rights. *De lege ferenda*, it is useful to consider whether and to what extent the establishment of the single market in 1993 will place new challenges to and perhaps strains on, the relationship between member states' human rights policies and the new Community imperatives of free circulation of persons and of deeper economic integration required by the building of the internal market. Such strains can already be identified in areas such as race relations – due to the increased mobility of persons – and in the field of economic and social rights – for the foreseeable negative impacts that the single market will produce in economically less competitive regions, especially with regard to unemployment and the attendant strains on the right to work recognized by the Italian Constitution article 4 (Cassese, Clapham and Weiler, 1990, pp.8–12).

The purpose of this chapter is not to address all such future problems ,whose complexity would require their systematic treatment in a series of specialized studies. It is rather to identify how, under the present system, the division of competences between the Community and member-states will affect the manner in which fundamental human rights may be protected in Italy. I will, therefore, first outline the essential features of the Italian system of protection of fundamental rights. Then I will briefly trace the development of Community competence in the field of human rights, especially in light of the European Court jurisprudence. Finally, I will try to assess what advantages and pitfalls the transfer of competence from member-states to the Community may entail in the field under consideration.

10.2　Constitutional and international law for the protection of fundamental rights in Italy

The Italian Constitution adopted in 1947 and entered into force on 1 January 1948 gives a prominent position to fundamental rights. Article 2 speaks of 'inviolable rights of the human person' which signifies that they may not be overridden by majority vote law-making, and perhaps not even by way of constitutional revision in so far as they constitute the indispensable mainstay of the democratic form of government. These rights are defined in detail in the Constitution and they comprise the traditional civil rights – personal liberty, freedom of movement, of expression, association, worship as well as of remedies before a competent court of law (articles 13–28). These rights are, with a few exceptions (e.g. association and movement), guaranteed to all individuals within the Italian jurisdiction regardless of citizenship. Ample room is also given to economic, social and cultural rights which are dealt with in articles 35–47. Article 4 recognizes the right to work for 'all citizens' and promotes the conditions that may render this right effective. Articles 48–54 guarantee political rights which are generally reserved to citizens. The above provisions are set against the background of a 'rigid' constitution, i.e. a constitution that may not be amended or modified by ordinary laws adopted by Parliament, but by a special procedure and special majorities within the Chamber of Deputies and the Senate (article 138). The ultimate custodian of the Constitution is the Constitutional Court, an organ which is capable of acting as the judge of the legislature in so far as it may strike down statutes and laws that have been found to be in breach of the Constitution. Individuals who claim that one of the fundamental rights recognized by the Constitution has been infringed upon by laws, statutes or acts having equivalent force (article 134) do not have direct access to the Constitutional Court but must raise the constitutional question before the court to which the claim is presented. The court will then refer the question to the Constitutional Court by way of preliminary ruling.

Besides the constitutional provision mentioned above, the system of human rights protection in Italy embraces a large number of international treaties and conventions, both multilateral and bilateral. Among the multilateral treaties, a special position is occupied by the 1950 European Convention on Human Rights and Fundamental Freedoms which was ratified by Italy in 1955. Italy also accepted the optional clauses in articles 25 and 46 of this Convention conferring jurisdiction, respectively, on the European Commission to receive complaints directly from individuals and on the European Court of Human Rights to interpret the Convention. The European Convention covers only standard civil and political rights. Economic, cultural and social rights are covered by additional protocols (First Protocol of 20 March 1952, concerning the right to own and enjoy property and the right to education) and by *ad hoc* conventions such as the European Social Charter and the many conventions adopted within the ILO framework which have been ratified by Italy (for a collection of these instruments, see ILO, *International Labour Conventions and Recommendations*, 1982, and for their effects in Italy, OFFEDDU, *Le convenzioni internazionali del lavoro e l'ordinamento giuridico italiano*, 1973). Besides these treaties, Italy ratified the 1966 United Nations Covenant on Civil and Political Rights, and on Social Economic and Cultural rights, as well as the Optional Protocol annexed to the Covenant on Civil and Political rights which confers jurisdiction to the Human Rights Committee in relation to individual communications alleging breaches of the Covenant.

With regard to the right to freedom from discrimination, two important conventions deserve mention here. They are the 1966 Convention on the Elimination of All Forms of Racial Discrimination (ratified by Italy on 5 January 1976) and the 1979 Convention on the Elimination of All Forms of Discrimination Against Women (ratified by Italy on 10 June 1985).

Human rights provisions are also contained in the 1947 Peace Treaty between Italy and the Allied and Associated Powers (article 15), and in the bilateral minorities agreements signed by Italy with Austria in 1946 to guarantee the special autonomy of the German-speaking community in Alto Adige/South Tyrol, and with Yugoslavia in 1954 and in 1975 (memorandum of understanding, London, 1954, and Treaty of Osimo, 1975; Caggiano, 1976, pp. 248ff.), by which the contracting parties undertook to guarantee minority protection in the context of the boundary settlement in the territory of Trieste.

Although there is some doubt that customary international law may add something new to the fairly complete system of human rights that prevails in Italy, customary norms may nevertheless have an impact on the way Italian law provides for the protection of human rights (for a contrary view, see Cappelletti and de Witte, 1986). First of all, customary norms of international law are incorporated into the Italian legal system by article 10, para. 1 of the Constitution and are thereby treated as constitutional norms. This circumstance may reinforce the normative intensity of those provisions on fundamental rights contained in domestic law and in treaties to the extent that they coincide with customary international law. A complete catalogue of rights guaranteed by customary international law cannot be formulated here. There is sufficient authority, however, for maintaining that a hypothetical catalogue would contain the right to be free from torture, slavery, extrajudicial executions or enforced disappearances, from prolonged arbitrary detention and from systematic racial discrimination and racial segregation (see the United States Restatement of the Law, Third, on the foreign relations law, Sec. 702, 1987, pp. 161ff.). With regard to such rights, the protection afforded by the Italian legal system would be reinforced as a consequence of its 'constitutionalization' by way of the already mentioned article 10, para 1.

10.3 Methods and procedures for the implementation of human rights in Italy

Besides the substantive aspects examined above, the assessment of costs and benefits of Italy's membership in the EC requires that we take into consideration the means and procedures through which the protection of fundamental rights can be assured in Italy.

With regard to the range of rights guaranteed by the Constitution, not only can they be invoked before the courts, but they may give rise to incidents of constitutionality whenever laws, statutes or acts having the force of law are deemed to be inconsistent with them, which ultimately may lead to the striking down of specific provisions which have been found by the Constitutional Court to be an infringement of such rights. It is to be noted that as a matter of principle the Italian Constitutional Court has agreed to review the constitutionality of national legislation incorporating and implementing international treaties. Therefore, in the unlikely event of a conflict between a right protected by the Constitution and a right guaranteed by a treaty to which Italy is a party, the theoretical possibility exists that the Constitutional Court may declare the latter unconstitutional and thus deprive it of any effect within the Italian legal system. This conclusion requires some modification with regard to the treaties establishing the EC, as we shall see later (section 10.4).

With regard to fundamental rights guaranteed by the international instruments to which Italy is a party (see section 10.2), although the Italian system adheres to the so-called 'dualist' approach to the relationship between municipal law and international law, nonetheless human rights treaties become part of the domestic law and may as such be enforced by ordinary courts of law. The situation is different, therefore, from the one prevailing in countries such as the United Kingdom or Denmark where human rights treaties are not incorporated into domestic law. Further, although the measure implementing the treaty in Italian law is usually an act of Parliament – which could therefore be superseded by subsequent statute – several techniques have been developed in order to reduce the vulnerability of international treaties *vis-à-vis* subsequent inconsistent legislation. The first technique is the so-called 'presumption of conformity', which involves a judicial interpretation of an apparently inconsistent domestic law provision in such a way as to render it compatible with international obligations (for examples of such practice, see Court of Cassation, 21 May 1973, no. 1455, and 11 October 1979, no. 5274). This technique should be particularly fruitful in the field of fundamental rights, since it is hardly conceivable that the Italian legal system would produce statutes that deliberately run counter to previously accepted treaty obligations on human rights. A second technique goes even further and consists in adopting the *speciality* criterion in favour of treaty obligations (*legi speciali per generalem non derogatur*). Under this criterion, a treaty provision on fundamental rights will survive even subsequent contrary provisions of a domestic statute unless the statute in question expressly intends to supersede the international obligation. In this case the judge will have no choice but to apply the domestic law and leave the matter to the Executive for the ensuing international responsibility arising from the breach of an international obligation.

Two special categories of human rights escape this rule. The first is the one regarding the rights of aliens, article 10, para. 2 of the Constitution gives a constitutional underpinning to these rights whether they derive from customary norms or from treaties. Among these rights one can include personal liberty, the right to enjoy property, the right of access to justice, and the general right to be free from the imposition of services or duties which are incompatible with the nationality bond of the alien with the state of which he is a citizen (Conforti, 1987; Nascimbene, 1988, pp. 77ff.; Cassese, 1975, pp. 461ff.).

The second category of specially 'reinforced' rights is represented by the fundamental rights protected by Community law. Although at an early stage (see decision no. 14 of 7 March 1964 in *Costa* v. *ENEL, Foro Italiano*, 1964, volume I: 465) the Italian Constitutional Court held that treaties establishing the EC could not be considered as different from ordinary international treaties, with the consequence that later national statutes could validly derogate them, later case-law has recognized the special status of Community law and its supremacy over conflicting national legislation (*Frontini* case, 27 December 1973 no. 183, *Foro Italiano*, 1974, volume I: 314ff.; *Società industrie chimiche Italia centrale* v. *Ministero commercio estero*, ibid. 1975, volume I: 2661). The supremacy of Community law, and therefore also of Community law on fundamental rights, has been recognized by reference to article 11 of the Italian Constitution which 'allows limitations of sovereignty necessary to the establishment of a system that guarantees peace and justice between nations; and promotes international organizations aiming at such system'. Until 1984 the supremacy of Community law based on article 11 required that the Constitutional Court would declare by way of preliminary ruling the unconstitutionality of a conflicting national statute. This system involved practical problems – i.e. delays in ensuring the precedence of Community law – and apprehension on the part of the European Court of Justice that the separation of the Community legal system would not be sufficiently safeguarded (*Simmenthal* case ECR 1978: 629). Since 1984 Italian case-law has accepted the principle that ordinary courts may simply set aside national legislation incompatible with Community law without the need any more for the Constitutional Court to declare such legislation unconstitutional under article 11. (*Granital* case, decision of the Constitutional Court of 8 June 1984, no. 170, *Foro Italiano*, 1984 volume I: 2062).

This privileged status of Community law in the Italian legal system makes it all the more important to assess in the following section the implications of the policy of fundamental rights protection as developed by Community organs and especially by the Court of Justice.

10.4 The nature, foundation and objectives of Community protection of human rights

As we have already pointed out, the treaties establishing the EC did not contain a charter of fundamental rights. The EC, unlike its earlier counterpart, the Council of Europe, was set up as a group of economic entities aiming at market integration and not at the establishment of uniform protection of individual rights in Europe. In this situation it would have been perfectly conceivable for the Community's organs to have shunned individual rights concerns in their law-making process. Indeed, this could have been facilitated by the fact that the Community's legal system was founded and developed as a derogation to member-states' rights, and therefore the main task of judicial review in the EC was intended to be the protection of member-states against *ultra vires* acts by the Community. Instead, as is well known, a law on fundamental rights began to be developed by the European Court of Justice in the late 1960s and it has been expanded up to the present as a body of unwritten principles supported by political decisions of other Community institutions, especially the European Parliament. To put it as concisely as possible, the stages through which the European Court developed its fundamental rights jurisprudence are the following.

First, the Court recognized that fundamental rights form an integral part of the general principles of Community law and claimed for itself the power to determine when such rights have been infringed upon by Community legislation. This early stage coincides with the *Stauder* case (*Stauder* v *City of Ulm*, ECR 1969: 419), in which a German national had complained that Community legislation, requiring disclosure of personal information in order to be admitted to benefit from the distribution of subsidized butter, amounted to a breach of his privacy rights. The Court held that the legislation in question did not violate fundamental rights, but unambiguously acknowledged its competence to determine such violations in the light of general principles of Community law.

The second stage coincides with the search for principles of reference outside of the self-contained system of Community law. In the well-known judgment of 17 December 1970 in the *Internationale Handelgesellschaft* case (ECR 1970: 1125) – concerning the right not to be deprived of proprietary interests in relation to the forfeiture of a compulsory export licence deposit – the Court admitted that in order to clarify the basis of human rights protection within the Community system, recourse could be made to constitutional traditions and basic common principles (*fontes cognoscendi*) of the national systems of member-states. This step was facilitated by the attempt made by the German courts, in referring the question under article 177, to obtain a review of Community legislation directly in the light of national constitutional principles. Moreover the enunciation of the Court as to the legal basis of Community's fundamental rights remained a theoretical one. It fell short of considering the Community measures as incompatible with applicable principles on the protection of human rights, something that later on led the German Bundesverfassungggericht to the controversial decision that national fundamental rights could represent the ultimate test of the validity of Community legislation as reviewed by national constitutional courts (decision of the Federal Constitutional Court of Germany, 1974, 2 CMLR: 540).

The third stage of the Court of Justice jurisprudence is marked by a reference to international treaties on the protection of human rights, particularly the European Convention of 1950. Early decisions at this stage are those in the *Nold* case (4/73, ECR 1974: 491) and in the *Hauer* case (44/79, ECR 1979: 3727), both concerning alleged infringements on economic rights (right to pursue economic activities in the former, right to property in the latter). A host of subsequent cases has reaffirmed the principle that the European Convention on Human Rights and other international human rights treaties applicable to member-states constitute a source of principles under which the legality of Community legislation may be reviewed. Although it is impossible here to review the various areas in which the question of consistency in Community law with regard to fundamental rights has been raised, such areas include sex discrimination (in the *Defrenne II* case, 15 June 1978, 149/77, ECR 1978 1365, the Court buttressed its recognition that 'the elimination of discriminations based on sex is part of [Community's] fundamental rights' by reference to the European Social Charter of 1961, and the ILO Convention no. 111 of 25 June 1958 on employment and professional discrimination; the right to a fair and public hearing (*Pecastaing* case, 98/79 ECR: 1980); the right not to be subjected to retroactive regulations as provided by article 7 of the European Convention on Human Rights (*Kirk* case, 63/83, ECR 1984: 2689); the inviolability of domicile and respect of privacy in relation to inspection required by the implementation of Community anti-trust law (cases 97/8, 99/87).

A striking feature of the case-law referred to above is that the judicial activism manifested by the Court in fashioning an unwritten bill of fundamental rights has not apparently been balanced by a concrete readiness to enforce such rights *vis á vis* Community policies. Invariably, the Court has either held that Community legislation must withstand scrutiny under international human rights standards because such standards are not 'sufficiently precise' (*Hauer*), because the right in question, e.g. privacy, applies only to individuals and not to commercial entities (cases 97/87, 98/87, 99/87), or because the adverse effects of Community legislation on fundamental rights are consistent with permissible restrictions recognized also by international human rights treaties (e.g. *Rutili* case, 36/75, ECR 1975: 1219ff., concerning the French denial to an Italian national of his right to choose his residence on grounds of 'ordre public').

10.5 Opportunities and benefits for Italy of autonomous protection of fundamental rights through EC membership

From an Italian point of view, the assessment of benefits deriving to Italy from the above mentioned judicial approach to the protection of human rights must take into consideration the following facts:

- Italy has a fairly detailed constitutional charter on fundamental rights whose content, as we have already pointed out (section 10.2), ranges from the traditional civil and political rights to the economic, social and cultural rights typical of a welfare state;
- with regard to remedies, Italian citizens and other individuals under Italian jurisdiction may obtain judicial review of legislation which is deemed inconsistent with such rights by virtue of the incident of constitutionality in ordinary judicial proceedings and by the consequent possibility that the Constitutional Court may strike down such legislation as unconstitutional;

– further, even a decision of the Constitutional Court may be reviewed by way of the international judicial or quasi-judicial procedure that guarantees the enforcement of human rights recognized in international treaties to which Italy is a party. These procedures are those available under the European Convention before the Strasbourg Commission and Court, and those provided under the optional protocol attached to the Covenant on Civil and Political Rights.

The most important implication of the development of a human rights protection policy by the Community is that the above paradigm must be set aside and replaced by the system of judicial review by the European Court of Justice in all the areas that have been occupied by the Community's law and policies. Since the European Court has asserted in its case-law that member-states may not engage in judicial review of Community law under the national fundamental rights standards (*Internationale Handelgesellschaft*, op. cit. section 10(4)), judicial protection of fundamental rights within Community law would acquire the character of an exclusive and self-contained system.

The obvious advantage of such a system for Italy, as for other member-states, is that it enriches the fundamental rights categories accepted at the national level by adding to them the Community law dimension. A vague and, perhaps, non-justifiable principle on non-discrimination based on sex in national law could acquire a more precise content in the context of Community law and thus become directly applicable in Italy and capable of overriding inconsistent national legislation by way of the supremacy of Community law.

Another possible advantage of the system that is now developing is that the consolidation of a bundle of fundamental rights in Community law might eventually lead to their incorporation into national law, thereby expanding the catalogue of fundamental rights provided by the Constitution and other national legislation. This process, as we all know, has taken place at some point in the life of federal states such as the United States, when the bill of rights becomes 'incorporated' into the law of the individual states. This process has not yet taken place in Europe and the protection of fundamental rights remains at present characterized as a system of judicial review of the legality of Community law, and not of member-states' action. However, since the creative jurisprudence of the European Court tends to build a true core of higher human rights law, not only within the autonomous sources of community law but also by reference to the heteronomous sources of the Common constitutional principles of member-states and of the international human rights treaties to which they are parties, it is perfectly feasible that new fundamental rights that are not originally part of the Italian constitutional system may be created by Community actions. To give an example, it is far from certain that the often-quoted principle of 'proportionality' that has found its way into Community law, mainly by way of derivation from German law, constitutes part of the Italian heritage of fundamental rights.

The safest way to achieve this incremental result in the range of rights protected would be for the European Court to interpret its reference to the 'constitutional traditions common to member states' in such a way as to choose as a parameter of reference the state providing the highest form of protection in any particular case.

This would permit an osmosis of different principles among the member-states and the setting-up of the highest level of human rights protection within the structure and scope of Community policies (this is suggested in literature by several authors; see, for example, Pescatore, 1974, p. 499; Hartley, 1988, p. 136). However, there are no indications in the case-law that the European Court of Justice aims at this result. Nor is there any indication of a serious exercise by the Court in comparative analysis in order to determine what would be the most effective national form of protection. Besides, as has been emphasized (Gaja, 1988, pp. 578f.), the mechanical adoption of the highest national standard for certain individuals could correspondingly involve the lowering of protection for other individuals, something that in the context of Community law may give rise to the delicate issues of balancing between competing interests, such as property and free trade versus limitations of production in the interest of the common market (*Nold, Hauer*), free movement of workers versus the right to work guaranteed to citizens under article 4 of the Italian Constitution, and the like.

Notwithstanding these problematical aspects, the certain benefit accruing to Italy from the continuing development of an independent Community system of human rights protection is the progress towards the perception of a European ethos, that is towards identification by Italian citizens with a core of principles and values that will mark their identity as European citizens. It is submitted that in an epoch where the notion of individual rights dominates every aspect of modern societies, the contribution of the European Court and the Community organs to the development of an unwritten charter of fundamental rights may be the most important factor in developing a true European polity beyond the 'utilitarian' model of the 'common' or 'single' European market.

10.6 Weaknesses and pitfalls of the EC approach to the protection of fundamental rights

If we turn now from the bright side to the shadows and weaknesses inherent in the protection of fundamental rights by the Community, the following shortcomings and risks may be briefly evaluated.

First of all, from the Italian point of view – that is, from the point of view of a state adhering to the dualist concept of the relationship between domestic law and international law and of a centralized system of judicial review based on the rigidity of the Constitution – it is easy to understand how difficult it is to accept the idea that the guarantee of fundamental rights and freedoms may be delegated to the European Court. This delegation, of course, would occur only in areas occupied by Community policies. Yet the increasing expansion of Community competences renders these areas subject to uncertain boundaries. Should, for instance, a provision of Italian legislation concerning the regulation of extra-Community workers become automatically subject to exclusive review by the European Court under article 177 simply because it is related to an emerging Community policy on the matter? The Court has taken a restrictive approach in recent case-law. In the *Demirel* case concerning the right of Turkish workers to reunite with their families (case no. 12/86, 1987), it has refused to review national legislation under a general principle applicable to the protection of human rights (the right to the respect of family life recognized also by article 8 of the European Convention), because in the specific circumstances the subject matter was regulated only by national law and such law was not related to the implementation of any provision of Community law. So that the Court can enforce fundamental rights against member-states' action, it is thus necessary that the field in which such action has taken place be already covered by Community legislation (see also the decision rendered in the case *Cinétheque,* nos. 60 and 61/82, ECR 1984: 1510ff., refusing to review French legislation imposing a waiting period between the release of a film and its commercialization on video-cassettes under the principle of freedom of speech recognized by article 10 of the European Convention).

Although so limited in its scope of application, the transfer to the European Court of the exclusive competence to review the compatibility of Community law with fundamental rights has been criticized in Italy (Conforti, 1987), especially on the basis of the legitimacy argument (i.e. the Community is not a federal state and the guarantee of individual rights must remain rooted in the national systems for as long as the Community remains an economic entity characterized by the lack of a true charter of rights). The Italian Constitutional Court, after early oscillations – ranging from the explicit recognition of the admissibility of constitutional control over the European Coal and Steel Community law (judgment no. 98 of 27 December 1965) to the outright rejection of such control on the theory that Community law is a separate system already endowed with its own judicial remedies (judgment no. 183 of 27 December 1973) – has recently taken the view that it retains the competence to 'ascertain … whether a provision of the [EC] Treaty, as interpreted and applied by the Community's institution, be in conflict with the principles of our constitutional system or with the inalienable rights of the human person … ' (*Spa Fragd* v. *Amministrazione delle Finanze,* case no. 232 of 21 April 1989). The principle involved in this case was that of article 24 of the Constitution concerning the right of judicial protection and to obtain a remedy. In this decision the Italian Constitution Court signalled that the national loss of judicial review competence in favour of the Community system cannot be pushed beyond a critical threshold that is marked by the absence of an alternative effective remedy in Community law against the clear infringement of a fundamental right guaranteed under the Italian Constitution. This doctrine must be approved not only because it is consistent with the ultimate safeguard of the nucleus of inalienable rights guaranteed by national constitutions – such as due process and access to justice – but also because, as a matter of policy, it is the best incentive to the further development and refinement by the European Court of its independent system of judicial review of Community action under human rights standards.

If we move now from the functional–institutional level to the substantive law level, a more subtle national loss may be identified with regard to the net result of the balancing between individual rights and limitations on such rights required in the 'public interest'. As already mentioned, the tendency of the European Court is generally to proclaim *in abstracto* the fundamental right at stake but then to uphold the Community action or the national action in the implementation of a Community policy, either because the human rights principles are not applicable (*Defrenne*), or because the alleged infringement does not arise in an area covered by Community law (*Cinéthèque*), or because the fundamental right to be protected – be it the common core of member-states' constitutional principles or their human rights treaties – is fairly general in content and subject to limitations both in community law and in national law (Rutili, Hauer). The reference to permissible limitations raises the question: what is the 'public interest' in the light of which the legality of the limitation must be assessed? Is it the Community interest? Is it the social, security and national interest of the member-state? The indications offered by the European Court jurisprudence so far point to the general Community interest. It could not be otherwise, since the Court is not the judge of national interests. Thus, in cases involving the problematic balancing of property rights against the public interest to impose limitations on such rights in the general social and economic interest, the Court has gauged such interest at the level of Community policies and objectives. In Hauer, the question was whether Community legislation restricting the freedom of planting new vineyards, which was intended to limit excess production of wine in the Community, could amount to a breach of the fundamental right to property and to the free pursuit of economic activities of the German owner. The Court based its negative answer to this question on the finding that under the constitutions of member-states (specific reference was made only to the Italian, German and Irish Constitutions), and under the First Protocol to the European Convention, the rights in question were not absolute but carried permissible limitations in the general interest similar in kind and intensity to the Community legislation at issue.

What is the cost sustained at the national level as a consequence of this method? Quite simply, it consists in the possibility that the 'public interest' justifying the sacrifice of the individual right exists only at the European level and not at the national level. To remain within the factual circumstances of Hauer, the general interest to limit wine production can hardly be a national interest for Germany, a net importer of wine. By the same token, the imposition of restrictions on the production of milk in Italy is certainly not in the national public interest of a country heavily dependent on imports of such a commodity. The Court's approach makes sense in the specific field of limitations of production or quotas required by the achievement of Community policies. However, it carries the subtle risk of giving the Community institutions a blank cheque for holding as 'reasonable' any restriction on human rights required by a Community objective regardless of compelling 'local' considerations.

Another weakness of the present system of Community protection of human rights is the lack of uniformity due to the absence of the 'incorporation' of the emerging corpus of community rights into the legal system of member-states. At present this lack of uniformity is hardly bridged by the judicial activism of the European Court. Despite the increasing number of decisions making reference to the common constitutional principles of member-states, the jurisprudence of the European Court has not yet resulted in a systematic regime of distillation of truly common principles with regard to the twelve states whose constitutional traditions remain quite different, including differences in emphasis with regard to social and economic rights.

It is true that the frequent reference to the European Convention on Human Rights works as a unifying element. However, the Convention has never been formally adopted in the Community legal system. It simply works as a material source of inspiration for the fashioning of Community rights on a case-by-case basis. Furthermore, as a recent Italian study has cogently demonstrated (Gaja, 1988, pp. 581ff), the European Court tends to construe the applicable right by a generic reference to the provisions of the Convention without undertaking a detailed analysis of the implementing practice of the Strasbourg organs. This shortcoming might prove fatal, especially in the area of permissible limitations on rights, were the European Court to decide in favour of the legality of a restriction which later was declared incompatible with the European Convention by the Strasbourg organs (see Gaja, ibid.). This uncertain interaction between the Community rights and the European Convention on Human Rights might have been cured by the Community's adhesion to the European Convention. However, this possibility seems at the moment to have lost political momentum so that the burden remains for the European Court of Justice to clarify and refine the scope of Community rights by reference also to the case-law interpreting and applying the rights and freedoms contained in the European Convention.

10.7 Conclusions

Anticipating the process taking place in the evolution of the constitutional structure of federal states, the European Court and the political organs of the Community have supported the making and development of a substantive and jurisdictional system of human rights protection. This system, applied originally as a form of administrative justice intended to prevent the Community organs from overstepping their competences, is liable to experience progressive evolution towards judicial review of the legality of state action in areas covered by Community law or related to its implementation. In the future it may even crystallize into a system of higher law applicable even to the review of member-states' action in areas not covered by Community law (indications in this sense emerge from the *Klensch* cases, nos. 201 and 202/85 of 25 November 1986, commented on by Weiler, 1987, p. 824).

The effects of this Community policy on the Italian legal system may constitute some costs. At the jurisdictional level, the main cost is to be evaluated by reference to the centralized system of judicial review embodied in the ConstitutionalCourt. At the present stage, a complete loss of control by the Constitutional Court over the observance of fundamental rights would be too high a price to pay for the nascent Community human rights system. The above analysis shows that recent case-law of the Italian Constitutional Court tends to resist the complete transfer of jurisdictional powers to the European Court in this area.

At the substantive level, some disadvantages may arise from the present system as a result of the uncertain scope of Community rights, the possibility that reference to the common tradition of member-states may set the substantive standard of protection at the lowest common denominator, and the uncertain interaction between community rights and the European Convention on Human Rights.

Also the notion of 'general interest' of the Community, as a source of permissible limitation on fundamental rights, may lead, if not properly balanced with the national interest of the member-states, to an overly broad construction by the European Court under the pressure of compelling Community policy objectives.

Ultimately, however, one must recognize that the most significant benefit accruing to Italy from the current Community attempt to develop a system of human rights protection is its value as a catalyst for further integration. In this area the emerging of a common legacy of fundamental rights offers a unique opportunity for Italy to join in an enterprise that aims at building a European polity, not simply a single market.

Bibliography

Cappelletti, M. and De Witte B. (1986), *Enforcing the International Law of Human Rights: The Case of Italy*, Italian National Reports to the XII International Congress of Comparative Law, Sydney, 1986, Milan: Giuffré, pp. 319–35, at p. 335.

Caggiano, G. D. (1976), 'Some reflections on the Treaty of Osimo between Italy and Yugoslavia', *Italian Yearbook of International Law*, 248ff.

Cassese, A. (1975), 'Commento agli art. 10 e 11' *Commentario della Costituzione*, vol. I: Bologna, 461ff.

Cassese, A. (1984), *Il diritto internazionale nel mondo contemporaneo*, Bologna, Il Mulino.

Cassese, A., Clapham, A., Weiler, J. (1992) – *What are our Rights? Agenda for a Human Rights Action Plan*, European University Working Paper No. 90/2, Florence, 1990.

Conforti, B. (1987), *Diritto Internazionale*, Napoli, ESI.

Gaja, G. (1988), 'Aspetti problematici della tutela dei diritti fondamentali nell' ordinamento comunitario', *Rivista dir. int. le*, 574ff.

Hartley, T. (1988), *The Foundations of European Community Law*, 2nd ed., Oxford.

Nascimbene, B. (1988), *Lo straniero nel diritto italiano*, Milano, Giuffré.

Offeddu, M. (1973), *Le convenzioni internazionali del lavoro e l'ordinamento giuridico italiano*, Padova.

Pescatore, P. (1974), *Les exigences de la démocraticité et la legitimité de la Communauté Européenne*, Cahiers de droit européen, 1974, 499ff.

Weiler, J. (1982), 'The European Court at a crossroads: Community human rights and member states action', in *Du Droit international au droit de l'integration, Liber amicorum Pierre Pescatore*, Baden-Baden.

Chapter 11

European integration and the Italian political system

Maurizio Cotta

11.1 The analysis of political costs and benefits of European integration

What are the effects of the process of European integration on national political systems? How does the special character of each country – in our case Italy – affect the net balance of costs and benefits? The attempt to provide some answers to these questions is most timely, in this historical moment, which will probably be remembered as a major turning point in the building of a supranational European community.

The process of European integration is a long-term process and its pace is far from continuous and unilinear. Periods of stagnation are followed by acceleration that in turn are followed by deceleration. The end of the 1980s and the beginning of the 1990s have seen a concurrence of internal and external factors that might create out of this period an important phase of growth and transformation. The implementation of the goal of a fully open European market by 1992 and the agreements reached to build supranational institutions for the regulation of European currencies and of a common monetary system, on the one hand, and the important challenges originating from the new international order developing out of the collapse of the Soviet bloc, on the other, are undoubtedly going to put to the test the ability of the European Community to cope with two of the most critical functions of any political system – regulation of the economy and action in the international arena. It is still too early to forecast whether the European Community will be able to accept the challenge and fully exploit the extraordinary opportunities at hand, but important changes will in any case take place.

For all these reasons, the present historical moment encourages a twofold appraisal of the effects of European integration: an evaluation of past effects and also speculations about the future.

In the economic field it has become fashionable, when analysing the effects of European integration to speak of costs and benefits. As a consequence quantitative measures of the net benefits or costs of past and future steps in the process have been offered. Can we adopt this approach in the political field as well and in a similar way evaluate the political costs and benefits of the integrative process?

A word of caution is required. We must not forget the important limitations that this method faces when transposed to the political field. Evaluating an effect as a cost or benefit obviously requires a criterion for determining its negative or positive value. And to assess the net aggregate benefit of a complex political process (as for instance European integration) would require a criterion of evaluation shared by most observers as well as by the actors involved in the political process and a common unit of measurement. These conditions exist at least to some extent in the domain of economic reasoning. The growth of national and individual income is generally considered a good thing (and therefore whatever produces that increase can be seen as a benefit and the opposite as a cost), and we have the instruments for measuring such quantities. Admittedly, if we go deeper than that, a number of difficult problems arise in the economic field, too. But in the political domain calculating costs and benefits is bound to be much more controversial from the outset. We do not have a dominant criterion as clearly established as the growth of national income to evaluate whether progress is being made or not. On the contrary, criteria of evaluation can be manifold; they may vary from country to country and, within countries, from one actor to another. As a consequence, what is for some countries or actors a benefit may be for others a cost. Finally, a quantitative measurement is often impossible.

This said, however, we should not forget the fact that the language of costs and benefits is often used in the political field. Calculations of political costs and benefits are obviously made by the relevant political actors. It is difficult to believe that only economic evaluations are made and that the political effects are not assessed and judged. It is reasonable to assume that the results of a retrospective and prospective calculation of political costs and benefits are reflected in the attitudes expressed *vis-à-vis* future steps of European integration by different actors. Moreover, developments of the integration process and in particular the pace with which it proceeds will be affected by the results of this calculation.

Therefore, even if it proves difficult finally to attain a global evaluation of the political costs and benefits of the process of European integration, it may be possible to come up with a number of more partial views that provide some understanding of how the effects of the process are judged (or will be judged) by the relevant actors in a political system.

In this perspective a starting point for the discussion of the Italian case can be offered by looking at the attitude and behaviour of the most significant Italian political actors at the élite and mass level *vis-à-vis* the problem of European integration. We may try to use them to understand what calculation of costs and benefits has been made by them in the past and what criteria of judgement have been employed. We may then try to project this analysis into the future and speculate about the consequences of the next steps in the process of integration.

The signs that in Italy the calculation of costs and benefits yields a positive result for a very large majority are rather strong.

If we look at mass attitudes, Eurobarometers, which since the 1970s have examined them regularly, offer a very consistent image: over the years and compared with their counterparts in the rest of Europe, Italians have always been among the most favourable to European integration; they are among those who are more convinced that their country has benefited from it and among those who would be more sorry if the European Community were not continued

(Eurobarometer, 1990, n.33). They also show very high rates of approval for any proposal for increasing the powers of European institutions (such as the European Parliament or the European 'currency') (Eurobarometer, 1990; Merusi, Padoan, Colasanti and Vilella, 1987, pp. 210–13).

The results do not change much when we move from the mass to the élite level. It is enough to consider the frequent pronouncements of all major political actors in favour of European integration. Indeed, since the 1970s, no Italian party has adopted an anti-European platform. On the contrary, all share a very pro-European position. A more specific analysis of a subset of the Italian political élite, the members of the European Parliament, shows an extremely high rate of support among them for European integration when compared to the attitudes of members from other countries (Bardi, 1989, p. 92).

If we shift our attention from attitudes to behaviour, the picture is further strengthened by the fact that Italian governments have rather consistently approved all the steps towards tighter European integration. In no case have they opposed them. In the field of behaviour there is, however, a somewhat contradictory sign: when we turn from grand decisions to implementation, the degree of Europeanism declines. Italy has indeed often been faulted for being 'lazy' in putting European rules and regulations into practice. As a consequence, the number of judicial proceedings against Italian authorities for violations of European directives has been rather high. And in another area, that of monetary integration, Italy has participated until recently in the EMS only under special conditions.

How can we interpret this basic information? First and foremost, it indicates significant concordance on the net benefits that are to be gained by Italy from participating in European integration. There are also some indications that certain aspects of integration are perceived as not being without costs. These costs, however, are mostly kept away from open discussion and do not affect the general attitudes towards Europe. They only produce special strategies (mainly originating from state bureaucracy and interest groups) directed at minimizing their impact.

The next step is to discuss what have been the main criteria of evaluation behind this very positive assessment of the benefits of European integration. Aside from the economic aspects (primarily the assumption that joining company with richer countries will also favour internal growth), which have naturally played a very important role, two fundamental political reasons have been at the root of the strong pro-European feelings shared in the Italian political system. Even if they have not always been articulated in a very explicit way, their substance is not too difficult to understand and is strictly connected with the two main types of effects of the process of supranational integration. The first reason rests on the anticipated impact of European integration upon the role of the country in the international arena: integration with countries that have a higher international status is perceived as providing important opportunities for Italy to enhance its position. The second is based upon the expected effects of the new supranational community on the internal structure of the national political system: joining more stable countries is seen as a way of strengthening the internal stability of democratic institutions.

From this preliminary assessment, one point stands out clearly. When we discuss the global effects (or costs and benefits) of a transnational process such as European integration, we should be aware that they are the result of both 'common' and 'country-specific' factors. The build-up of supranational rules, institutions, decision-making arenas, authorities, etc., is obviously 'common' to all the countries involved. But the consequences that all this has for national units do not depend mechanistically on the nature and scale of supranational developments but also on many specific conditions of each country (such as its international role, internal political stability, degree of legitimacy of political élites, effectiveness of policy-making institutions, etc.). This means also that when we try to forecast the future effects (benefits and costs) of the process of European integration we should take into account not only progress at the supranational level but also the changing political conditions within each national unit.

In the following pages I will discuss how common and country-specific effects of supranational integration have blended together in the Italian case and, as far as possible, I will try to assess what the future results of this function will be and to what extent they will differ from the past in the hypothesis of a sustained growth of integration. In this analysis I will treat the international and the internal dimensions of the problem separately.

11.2 The international dimension of European integration

A process of supranational integration is, by its very nature, bound to change the system of international relations in many ways and in particular to affect the role and status of member-countries within that system. From the point of view of member-countries, its effects will take the form both of opportunities and constraints and will concern, on one hand, the relations of member-countries among themselves, and, on the other hand, those relations of member countries with other units of the international system.

With regard to relations among member countries, supranational integration is both a sign and sanction of friendly and co-operative relations with the aim of excluding serious conflicts among them. This was an important aspect at the beginning of European integration, particularly with regard to the German–French relationship. This aspect did not play such a significant role for Italy, which did not have major open conflicts with any of the other member-countries (if there were any potentially irksome problems with neighbouring countries, they were historically with Austria, which, however, has remained outside the European Community). More relevant from the Italian point of view was the fact that European integration blurred the distinction between winners and losers of the Second World War. The Common Market (and other international organizations such as NATO) helped Italy as well as Germany to leave the ghetto of the losers and to join on an equal footing countries such as France and, later, the United Kingdom, which were considered the winners.

But probably a crucial component of Italian support for European integration has been the expectations about its positive effects on the international status and role of the country. What were the grounds for such expectations? In order to understand them, we must discuss briefly some implications of the process of supranational integration.

The process of supranational integration necessarily entails some degree of co-ordination of the international behaviour of member-countries and at least a partial transfer of competences in the field of international politics from national units to supranational authorities. The consequences are not bound to be the same for all countries. Indeed, perceptions can vary greatly. We may reasonably expect that countries that already enjoy a high status in the international community stand to gain less from this transformation than countries that have a lower status. For the latter, joining a larger group may mean stepping at least indirectly (through the supranational union) into the 'big game' of international politics. This may well compensate for the obvious constraints that derive from the integrative process. The opposite is going to be true for the former. What they gain from integration may not seem to be much more than what they already had and what they lose in terms of freedom of action may appear substantial, unless, of course, they are able to take a leading role within the supranational unit. Finally, there may be countries whose international status is much less clear.

We need not discuss here the factors (size, population, economic resources, history, etc.) that may determine the international status of a country. It is sufficiently clear, however, that countries with differing status belong to the European Community. There are, on the one hand, countries such as France and the United Kingdom which have historically belonged to the rather exclusive club of 'great powers' and which still have this role acknowledged through their permanent membership in the Security Council of the United Nations. On the other hand, there is a number of small countries – Belgium, Luxembourg, the Netherlands, to which were later added Ireland, Denmark and then Greece and Portugal – which, because of their size, have been only secondary players on the international scene (and have to a large extent accepted that role, making the best of the advantages that go with it). In between there are countries that for different reasons have a more uncertain status. Germany is a case in point: with the past role of a great power and the present one of an economic giant it has seen its international political status hampered by memories of its imperialistic attempts under Nazism and of its disruptive defeat in the Second World War. For different reasons, Italy shares a similarly ambiguous position: too big to be satisfied with the status of a small country, but at the same time never able to make it into the 'big league'.

If we look at how countries have reacted to the impact of supranational integration on their international role, it is not difficult to relate differences between countries to their specific international status. The countries which already had a high status have not been particularly keen to promote a strong international EC role and have generally tried to preserve their own autonomous role. It is enough to mention the special relationship of the United Kingdom with the United States and also the rather independent role of France in many areas of international relations. On the other side, the small countries have generally favoured an increased international role of the European Community (except when they feared that it might affect their own distinctive identity). The balance of costs and benefits for the countries with a more ambiguous status could in theory be less clear. In the Italian case it is quickly seen why benefits are perceived as outweighing costs. It is true that Italy is for its size and population one of the big countries within the EC; however, in spite of its size it has never belonged to the group of first rank countries in Europe. For many reasons, in particular its late unification and delayed industrial development, it has been confined to a second-ary rank in the international arena. Being a large country without the correspond-ing rank has often become a source of frustration for Italy during the last century. This was particularly evident after the First World War when, at the peace conference, it could not get what many of its leaders thought it deserved to obtain. And new frustrations followed when the nationalistic exaltation of the Fascist period produced the humiliating defeat in the Second World War. Belonging to a supranational union based on the principle of parity among member-countries (and on the assumption that this union would gain a role in the international scene) could be seen in Italy as the best way to solve this old and recurrent frustration.

To support this interpretation we need only look at the extent to which the 'Italian semester', when the *pro tempore* leadership of the community falls upon the shoulders of Italy, has been perceived by politicians and the mass media as a moment when the Italian government could be acknowledged as a significant player in the world arena. As could be expected, the emphasis on the Italian semester was particularly strong in 1990 when a critical international situation – the occupation of Kuwait – gave special priority to international politics.

Obviously the importance of these benefits (but also of the potential risks of a stronger international role) has been curtailed by the fact that until the Eastern European upheaval the two dominant actors in the international scene were the United States and the Soviet Union, while the European Community lacked specific competence in the field of foreign policy and produced only voluntary processes of consultation.

The international aspect of European integration is bound to be much more important with the far-reaching international realignment that is now under way. The new order that the whole of Europe ('West' and 'East' now having lost much of their meaning) awaits is a source of unforeseen challenges for the European Community, not only at the economical but also at the political level. There is little doubt that demands for stronger co-ordination of the foreign policies of member-countries in this area will increase. In another sphere as well – that of the Middle East, with the Gulf War over but a stable peaceful settlement far from achieved – European countries are equally stimulated to meditate over the limits, set by their weak instruments of supranational co-ordination in the fields of foreign and military policy, to their international effectiveness (both political and military) in an area so close to their borders and to their vital interests.

All this means that there is a good chance (although not a deterministic expectation) that the European Community will in the future have a stronger voice in the field of international relations, increasing as a consequence the benefits of participation for lower-status countries. It is interesting to mention that in 1990 it was suggested (by some Italian leaders as well as by others) that in the future, instead of two of its member countries (France and the United Kingdom), the EC itself should have a permanent seat in the Security Council of the United Nations.

What is going to happen with the future progress of integration? The potential benefits deriving from integration will indeed grow, but it is reasonable to assume that costs also will become greater. Even for a second-rank country like Italy, costs arising from participation in a larger integrated unit may become substantial. In the first place, some degree of freedom of manoeuvring may be lost. A good example of this may be what happened during the Kuwait crisis; Italy, having the *pro tempore* presidency of the EC, had to take a much more clear-cut position *vis-à-vis* Iraq than it would have otherwise probably held. Furthermore, the potential for conflict between participation in the international activities of the Community and previous international linkages of a member country is bound to increase. And, finally, the internal costs of foreign engagements (both in terms of budgetary choices and of public support) may also become more significant.

Another point has to be mentioned in this perspective. The more important the international role of the European Community becomes (probably more slowly on matters of war and peace, but more substantially on matters of international economic, commercial and monetary policies), the greater the political stakes become. We may therefore expect that the struggle among member-countries (but also among other actors such as interest groups that may cut across national boundaries) to influence the European decision-making process will become more acute. Considering the limited attention that in the past the Italian political élite has given to problems of international politics, compared to political élites of the other bigger European countries, the risk that Italy might play only a secondary role in the making of European international policies should not be discarded lightly. A reasonable forecast is therefore that the positive balance between benefits and costs might become less clear in the future.

11.3 The internal effects of integration

But as we have said before, the process of European integration is not only relevant for the way it changes the international environment and the status of a country within it. It should be evaluated also for its potential effects upon important aspects of the internal political scene.

From this point of view the favourable attitudes *vis-à-vis* the process of European integration, shared in Italy initially by a large majority (against a sizeable dissenting minority) both at the élite (Walker, 1976) and at the mass level, and with the passing of time by a near unanimity, have historically found solid ground in the problem of democratic stability. In a country, such as Italy, where the new democratic institutions after the Second World War had to face a difficult process of consolidation (Morlino, 1981; Cotta, 1990) and the challenge of a strong anti-system opposition (Sartori, 1976), the integration within a larger supranational system, of which other more stable democratic countries were part, was perceived by large components of public opinion as a useful 'insurance' against the risks of a democratic breakdown. In this perspective the governing parties could make their decision to bring Italy into Europe and their linkages with some of the major European political forces (Christian Democratic, Socialist and Liberal) very important instruments for strengthening and consolidating their electoral support against the attacks of the opposition.

One might suggest that the European variable (at the same time a legitimating and a constraining factor) helps significantly to explain the ability of such a polarized political system to survive, in spite of the unfavourable odds, and then to overcome its major original weakness.

This role of European integration as a buttress of the political and socioeconomic system was in the past also the main reason behind the only strong dissenting opinion on Europe, that of the largest opposition party (Walker, 1976; Galante, 1988). The initial hostility of the PCI to European integration had very much to do with the strong identification of that party with the Soviet Union and its political and social system. European integration was perceived as a major obstacle for the transformation of Italy in this direction.

With the passing of time, the decreasing identification of the PCI with the Soviet Union, along with its increasing propensity to accept the fundamental aspects of pluralistic democracy and market economy have brought this party, too, to share the general pro-European mood. Furthermore, beginning in the 1970s, Europe has come to play a very significant role in the strategy of this party which has been directed at obtaining its full legitimation within the Italian political system. By actively seeking (and publicizing) co-operative relations with other parties of the left within the European Community, in particular with the German SPD, at a time when its own relations with the national Socialist Party were by far more difficult, the Communist Party has tried to present itself to Italian public opinion as a 'normal' left-wing party. This is another interesting example of how the supranational political arena can be used for national political purposes.

With the decreasing importance of the problem of democratic stability, one of the reasons for the strong Europeanism of Italians has lost some of its relevance. But other reasons have continued to bring the European theme into internal politics. A major reason, which deserves special attention, has to do with the features of the policy-making process in the Italian political system. Given the high level of fragmentation of political actors (and particularly of governmental majorities), the policy-making process has been strongly and consistently biased in the direction of distributive (in the sense of Lowi, 1972) and micro-sectional outputs (Di Palma, 1976) designed to placate all interests. The effects of this type of policy-making are sufficiently clear: among them the large public deficit is the most prominent. It is well known, however, that, since public resources are limited, there are limits also to distributive policies. And constantly in order to re-equilibrate the financial situation, there is a need to adopt more severe policies that cut benefits and reallocate costs (Regonini, 1985). Faced with such a situation, Italian political élites (and more specifically the governmental leadership) have had to find special ways to legitimize their action. International constraints, such as recommendations of the IMF, have often been used in order to justify unpopular fiscal and monetary measures. It is easy to see, even without a systematic analysis of the policy-making process, that Europe has come to play an increasingly important

role along these lines, partly because, with increasing monetary integration (originating from participation in the EMS), constraints have become real, but also,
beyond such real factors, because more symbolic and less easily measured influences could be evoked and brought into play. It must be noted that Europe has
become a strong symbol of legitimation. In the mass media and in public opinion
the standards of European countries have to a great extent replaced American
standards as a yardstick of accomplishment. The need to keep within the fold of
European integration and to avoid being left behind by the leading European
countries is therefore often brought into the political debate by political élites in
order to increase the legitimacy of austerity measures. We might interpret this as a
way of reducing the internal costs of a policy by appealing to its supranational
benefits.

The question that has to be raised is what role the 'European Card' will play in
the national policy-making process once supranational integration reaches a higher
stage. The fairly easy forecast is that the symbolic and somewhat elusive aspects
that were important in the past will play a gradually less important role *vis-à-vis*
more substantial and real constraints. A number of 'difficult' decisions will have to
be taken not only to pursue the persuasive and ill-defined goal of 'keeping up with
the Europeans' but also in order to implement precise policies decided at the
supranational level. This means that the 'European card' will play a greater role in
the national decision-making process but at the same time will be less amenable to
manipulation by national politicians.

To the extent that the linkages between supranational and internal decision-
making processes will gain greater weight and the effects of European constraints
upon national decisions will become stronger, we may expect also that the
assessment of costs and benefits will be based less on symbolic and more on down-
to-earth criteria of evaluation. Together with benefits, supranational costs will also
become more real and visible. It will be less easy to exploit only the advantages of
being part of Europe and to conceal the negative sides. To some extent this will be
due also to the changes that are to be expected in the European policy-making
process. In order to solve some of the problems of integration, the typical
distributive policies that in the past have played such a dominant role in the
European Community (the Agricultural policies of the EC are the clearest example) and that have produced highly visible benefits but concealed the costs will
have to be complemented with other types of policies. And these policies will not
have a costs/benefits combination so favourable for political élites.

The next question that has to be asked is whether we may expect in the future a
more structural impact of the process of supranational integration upon the
political systems of member countries. Any forecast is obviously made more
difficult by the very uncertainty of the process of supranational integration. To
what extent the supranational arena will gain prominence over national politics
within five or ten years is not easy to anticipate. It is sufficiently clear, however,
that regulation of the economy, i.e. one of the major policy domains for all
contemporary states and a domain crucial for the popular evaluation of performances of any democratic government, will increasingly fall under the control of
supranational decision-making bodies (the European Council, the Commission,

and the new monetary institutions that will be developed in the near future). At the same time national authorities will lose a substantial amount of autonomous control over crucial decisions. It is worthwhile exploring (albeit necessarily in a very hypothetical way) what effects these developments could have on the performances of national political systems and, in connection with this, on the legitimacy and the political weight of national élites and institutions.

On the one hand, the fact that an increasing number of decisions are being taken away from the national decision-making system (i.e. from the parliament–government–parties circuit) could be seen, from an Italian perspective, as a benefit. If not political élites, at least Italian public opinion, which surveys show to be the least satisfied in Europe with the working of the national political system (Eurobarometer, 1990), would certainly agree. In any case it could be suggested that, given the low performance of the Italian system, freeing it from some burdens might potentially leave it with greater capacities to cope with the competences that are left. We should not forget, however, another side of the problem. The loss of control over a range of important issues will also deprive the national policy-making system of some crucial political resources, thereby reducing its legitimacy and the level of public support it enjoys. Given the fact that the situation of the Italian political system is from this point of view already far from brilliant, the negative consequences might be severe. We should not underestimate the possibility that as a result the national political system could be left seriously weakened and as a consequence unable to face effectively the duties that will still have to be performed at that level. Countervailing strategies might become necessary. A well-organized redistribution of decisional competences also in the direction of the regional level could probably help create a less congested and more efficient national level. But in the end the real answer could come only from a serious reform of some of the central components of the national policy-making institutions and of the way they work – a reform that should in the first place reactivate popular support for these institutions.

Since the supranational decision-making process will be based to a large extent on the participation of national élites, the net effects of these transformations for Italy will depend to a significant extent also on the ability of the Italian political élite to perform successfully in the supranational arena when national interests are at stake. If national politicians can in the supranational decision-making arenas stage a successful representation and defence of Italian interests, they will 're-legitimate' themselves also in the national political system, via the supranational role. If, however, they are perceived by public opinion to be too often on the losing side in European decisions, they will also face a difficult situation at home. Their ability to lead and govern in the national policy-making arena will be further diminished by supranational failures. Interests will look for alternative channels of representation and in any case will become less easy to control.

In order to forecast the effects of further steps in the integrative process, a crucial question therefore concerns the linkages between national and supranational levels, and, in particular, how the different national élites that to a great extent make up the supranational policy-making system (truly supranational élites being still a minor component of it) will interact. A further question is what balance of power will emerge from that.

Which national élites will become more influential and which will be on the losing side in the supranational arena? An answer is obviously difficult. Some of the characteristics of the Italian political élite suggest, however, that it will find itself at a disadvantage unless important changes in its structure take place. In particular, its high level of fragmentation and its limited ability to produce strong and stable leadership and long-term agreements will prove serious weaknesses in the competition with the political élites of the other big countries of the European Community, all of which share lower levels of fragmentation and stronger leadership.

11.4 Conclusions

Although much of our discussion has been by necessity highly hypothetical, it seems sufficiently clear to conclude that the rather simple balance of political costs and benefits of participation in the process of European integration, which has sustained the strong pro-European feelings of Italy in the past, is bound to change in the future. If in the past political costs were extremely limited and clearly outweighed by benefits, in the future, as a consequence of significant developments in supranational integration, some substantial political costs will probably materialize. The potential increase of benefits will also be relevant, but the net balance might not be as clearly positive as in the past. It may also happen that the balance of costs and benefits will yield different results for different actors within the national political system.

In the end I do not think that such divergencies will be able to reverse the dominant support of European integration expressed today by Italian masses and élites. But the theme of Europe will probably lose the aura of unanimity it presently has and will be subjected to the scrutiny of political debate in a more controversial way.

Bibliography

Bardi, L. (1989), *Il Parlamento della comunità Europea*, Il Mulino, Bologna.

Cotta, M. (1990), 'The "centrality" of Parliament in a protracted democratic consolidation: the Italian case', in Ulrike Liebert and Maurizio Cotta (eds), *Parliament and Democratic Consolidation in Southern Europe*, London: Pinter.

Di Palma, G.(1976), *Surviving Without Governing*, Berkeley: University of California Press.

Eurobarometer (1990), 'Directorate general Information', n. 33, Communication, Culture of the European Commission, Brussels.

Galante, S. (1988), *Il Partito comunista italiano e l'integrazione europea,* Padua: Liviana Editrice.

Lowi, T. J. (1972), 'Four systems of policy, politics and choice', *Public Administration Review, vol. 32: 298–310.*

Merusi, F., Padoan, P. C., Colasanti, F. and Vilella, G. C. (1987), *L'integrazione monetaria dell'Europa*, Bologna: Il Mulino.

Morlino, L. (1981) 'Del fascismo a una democracia débil: el cambio de régimen en Italia (1939–1948)', in Julian Santamaria (ed.), *Transicion a la democracia en el sur de Europa y America Latina*, Madrid: Centro de Investigaciones Sociologicas.

Regonini, G. (1985), 'Le politiche sociali in Italia: metodi di analisi', *Rivista Italiana di Scienza Politica*, vol. 15, no. 3: 335–77.

Sartori, G. (1976), *Parties and Party Systems*, Cambridge: Cambridge University Press.

Walker, R. (1976), *I partiti politici italiani e l'integrazione europea*, Il Mulino, Bologna.

PART IV: SOCIAL POLICY

Chapter 12

Community objectives and national goals in the field of social policy

Grazia Atanasio

12.1

In Italy the impact of a Community social policy and the debate on the social dimension of the internal market become part of a wider context of discussion on the reform of the Italian model of the welfare state (Ferrera, 1985) and of the 'new deal' of Italian labour policies (CNEL, 1985; Galantino, 1985; Giugni, 1986).

By the 1980s, the welfare state concept that had developed out of the post-war experience had reached the point of crisis, culminating in a necessary reform of the Italian model which had proved to be inadequate and ineffective not only as a result of the economic crisis but also of two constant, opposing ideas about social security. One was intended as a guarantee against need, providing a minimum wage and extended to the whole population by means of general solidarity (the so-called 'universalistic' model of the United Kingdom); the other was intended as a guarantee of income by way of an insurance system or categories contribution (the 'particularistic' model of France and Germany) (Piccininno 1989, p. 20).

The reform of 1983–7 aimed at establishing a more selective system of defining taxes by reference to the family income, and, as a consequence, at increasing the number of beneficiaries. In order to achieve this goal and to reduce the discretionary powers of central administration in managing the distribution of services and the definition of taxes, a main feature of the reform was decentralization (Treu, 1987).

Although in the field of health services the reform increased administrative ineffectiveness, decentralization at the regional level, as regards vocational training and employment agencies, seemed a better solution to the needs of local production.

The new course of Italian labour legislation, which has been described as the passage from *garantismo* to control (Cessari and De Luca Tamajo, 1982), represents a deep change in the system of industrial relations and management of the labour market. Italian labour law was characterized by a certain rigidity, aimed at securing the protection of employees' individual rights (*garantismo*), until the second half of the 1970s when the instrument of the law was substituted by trade-unions and state control, by deferment to collective bargaining, with an integrative function, but sometimes also by way of derogation of the content of the law itself. Since the 'crisis laws' of the emergency phase the introduction of greater 'flexibility' has proceeded rapidly. Direct state intervention has tended to be replaced by an extension of tripartitism and the articulated use of collective negotiation as a conscious social mechanism of change and adaptation (Mengoni, 1988).

In such a scenario which is progressively changing, the impact of Community issues is very strong. National objectives of labour policy must be evaluated from the perspective of social harmonization at Community level, though limited as regards its automatic effects, by means of the actual purport of the Single European Act, which does not consider social harmonization to be a preliminary condition to the completion of internal market, according to article 8A.

12.1.1

Indeed, it cannot be affirmed that a common social policy in proper terms exists in the European Community: member-states are principally responsible for Community social policy. According to the Treaty of Rome, Community power is limited to 'promoting close cooperation between Member States in the social field' (article 118). To this end the Treaty does not provide that the Commission shall issue any binding act, but only opinions; the legal *impasse* could be avoided by resorting to articles 100 and 235 with the obvious consequence of coming up against another *impasse,* that of Council unanimity. However, it is on the this ground that over the years, especially since the Paris summit in 1972, a Community social policy has developed (Pocar, 1983).

The most important steps have been taken in the field of employment, harmonization of working conditions and industrial democracy, even though the results have not always been satisfactory as a result of resistance among the Council of Ministers.

The new social policy envisaged by the Single European Act confined itself to two social provisions of some significance: article 118A, which represents a new legal basis for harmonization relating to working conditions and the health and safety of workers, although it is limited in its content by referring only to 'minimum requirements'; and article 118B, which introduces the notion of social dialogue at European level, but reduces its scope by adding that relations based on agreement between social partners shall depend on the goodwill of the partners.

As a result of the SEA, Community action is limited to the working environment with regard to the safety and health of workers, while the scope of application of EC social policy rests in the field of co-operation between member-states. In addition, it expressly provides the maintenance of unanimity rule as regards Council decisions concerning provisions relating to the free movement of persons and to the rights and interests of employed persons (article 100A, para. 2).

Except for the possibility of promoting social dialogue at European level and the development of economic and social cohesion by the action of the Structural Funds, the SEA has not introduced clear objectives of social policy in the Treaty (Vogel and Polski, 1989).

12.1.2

However, in view of the completion of the internal market, the debate on the need for a social policy has become more intense since it is closely linked to that of economic integration. The increased competition across the Community, as a result of the complete liberalization of the market, could have in the short term negative effects in weaker areas and sectors of the Community and could accentuate structural imbalance and regional disparities (see *Cecchini Report on the Cost of Non-Europe*, SEC/88/324 FINAL, and *Marin Memorandum on the Social Dimension of Internal Market*, SEC/88/1148 FINAL). Any significant differences in working conditions between the member-states raises the possibility that such differences could distort competition and give rise to concerns of 'social dumping'. In order to avoid such risks, greater importance has been attached to the implementation of a social policy at Community level.

In the context of the debate on the social dimension of the internal market, however, there are great differences of opinion among the social partners, on the one hand, and among the member states, on the other.

The recent adoption by the Commission of a Draft Charter of Fundamental Social Rights (COM/89/471 FINAL), presented to the summit of EC heads of state in Strasburg in December 1989 and evoking much reaction, shows how difficult the problem of Community social policy is.

The Charter, which aims to define basic rights, including minimum-wage guarantees and workers' participation in corporate decision-making, for all EC workers, is vague enough to allow for national differences in labour law, although it is not intended to be without effect. For this reason, given the British refusal to approve the Charter, the Commission has prepared an action programme (COM/89/568 FINAL) of EC legislation to ensure that the rights enshrined in the Charter are put into effect at the national, regional or local level. According to the Commission, responsibility for the initiatives to be taken as regards the implementation of social rights lies with the member states, that is, with their constituent parts of the two sides of industry as well as with, within the limits of its powers, the European Community. Thus the Commission introduces the principle of subsidiarity according to which the more suitable level for decision-making is the lowest at which the set objectives can be reached most effectively. Faced with one side of industry which considers the fixing of social policies at Community level untimely, given that market forces would ultimately determine their convergency, and the other side which claims the guarantee of fundamental social rights and the definition of minimum rules of labour and social security law, the Community position expressed by the Commission in the debate on the social dimension of the internal market appears to be a middle course between the conservative view of employers and the progressive view of trade unions.

By regulating social matters at Community level the scope of intervention of social partners could be reduced and the balance between the two main instruments of settlement on the labour market – law-making and bargaining – could be broken.

The idea of a minimum base of social rules enshrined in the Charter answers the need for the harmonization of national law in the field of labour and social security in order to avoid the situation whereby differences in financing social protection regimes – as is the case of compulsory contributions of employers varying from 53 per cent in Italy to 10 per cent in Denmark – could affect the localization of enterprises by provoking the effects of social dumping. The considerable development of very varied forms of flexible and atypical employment contracts, such as temporary work, part-time work and fixed-term contracts, also calls for a Community framework ensuring a minimum of consistency between these various forms of contract in order to avoid the danger of distortion of competition and increase the transparency of the labour market at Community level.

The Commission's choice of promoting a sort of 'framework agreement', stressing the principle of subsidiarity, can be a way to overcome the contrast between trade unions and employers, concerning the binding character of the Charter, the potential developments of social dialogue at Community level, and some member states' opposition. At the same time it is a clear affirmation that for the progressive establishment of a Community system of industrial relations, necessary to control and manage by mutual consent the economic, technical, social and production changes caused by the achievement of the internal market, it is crucial to secure complementarity between institutional law-making and the autonomous relations of social partners (Ripa di Meana, 1989, p. 69).

12.1.3

Italian ministers within the Council supported the Charter of Fundamental Social Rights and demanded, in the event it is not binding and defers to national legislation and practice, a concrete implementation through the adoption of an action programme, especially as regards 'the determination of paid leave; the continued payment of remuneration during holidays and during sickness; the protection of children and adolescents; the situation of pregnant women and of mothers with children of an early age; the professional insertion of the disabled; protection of health and safety at the workplace; vocational guidance; mutual recognition of qualifications and temporary work' (SI/89/792/2).

One reason underlying Italian support for the aims that the Community is going to propose is that, notwithstanding the recent trend towards 'deregulation' in Italian labour policy, the legal system rests firmly anchored to the protection of workers' interests; moreover, the Italian Constitution enshrines fundamental social rights and freedom. Another reason can be found in the lip-service approach to Europeanism on the part of the Italian government, even if this does not always correspond to a comparable commitment in terms of participation in the EC decision-making process and despite the frequent failure promptly to comply with EC directives (this latter, however, is not entirely an Italian problem).

But it would be rather superficial only to evaluate the reactions evoked in Italy by the recent debate on the *espace social européen*. An assessment of the compatibility between Community objectives and Italian goals in the field of social policy must take into account the impact that EC membership has had and the effects of probable developments on Italian policy positions. To this end the analysis will now be focused on the main issues of employment policy, industrial relations and worker participation.

12.2

Employment policy is a central objective of EC social policy: in this field and in that (closely linked) of vocational training, the Treaty provides the main instrument of direct Community intervention in the social field, the European Social Fund (article 123). The evolution of ESF activity, from the outset to the reform of the 1970s (Pocar, 1983, pp. 213ff.), together with the recent reform of the Structural Funds in 1988 (Santaniello, 1989), answers the need to promote and co-ordinate at EC level employment and worker mobility more concretely. From the ESF's initial function as a mere instrument of compensation for member states' expenditures in the social field to the restrictions on automatic intervention in order to develop Community action in the field of employment and worker mobility, the pattern appears to be that of creating a more flexible instrument in the context of a serious economic and employment crises. The recent reform aims especially to overcome the problems raised by two aspects of the present situation: the differences in demographic structures, employment and income between the Community's various geographical areas; and the problems encountered by specific groups in gaining access to the labour market, especially women and young people, in relation to equality of employment opportunities. The concentration of the Fund's activities on a limited number of priority objectives should make a major contribution to the growth of employment: on the one hand, because of the horizontal intervention undertaken by the ESF in the context of the fight against long-term unemployment and the promotion of the professional insertion of young people; on the other hand, in the context of interventions undertaken in relation to less advantaged regions, regions suffering from industrial decline and rural areas, by promoting stability of employment and developing new employment opportunities for people threatened with redundancy or already unemployed. As regards its first area of operation, the ESF has the role to provide backing or encouragement for the implementation of policies designed to promote employment, more especially by facilitating the occupational integration of young people and combating long-term unemployment. However, in the second area of its operation the ESF may intervene on a wider scale, especially in the late-developing regions, to assist categories of people who contribute to the economic development of the regions and areas concerned.

According to a quantitative analysis, if we consider the Italian share in the allocation of ESF's resources in recent years, the balance of benefits is doubtless positive (20.6 per cent of resources allocated in 1987 and 18.6 per cent in 1989. *16th and 17th Report on the Activities of the European Social Fund*, SEC/89/2200 FINAL), especially in comparison with the first period of ESF activity when most of the Fund's contributions were allotted to the Federal Republic of Germany instead of Italy which was supposed to be the main beneficiary.

Thanks to the reform of the 1970s, Italy became the preferential beneficiary of ESF intervention: during the period 1973–83, the Italian share increased at an average annual rate of 31 per cent, thus representing the most important national amount (Papo, 1984).

From another point of view, delays and difficulties in the utilization of appropriations and the trend towards non-specific intervention, in particular in the case of the Regions as a result of the characteristic dualism of Italy, rendered Italian performance less positive. As a consequence, Italy was no longer the main beneficiary of the Fund's financing. Recently Italy was overtaken by the United Kingdom whose share in 1988 amounted to 19.1 per cent. Because of the lack of a legal framework in relation to labour policies, Italy has never taken an interventionist approach characterized by specific ends such as facilitating the access of young people to the labour market. Thus Community resources have been prevalently devoted to the normal vocational training activity carried out by regional administrations (Papo, 1984, p. 41). If the lack of programming at national level prevented Italy from fully exploiting – from a qualitative point of view – ESF's potential, then it is to be hoped that the reform introduced by Act no. 56 of 28 February 1987, regulating the labour market, may contribute to a better utilization of ESF's resources by Italy. A review of the role and functions of public employment services has been undertaken for the purpose of developing labour market 'observatories' at a local level in order to detect emerging training needs and to avoid skill shortages. In addition, a special focus on youth as a target group characterizes another recent initiative aimed at introducing and regulating new forms of employment contracts such as fixed-term employment, employment-training contracts and part-time work (Act no. 863 of 19 December 1984).

Assuming that necessary measures are taken at national level in order to establish a new administration for the labour market which would aim to achieve higher levels of employment by the introduction of greater flexibility and decentralization, it would be interesting to ascertain whether the ESF's policy may help to eliminate the actual causes of unemployment or whether it aims merely to contain the problem of employment disparities unresolved by national and Community economic policies (Zedda, 1988). Job creation and vocational training could have, in fact, a twofold role of development instrument and welfare support. If one considers Italian economic dualism, one can share the worries of Italian trade unions that the increase in jobs as a result of the removal of trade barriers and the opening up of frontiers could also mean in the short term a cut in jobs in weaker production areas and in less-developed areas (Benvenuto, 1989, p. 41): the so-called 'J' effect of Community integration in Italy would affect the steel sector and the regions of *mezzogiorno*.

For this reason, it is essential to consider the relation between economic and social policies for employment. The priority objectives set out by the Regulations reforming the Structural Fund answer the problem in a very consistent way, but the ultimate result depends on their implementation. Some criticism has been raised as regards a certain rigidity in fixing definite and precise objectives (Garonna, 1989). There is a risk that, for example, in those areas not covered by priority objectives intervention in favour of the short-term unemployed would be impossible and that horizontal intervention affecting the 'industrial atmosphere' as a whole might be neglected, as well as the development of continuing training policies over and above the priority objectives areas. With regard to Italian participation in the ESF, the fact that regional priority is subordinate to the implementation of specific interventions questions the justification of Community financing in those less-developed regions where administration is at its weakest. Another problem concerns the Fund's intervention in regions suffering from industrial decline and the indicators chosen to define these areas (GNP and unemployment rates). The Italian system of wage guarantee in case of crisis within a firm founded on the Work Compensation Fund (*Cassa Integrazione Guadagni*) implies the keeping of employment by the firm: this carries the risk that a reduction in the unemployment rate might lead to an underestimation of employment problems in areas suffering from industrial crisis.

Moreover, the main objection to the system concerns the identification of structural objectives and the programming aim that is central to the Fund's reform. Planning policy can be effective in so far as it is 'indicative', with the ultimate end of promoting and stimulating without creating close ties and rigidity (Garonna, 1989, p. 79). However, planning policy cannot undermine the application of the subsidiarity principle that is considered a fundamental principle of European integration.

12.2.1

The need for greater flexibility in the labour market has become an imperative of economic policy (Faustini and Tresoldi, 1984): modern economy demands a special speed of decision and adaptation together with resilience and variety of the institutional models wherein it operates (Giugni, 1982, p. 406). In order to adapt labour law for purposes of flexibility, policy demands 'deregulation', an end to 'burdens on business' and the replacement of the 'going rate' by the 'market rate' (Wedderburn, 1988, p. 191).

In this field Community goals are very clear: by proposing a Community Social Charter the Commission's underlying purpose is to create a single and flexible labour market in the European Community. The Single European Act through article 118A, providing that directives on health and safety minimum requirements 'shall avoid imposing administrative, financial and legal constraints in a way which would hold back the creation and development of small and medium-sized undertakings', represents 'une consécration, au niveau communitaire de la politique de dérégulation et de flexibilité du droit du travail' (Vogel-Polski, 1989, p. 183).

Let us see how the Italian system, which starts from a strong legalistic base, has dealt with the problem of introducing more flexibility in the labour market, at the same time maintaining the fundamental values and guarantees of protection inherent in domestic labour law. After all, it is just a question of flexibility – flexibility of the Italian legalistic system, flexibility of *garantismo* (Perulli, 1989).

Traditionally, Italian labour law was characterized by strict legal regulations establishing the individual rights of wage-earners (*garantismo*); employment contracts were essentially conceived as open-ended and full-time; employers' freedom to hire people was firmly limited. Thus, workers' protection was detrimental to the interests of unemployed persons and young people looking for a first job. In the mid-1970s, the emergency phase of labour law tried to answer the economy's needs demanding changes in labour legislation by the first deregulation under the control of trade unions and the state. Act no. 903/77 is a significant example: it eliminates the restrictions on women's work which made the cost of female labour higher, but, as regards night work and certain heavy work, it refers to the arena of collective bargaining.

Among manpower measures undertaken by the Italian government to fight unemployment on the ground of lower cost and greater flexibility of labour, Act no. 863/84 seems to be of greater relevance as regards the provision regulating a new form of hiring based on 'employment-training contracts', already introduced by Act 285/77 (article 3), and that relating to part-time work (article 5).

For the purpose of promoting employment-training contracts, the law provides incentives to employers in the form of partial exemptions from social security contributions and the possibility of nominative hiring. At the end of the training period of two years, the government provides financial incentives to employers for hiring people on open-ended contracts.

Such a 'flexible' contract, justly considered as the 'metaphor' of the new course of Italian labour law policies (De Luca, 1989, p. 110), represents a consistent answer to the need to increase youth employment, notwithstanding its potentially controversial side-effects – any subsequent creation of jobs may well render employment more precarious.

From the perspective of social harmonization of the internal EC market and in terms of assessment of the impact of EC membership on Italian social policy, one must consider that such a manpower strategy, in addition to being expensive, leads to accusations of promoting unfair competition with the risk of falling into the category of state aids which are subjected to the provisions of articles 92 and 93 of the Treaty requiring prior authorization of the Commission before being implemented.

Recently, however, article 5 of Act 291/88 limited the right to reduced contributions to small- and medium-sized enterprises and to those enterprises located in the area of Mezzogiorno.

As regards provisions concerning part-time work, given the low diffusion of this kind of employment in Italy (6 per cent of employed people) in comparison with other member states, Act no. 863/84 represents an attempt to promote part-time contracts, overcoming the difficulties posed by Civil Code rules on working hours and social security provisions. Although its purpose was 'deregulatory', the law is to foreign eyes ultimately regulatory in that it requires prescribed form and content of part-time contracts and gives part-timers certain basic rights in relation to full-time employees (Wedderburn, 1988).

Italian commentators also consider the approach of the law in regulating part-time work as too rigid and complain about its strict legalistic content which causes the protection and guarantee aspects to prevail on those aiming at promotion (Tanini, 1989). One reason can be found in trade-union attitudes towards part-time work which has never been considered as a valid instrument of employment policy because part-time work in general has been perceived as a form of under-employment concerning mainly women.

However, in 1985–8 an increase in part-time contracts caused the extension of such a rule to the public sector (Act no. 554/88). Yet, considering that Italy maintains the highest levels of irregular work and the lowest diffusion of part-time work in Europe, such an increase in part-time contracts following the adoption of the law in 1984 may be the result of the emergence of a black economy which, after all, was one of the aims of the law.

To such ends and also for the purpose of shaping a framework ensuring basic rights for 'atypical' workers, two proposals for directives at Community level were submitted to the Council in 1982 (on voluntary part-time working and relating to temporary work and fixed-term contracts), but without results. Now, according to the Commission's action programme relating to the implementation of the Community Social Charter (COM/89/568 FINAL), a new directive on contracts and employment relationships other than full-time and open-ended contracts will be proposed. The eventuality, remote though it may be, of the adoption of such a directive should not concern Italian legislators, given the high level of protection granted to part-time workers by national legislation. Paradoxically, though, the fact that Italian labour law is the most advanced one as regards the guarantee of individual and collective rights among EC countries (Foglia, 1986, p. 429) has up till now not prevented Italy from receiving negative judgments on the part of the EC Court in the matter of compliance with Community rules in the field of industrial relations (see next section).

12.3

Two judgments of the European Court of Justice have found Italy in breach of its duty to comply with directive 75/129 on the approximation of the laws of the member states pertaining to collective redundancies (ECCJ. Judgment of 8 June 1982, case 91/81, and ECCJ Judgment of 6 November 1985, case 131/84). The outcry raised in Italy by the Court's first censure was founded on the firm belief that national law and practice relating to collective dismissals were highly protective of workers' rights. The instruments provided for in the industrial sector by collective bargaining in Italy (collective agreements of 1950 and 1965) are more incisive, indeed, than Community rules, while a punctilious implementation of the directive may paradoxically lead to a weaker protection of workers' rights. Nevertheless, inadequacies in implementation procedures in relation to Community standards, in particular as regards the agricultural and trade sectors and employers' obligations to inform, by written notification, union organizations and public authorities, make legislative intervention vital to implement fully the directive. Indeed, the Italian Court of Cassation recently denied the direct effects of such a directive in that its provisions are not specific and require a definite implementation act (Judgment of 26 May 1989, no. 2533), thus rejecting the solution accepted by some previous judgments (see Gennarelli Donahue, 1986).

The reluctant attitude of the Italian government may be explained – if not justified – by the hope of enacting comprehensive legislation that will regulate the complex matter of labour market mobility. With this aim, during recent legislature two different bills (Magrini, 1990) have been proposed. One, extending to all sectors the rules concerning the consultation process with trade unions operating in the industrial sector according to collective agreements of 20/12/1950 and 5/5/1965, and setting out an obligation to inform the Regional Commission for Employment, aims at the actual implementation of the directive. The other bill has a wider scope of application and relates to that legislation which, since 1968, has brought about the progressive expansion of employment protection through the Workers' Compensation Fund (*Cassa Integrazione Guadagni*), on one hand, and by increasing limitations on employers' power of dismissal, on the other, such as Act no. 164/75, which provides wage guarantee mechanisms, and Act no. 675/77, which is a relevant example of the so-called ('labour law of the emergency phase'. This act, which aims to replace collective dismissal as the traditional way of solving enterprise crises, obliges, through workers' mobility mechanisms, employers to inform Provincial Labour Offices of plans to make redundancies; yet it does not fulfil the standards required by directive 129/75 (Foglia and Saggio, 1989, p. 160).

However, the purpose of the bill presently under discussion in Parliament is to rearrange the laws now in force in connection with the Workers' Compensation Fund and labour mobility. In such a context, and in compliance with the EC directive, it introduces new rules on collective dismissal marked by the recognition of unions' rights to information and consultation and by the state's mediation (De Luca, 1989, p. 118). Thus, in view of the reform of the Italian labour market, such rules may significantly contribute to the effort undertaken by Act no. 56/87 on manpower employment for the purposes of a consistent labour law policy.

12.3.1

Present trends of Italian labour and social policy seem to be marked by both the guarantee of individual rights of workers and the safeguard and promotion of employment (De Luca, 1989, p. 119). Can there be compatibility between the options of labour and social policy at Community and national level? To this end it is interesting to see what are the aims pursued by the EC directive on collective dismissal. They are essentially two: to avoid the danger of distortions of competition among undertakings as long as different member states' laws concerning forms and procedures of collective redundancies may have negative effects on the operation of a common market; and to harmonize the guarantee of protection for workers. In fact, in view of the establishment of a Single European Market, the Commission is going to propose a revision of this directive so as to cover cases where redundancy decisions are taken by a decision-making centre or an undertaking located in another member state (see *Commission Action Programme* COM/89/568 FINAL).

Indeed the entire Community social policy, whereas it regulates labour relations, pursues such objectives (Mancini, 1985). Moreover, Community law seems to give preference to the first over the second. An example is the principle of equal treatment between men and women. The Treaty, after proclaiming that 'Member States agree upon the need to promote improved working conditions and an improved standard of living for workers, so as to make possible their harmonisation while the improvement is being maintained' (article 117), limits itself to affirming the principle that 'men and women should receive equal pay for equal work' (article 119), thus showing that concerns about differences in labour cost provoking distortion of competition were stronger than the desire to promote working conditions. Further developments in this field – directive 75/117 which introduced the principle of equal pay for 'work of equal value'; the equal treatment directive (76/207) aiming to overcome sex discrimination at the point of entry into the labour market; and the social security directive (79/7) which covers statutory social security schemes providing protection against the risk of sickness, invalidity, accidents at work, occupational diseases and unemployment, but not the retirement age which remains a matter for national governments – can be considered as aiming to eliminate the loopholes that endanger free competition among European undertakings. In the same view, other directives have contributed to enrich Community experience in the harmonization of member-states' labour law: in addition to directive 75/129, directive 77/187 on the approximation of the law of member states pertaining to the safeguarding of workers' rights in the event of transfer of firms, establishments, or parts of establishments, and directive 80/987 on the protection of workers in case of insolvency of employers.

It is necessary, however, to make some distinctions and to add some considerations relating to the activist role (Rasmussen, 1986) played by the EC Court in this field. With regard to the principle of equal treatment of men and women, the case-law of the Court gave significant impulse to the enforcement of such principle in the EC. One must recognize that, by widening the scope of the principles of workers' protection and guarantees provided by Community legislation, the Court has promoted the improvement of working conditions in the field of social policy and also in that relating to the free movement of workers.

To this end the contribution made by national judges through prejudicial deferment has been conclusive, provided that the Court's preliminary rulings give only indirect opinions on the controversial matter, that an eventual incompatibility ruling has no *erga omnes* effects, and that, different from infringement proceedings carried out by the Commission, an impartial national judge applies (Mancini, 1985, p. 491).

Concerning the directive on workers' protection in the case of employers' insolvency, it must be recognized that its main purpose is the protection of workers' rights, but, on the other hand, it leaves member states with the widest freedom in implementing its provisions in that it shapes a very vague framework and allows for the exclusion of particular categories of workers from its scope of application.

Italy, which has excluded all the workers benefiting from the Workers' Compensation Fund, was recently condemned by the EC Court for failure to comply with the directive (EECJ Judgment of 2 February 1989, case 22/87). As long as the directive's aim is to establish a common minimum standard of rules protecting workers in cases of a firm's crisis from a strictly patrimonial point of view, then the large number of Italian law provisions promoting employment stability in case of industrial crisis through such instruments of 'actual' protection for workers as the Workers' Compensation Fund or the Extraordinary Administration of Large-Sized Enterprises Under Crisis (*amministrazione straordinaria delle grandi imprese*) would not seem to fulfil the social policy objectives pursued by the European Community (Foglia, 1989). The scope of application of Italian interventions, however far-reaching they may be, neither embraces the agricultural and services sectors and small- and medium-sized enterprises nor managers (*dirigenti*), apprentices (*apprendisti*) and persons who work at home (*lavoratori a domicilio*). Ultimately, in this case national goals of achieving high levels of employment account for the narrowing of 'actual' areas of protection – the resultant functional option for the purpose of increasing productivity and competitiveness of small- and medium-sized enterprises. The proposals aiming at reforming the organization of the labour market, as we have seen, show that Italian labour policy tends to reconcile instances of *garantismo* and the goal of job creation and employment stability (De Luca, 1989). Such a view is consistent with the perspective of harmonization of national social policies at Community level in so far as, beyond the recognition of fundamental principles of social guarantee, there is an harmonization on the main objective towards manpower employment.

12.3.2

A final consideration must be made with regard to the directive relating to labour relations' rights which concerns workers' protection in case of transfer of enterprise. Again, a judgment of the European Court found Italy in breach of its duty to comply with the directive's provisions (10 July 1986, case 235/84) and, in particular, for a breach of its obligations relating to consultations and information involving union confederations. In fact, in Italy, proceedings on disclosure of information for unions are provided only by collective agreements, not binding *erga omnes*, and are therefore inadequate for the implementation of a directive. The Court's censure, besides overburdening the Italian position with regard to the implementation of Community provisions in the field of labour law, stresses the need to regulate organically unions' rights of information at present fragmented into different provisions, both of legislative and convention type and having, on the whole, a limited scope of application. Act 215/78, providing a relatively strong involvement of unions in the case of transfer of enterprise, has a sectorial character in that it applies only in the case of enterprise crisis. At the convention level; after the generalized extension of the collective right to information on industrial policies by the National Convention of 1976, the tripartite agreement of 22 January 1983, which represents a turning point in the Italian system of industrial relations, introduced unions' rights of information in the matters of industrial reconversion and technological changes; the agreement of 14 February 1984 or, in the public sector, the *IRI* Protocol of 18 December 1984 establishing consultation committees (*Comitati Consultivi Paritetici*), and, finally, the arrangement of 8 May 1986, which follows the trend towards new models of industrial relations, proceed in the same direction. The bill proposed by CNEL (*Consiglio Nazionale dell'Economia e del Lavoro*) on 25 March 1986 shows that the rights of information and consultation are a crucial issue in Italy and a legislative solution is welcomed in order to bring Italian labour law into conformity with Community initiatives in this field.

Another point of view, tends to fear a negative impact of a legal framework regarding information and consultation rights on the system of labour relations, (d'Harmant François, 1986a). According to this opinion, since industrial relations find their natural expression by way of collective bargaining, the need to respect general principles of national legal systems and the exigency of avoiding delays in implementing Community rules should lead to the consideration of the opportunity of introducing collective agreements in the scope of article 189 of the Treaty as an instrument liable to bring into effect Community provisions (d'Harmant François, 1989, p. 48). This implies general or at least diffuse effects of collective bargaining that presently has no *erga omnes* effects, since the provisions of article 39 of the Italian Constitution have never been put into effect. Legislative interventions tend to widen the scope of obligatoriness of collective bargaining (La Terza, 1989, p. 177), sometimes to the detriment of the homogeneity of workers' protection.

12.3.3

The recent adoption of the framework directive 89/391 on the implementation of measures to promote improvements in the safety and health of workers at work (Biagi, 1990) raises again the problem of the compatibility of the Italian legal system with Community standards. The framework directive, providing that 'employers shall consult workers and/or their representatives and allow them to take part in discussion on all questions relating to safety and health at work' (article 11), adds the obligation of workers' participation to those of information and consultation already introduced by the directive on collective redundancies and transfer of enterprise.

If one considers the inadequacies and lack of effectiveness of current Italian legislation concerning safety and health of workers (Smuraglia, 1988), it is highly doubtful that the standards of protection introduced by this directive and the others related to it can be fulfilled. Act no. 833/78, which should replace the already outdated legislation enacted in the mid–1950's, has for the most part not been put into practice as regards the goals of health safeguards.

If, in addition, one considers the Italian failure to comply with both directives introducing the obligation of information and participation, and failing a legislative framework regulating organically unions' rights of information and consultation, the provision for compulsory working consultation is not likely to be implemented into the Italian system of labour relations. Indeed, 'on the whole the

Italian system differs markedly or is in contradiction with the contents and general orientations adopted by the Directive' (Montuschi, 1990, p. 156). At the conventional level, however, there are examples of advanced agreements, such as the Chemical Workers' National Agreement of 6 December 1986, whose rules could be embodied in legislation in order to fulfil Community provisions.

From another point of view, such a provision may be seen as an attempt by the Commission to achieve, by other means and as a result of qualified majority rule of article 118A, the advancement of a 'social dialogue' aimed at a stand still by 5th Company Directive (Lonbay, 1989, p. 212). In the field of industrial democracy, in fact, Commission proposals envisaging participation models such as the 5th Directive and the draft regulation on the Statute of the European Limited Company, or entailing extended rights of information and consultation such as the Vredeling Directive, meet the resistance of member states within the Council of Ministers (Boyle, 1989).

Indeed, the Community pursued the objective of harmonization of company law through different approaches to participation issues. Only rights of information, consultation and negotiation relating to specific situations, such as collective redundancies, transfer of enterprise, company merger and, more recently, safety and health at work, found recognition through the instrument of directives, while the ultimate result was unsuccessful with regard to generalized rights of information and consultation or forms of participation in the management of enterprise. Concerning the Vredeling Directive, the adequacy of such an instrument for the purposes of harmonization of industrial relations systems, where information and consultation rights may find their source both in law and bargaining, is highly doubtful (Vadalà, 1985; d'Harmant François, 1986a).

However, from the perspective of 'social dialogue' envisaged by article 118B, the EC Commission intends to pursue the objective of promoting the development of information, consultation and participation practices through instruments that are more 'fluid' than directives (COM/89/568FINAL). In Italy, at least, there is preference for legislative interventions limited to establishing procedural rules and a legal framework calculated to exercise information and consultation rights rather than for solutions of direct participation in enterprise management (Foglia, 1985).

The Italian system of labour relations seems to be in a complex transitional period which may turn out to be the passing from a phase of conflicts to one of participation: industrial relations are no more marked by conflicts than in the 1970s, yet there seems to be little interest in workers' participation (Treu and Negrelli, 1987). Economic crisis and technological changes have over the years affected the evolution of the labour relations system from a model of pure pluralism to one of neo-corporatism and concerted action introduced by the agreements of 1977, 1983 and 1984, whereby the government, unions and employers engage to pursue common objectives in the field of economic and social policies (Runggaldier, 1985; Treu, 1985; d'Harmant François, 1986b). Major participation of unions in the labour market and industrial reconversion decisions at national level was not matched by a similar clear and regular trend towards union involvement at enterprise level.

The debate on industrial democracy initiated in the mid–1970s led to the recognition of information and consultation practices as collective rights of workers. Such a recognition has been included in collective agreements, but a legal framework regulating the matter is still lacking and the exercise of those rights has not been satisfactory and uniform. Reasons for weaker advancement at enterprise level compared to the concerted action at national level between social partners can be found in the priority of national actions to solve macroeconomic problems and in the traditional centralization of labour relations in Italy (Treu and Negrelli, 1987, p. 90).

The present trend towards fragmentation and diversification of Italian labour relations strongly reduces the role of centralized political bargaining (Ferraro, 1986, p. 683) and marks the probable decline of the traditional system. The consequent crisis could be overcome by changing labour relations from an instrument of guarantee and minimum protection of working conditions into one of participation and involvement in decision-making processes relating to economic and production management (Pessi, 1986, p. 755).

The Commission proposal on the Statute of the European Company which envisages three different models of participation (even though it has been firmly opposed by Italian *Confindustria*) may contribute towards developing the Italian debate on industrial democracy and shaping an alternative model of labour relations.

12.4

A substantial homogeneity between Community social policy and recent developments of Italian labour policies can be affirmed, although problems of compatibility may arise in relation to single aspects of Community options given the peculiarity of the Italian case in the European context.

In Italy the debate on flexibility and deregulation of the labour market resulted in actual legislative initiatives that brought Italy into consonance with European policies. Such evolution, consistent with technological, economic and production changes, developed first in the context of labour market policies. Italian labour law has been traditionally more concerned with protecting existing labour, promoting individual rights, granting minimum income to unemployed persons than with creating new jobs. The priority given to the objective of achieving higher levels of employment did not result in a pure and simple deregulation of the labour market, something inconceivable and incongruous with the general principles of protection granted by the Italian legal system, but led to the introduction of articulated forms of controlled and contracted flexibility. The demand for flexibility of the legal and contractual provisions regulating individual labour relations coupled with the need for resiliency of the Italian model of industrial relations. All contractual arrangements from 1984 to 1987 clearly begin to shape a modern system of industrial relations from a perspective very close to the European one.

Lacking formal institutions for workers' participation, at present the Italian system of labour relations is characterized by a lower degree of juridification of collective rights but a higher degree of juridification of individual rights, and it represents a rather rare case of self-regulation where social mechanisms of change and adaptation operate.

Suppleness of *garantismo* instances that the Italian legal system previously expressed through the rigidity of labour rules should be compensated by new institutional forms of worker participation. To that end, the development of a social dialogue at the European level could be useful in the debate on industrial democracy in Italy.

Bibliography

Benvenuto, G. (1989), 'Il sindacato e l'Europa', *Mondoperaio*, no. 7: 38–41.

Biagi, M. (1990), 'From Conflict to Participation in Safety: Industrial Relations and Working Environment in Europe 1992', *International Journal of Comparative Labour Law and Industrial Relations*, no. 6: 67–79.

Boyle, A. J. (1989), 'The Single Market: the Fifth Directive and the European Company Statute', *Studi Senesi*, no. 2: 175–90.

CNEL (Consiglio Nazionale dell'Economia e del Lavoro) (1985), 'Osservazioni e proposte sulla revisione della legislazione sul rapporto di lavoro', *Rivista Italiana di Diritto del Lavoro*, no. 4: 416–513.

Cessari, A. and Luca Tamajo, R. de (1982), *Dal garantismo al controllo*, Milan, Giuffré.

Harmant François, A. d' (1986a). 'L'informazione e la consultazione dei lavoratori nel progetto comunitario e nella regolamentazione italiana', *Affari Sociali Internazionali*, no. 1: 73–92.

Harmant François, A. d' (1986b), 'Dal 1975 al 1986: come cambia il sistema di relazioni industriali', *Il Diritto del Lavoro*, no. 2: 249–59.

Harmant François, A. d'(1989), 'Il Mercato Unico Europeo e l'armonizzazione degli ordinamenti del lavoro', *Rivista di Diritto Europeo*, no. 1: 33–79.

Luca, M. de (1989), 'Statuto dei lavoratori: prospettive del garantismo per gli anni '90', *Il Diritto del Lavoro*, no. 2: 109–21.

Faustini, G. and Tresoldi, C. (1984), 'Le prospettive dell'occupazione in Italia, al 1990', *Economia & Lavoro*, no. 4: 73–8.

Ferraro, G. (1986), 'Fonti autonome e fonti eteronome nella legislazione della flessibilitá', *Giornale di Diritto del Lavoro e di Relazioni Industriali*, no. 32: 667–707.

Ferrera, M. (1985), *Il Welfare state in Italia, sviluppo e crisi in prospettiva comparata*, Bologna, Il Mulino.

Foglia, R. (1985), 'La partecipazione dei lavoratori alla gestione delle societá nella proposta di V Direttiva CEE', *Le societá*, no. 2: 129–43.

Foglia, R. (1986), 'Trasferimento di imprese, tutela dei lavoratori e obblighi comunitari', *Il Diritto del Lavoro*, no. 3: 426–35.

Foglia, R. (1989), 'Tutela dei lavoratori in caso di insolvenza dell'imprenditore e disciplina comunitaria', *Il Diritto del Lavoro*, no. 2: 156–66.

Foglia, R. and Saggio, A. (1989), 'L'incidenza del diritto comunitario sul Diritto del Lavoro in Italia', *Foro Italiano*, no. 3: 149–68.

Galantino, L. (1985), 'Il diritto del lavoro e la societá dell'informazione', *Il diritto del lavoro*, no. 5: 323–48.

Garonna, P. (1989), 'Tre idee per l'obiettivo occupazione', *Mondoperaio*, no. 5: 77–83.

Gennarelli Donahue, M. (1986), 'La normativa italiana in materia di licenziamenti collettivi e la disciplina comunitaria', *Rivista di Diritto Europeo*, no. 4: 228–42.

Giugni, G. (1982), 'Il diritto del lavoro negli anni '80', *Gioranale di Diritto del Lavoro e di*

Relazioni Industriali, no. 15, 373–401.

Giugni, G. (1986), 'Giuridificazione e deregolazione nel diritto del lavoro italiano', *Giornale di Diritto del Lavoro e di Relazioni Industriali*, no. 30, 317–41.

La Terza, M. (1989), 'Tendenze legislative attuali in tema di efficacia generale del contratto collettivo', *Il Diritto del Lavoro*, no. 2: 171–7.

Lonbay, J. (1989), 'Free movement of persons, recognition of qualifications and working conditions', *International and Comparative Law Quarterly*, no. 1: 211–14.

Magrini, S. (1990), 'Licenziamenti individuali e collettivi: separatezza e convergenza delle tutele' *Giornale di Diritto del Lavoro e di Relazioni Industriali*, no. 46; 313–67.

Mancini, F. (1985), 'Diritto del lavoro e diritto comunitario' *Giornale di diritto del lavoro e di relazioni industriali*, no. 27, 477–93.

Mengoni, L. (1988), 'Il dibattito sulla revisione della legislazione del lavoro', *Rivista Italiana di Diritto del Lavoro*, no. 1: 3–13.

Montuschi, L. (1990), 'Health and safety provision in Italy: the impact of the EEC Framework Directive', *International Journal of Comparative Labour Law and Industrial Relations*, no. 6: 146–58.

Papo, M. (1984), *La politica sociale della Comunitá Europea*, Rome, Istituto nazionale per lo studio delle congiuntura.

Perulli, A. (1989), 'Diritto del lavoro e flessibilitá', *Lavoro e Diritto*, no. 3: 397–420.

Pessi, R. (1986), 'Innovazione tecnologica a sistema di relazioni industriali: la contrattazione delle trasformazione e il protocollo IRI', *Rivista Italiana di Diritto del Lavoro*, no 4: 723–73.

Piccininno, S. (1989), 'Le prospettive della tutela previdenziale dei dipendenti dagli enti di diritto pubblico nel sistema della previdenza sociale', *Il Diritto del Lavoro*, no. 1, 20–31.

Pocar, F. (1983), *Diritto comunitario del lavoro*, Padua, Cedam.

Rasmussen, H. (1986), *On Law and Policy in the European Court of Justice*, Dordrecht: Martinus Nijhoff.

Ripa di Meana, C. (1989), 'Lo Stato sociale europeo: tra mito e realtá', *Mondoperaio*, no. 5: 64–7.

Runggaldier, U. (1985), 'Tendances actuelles du droit du travail italien', *Droit Social*, no. 12, 856–62.

Santaniello, R. (1989), 'La coesione economica e sociale nella CEE: dal Trattato di Roma all'Atto Unico Europeo. La riforma dei fondi a finalitá strutturale', *Affari Sociali Internazionali*, no. 1: 157–79.

Smuraglia, C. (1988), 'La tutela della salute dei lavoratori', *Rivista Italiana di Diritto del Lavoro*, no. 4: 414–41.

Tanini, N. (1989), 'Analisi critica della disciplina sul lavoro a tempo parziale e prospettive di revisione', *Il Diritto del Lavoro*, no. 2: 156–70.

Treu, T. (1985), 'Evolution récente du droit du travail en Italie', *Travail et Société*, no. 1: 29–47.

Treu, T. (1987), 'Il quadro normativo ed istituzionale a sostegno della creazione di occupazione e di nuove imprese', *Rivista Italiana di Diritto del Lavoro*, no.3: 333–59.

Treu, T. and Negrelli, S. (1987), 'La participation des travailleurs et les politiques du personnel en Italie', *Revue Internationale du Travail*, no. 1: 87–102.

Vadalà, P. (1985), 'La proposta di direttiva CEE sui diritti di informazione e di consultazione', *Il Diritto del Lavoro*, no. 2: 215–31.

Vogel-Polski, E. (1989), 'L'Acte Unique ouvre-t-il l' espace social européen?', *Droit Social*, no. 2, 177–89.

Wedderburn (1988), 'Deregulation and labour law in Britain and Western Europe', *International Journal of Comparative Labour Law and Industrial Relations*, no. 4: 191–205.

Zedda, L. (1988), 'Osservazioni sul diritto al lavoro nell'Europa comunitaria', *Diritto Comunitario e degli Scambi Internazionali*, no. 3: 347–75.

Index